T0046740

ADVANCE PRAISE FOR

Barack Obama's True Legacy

"*Barack Obama's True Legacy* is an invaluable lens through which to gauge the immense damage the Obama Presidency inflicted on America, and the catastrophic harm the Biden administration is inflicting upon the nation. A remarkable achievement and a must-read."

—DINESH D'SOUZA, BESTSELLING AUTHOR AND FILMMAKER

"I rejoiced at the election of the first black president, but by Obama's second term, I announced that I regarded him as the most destructive president of the modern era. Reading this book provides the evidence for that assessment. For most Americans, *Barack Obama's True Legacy* will be eye-opening and profoundly disturbing. This is a truly important book."

—DENNIS PRAGER, NATIONALLY SYNDICATED RADIO TALK SHOW HOST, FOUNDER OF PRAGER UNIVERSITY, AND A *NEW YORK TIMES* BESTSELLING AUTHOR OF TEN BOOKS

"A masterful unveiling of how Barack Obama zealously worked to impair the fabric and national security of the United States—with devastating consequences for our nation and the world. The catastrophe reverberates all the more now that the Obama team is back in power. A ferocious and chilling read that needs to be in every household."

—MIKE HUCKABEE, GOVERNOR OF ARKANSAS FROM 1996-2007

"This comprehensive, powerful, and eye-opening indictment is the definitive account of Obama's White House perfidy—and the perfect gift for that person in your life who still thinks he was a great president."

—BRUCE BAWER, AUTHOR OF *WHILE EUROPE SLEPT* AND *SURRENDER*

"Every US President is given a choice of codename by the Secret Service. Barack Obama handpicked 'Renegade,' which is defined as a 'traitor,' 'deserter,' 'betrayer.' *Barack Obama's True Legacy* illustrates precisely how his code name was tailor-made for him. A most necessary account of his duplicitous, anti-America agenda, and a sobering look at his track record while in the White House."

—NOOR BIN LADIN, WRITER AND ADVOCATE DEDICATED TO DEFENDING FREEDOM AND THOSE THREATENED BY THE ADHERENTS OF OPPRESSIVE IDEOLOGIES.

BARACK OBAMA'S TRUE LEGACY

How He Transformed America

REPUBLIC

BOOK PUBLISHERS

BARACK OBAMA'S TRUE LEGACY

First Edition

Copyright 2023 Jamie Glazov

All rights reserved. No part of this book may be reproduced in any form or by any electronic or mechanical means, including information storage and retrieval systems, without permission in writing from the publisher, except by a reviewer, who may quote brief passages in a review.

All information included in this book is based on the author's recollections, opinions, and views. Publisher makes no representations, warranties, guarantees or otherwise with respect to the accuracy or completeness of the contents of this book.

ISBN 9781645720614 (paperback)   9781645720621 (ebook)

For inquiries about volume orders, please contact:

Republic Book Publishers

27 West 20th Street

Suite 1103

New York, NY 10011

editor@republicbookpublishers.com

Published in the United States by Republic Book Publishers

Distributed by Independent Publishers Group

www.ipgbook.com

Book designed by Mark Karis

Printed in the United States of America

CONTENTS

FOREWORD

by General Michael Flynn

SEVERAL WEEKS AFTER the highly questionable 2020 presidential election appeared to put his vice president, Joe Biden, on the path to the White House, Barack Obama told late-night talk show host Stephen Colbert that he would like to have a third term by proxy: "I used to say if I can make an arrangement where I had a stand-in or front-man or front-woman and they had an earpiece in and I was just in my basement in my sweats looking through the stuff and I could sort of deliver the lines while someone was doing all the talking and ceremony, I'd be fine with that because I found the work fascinating."[1]

Early on in Joe Biden's calamitous presidency, it became clear that

Biden was indeed someone's proxy, and that someone was likely Barack Hussein Obama. Even if Barack Obama is not actually directing Biden's actions from his basement, the Biden administration established itself immediately as the instrument for the resumption of the Obama agenda. What befell America during the Biden presidency was what Barack Obama envisioned for our nation and what he'd spent eight years setting into motion. Donald Trump did a great deal to reverse the disastrous direction in which the country was heading, but Biden's team worked energetically to undo all that Trump accomplished.

And so, by May 2021, the United States of America faced a number of crises that appeared suddenly, were largely self-inflicted, and which threatened its survival as a free nation more severely than at any time since the bombing of Pearl Harbor. All of these crises were entirely foreseeable and completely preventable. And, all of them were the direct result of the socialist, internationalist, and statist policies of Barack Obama.

After having attained the White House by means of an election that was full of irregularities, which were never fully investigated and buried beneath the media's insistence that only paranoid conspiracy theorists and diehard partisans thought that the election was anything but free and fair, the Biden administration set out to pursue a number of policies that could lead to nothing less than the end of the United States as a republic of laws governed under the Constitution.

Ignoring Congress, despite the fact that both the House and Senate had Democrat majorities, Biden immediately signed over fifty Executive Orders to reverse numerous Trump policies, relax border and immigration controls, subject the nation once again to onerous economic burdens designed to fight the phantasm of "climate change," exacerbate the hysteria and restrictions of freedom presented as measures to fight the coronavirus, and promote a far-left social agenda. Biden also restarted Obama's objective of "fundamentally transforming the United States of America" with a culture war waged from inside the White House against Americans. Obama had made Americans poor. Biden would leave them even poorer.

Daniel Greenfield states in this book that "Obama powered a historic economic shift that took power away from workers and gave it to Silicon Valley, that took American jobs and shipped them to China, and that took jobs from black teenagers and gave them to illegal aliens.

He oversaw a historic power slide away from America to China, Russia, and the Islamic terrorists of the world laboring to build their caliphates." During the opening months of the Biden administration, China rapidly became a massive threat to America's economic wellbeing and standing in the world. Biden's team emboldened the Communist Chinese to step up their activities toward economic, military, and technological domination of the entire world. This emboldening of China took place as Biden's team ended the Keystone Pipeline project that had enabled the nation to attain energy independence during the Trump administration. Gas prices soared, and Americans once again experienced gas shortages of a severity that had not been seen since the 1970s. This was the logical outcome of Obama's energy policies, which mandated the voluntary weakening of the United States and its increased dependence on foreign powers.

Obama had opened up the borders to demographically transform the country; Biden would go even further beyond that to build on his former boss's legacy. Biden's administration also worked to weaken national security by opening the southern border. As Matthew Vadum says in these pages, "An insecure border and growing disrespect for the nation's immigration laws is the ugly legacy that President Barack Obama left behind." Biden's team has determinedly taken Obama's open-borders policies as a blueprint, in a matter of months transforming a relatively quiet southern border into a hellhole of drug and human trafficking, with a massive humanitarian crisis caused by a lack of facilities to accommodate the influx Biden's team had invited.

As could have been predicted, jihadis also took advantage. The rapid fall of Afghanistan to the Taliban in August 2021 was the foremost example, but Biden's presidency also increased the jihad terror threat within the United States. In April 2021, US Border Patrol agents announced that they had arrested two Yemenis who were on a terror watch list as they tried to enter the United States.[2] Significantly, shortly after announcing this, US Customs and Border Protection (CBP) removed the press release from its website.[3] Apparently the CBP preferred that Americans not know just how serious the crisis at the border really was.

All of this and much more represented a reimplementation of Obama-era policies and programs. And Biden's team didn't stop there. Immediately repudiating Trump's deep and unshakeable support for Israel, the Biden administration returned to Barack Obama's stance of hostility toward Israel, with blithe disregard for the wellbeing of America's most reliable ally in the Middle East. The *Washington Free Beacon* reported in March 2021 that the administration was determined to fund the Palestinians with no regard whatsoever for what they planned to do with the money, up to and including the financing of jihad terror activity: "the Biden administration privately confirmed to Congress last week that the Palestinian Authority has continued to use international aid money to reward terrorists but said the finding won't impact its plans to restart funding."[4]

While betraying Israel as Obama did, Biden's team is also following in his footsteps in providing aid and comfort to one of the most formidable enemies America faces on the world stage: the Islamic Republic of Iran. The Biden administration appears prepared to make virtually any concession in order to induce Iran to return to Obama's disastrous nuclear deal, which—contrary to media myth—did nothing to hinder Iran's nuclear program, and a great deal to empower it.

All this is taking place amid unprecedented threats to our First and Second Amendment rights to the freedom of speech and to bear arms. The social media giants and the media have colluded with the Biden team to whitewash the numerous crises into which Biden has plunged the nation and to silence dissenting voices, most notably that of former President Trump, who has tried to alert the public to the gravity of what is really happening. The social media giants feel free to restrict Trump's speech and that of other Americans because of legal protections that were put in place during the Obama years.

And so, by November 2021, after enjoying four years of relative peace and prosperity during the administration of Donald J. Trump, the nation faces chronic unemployment and inflation, a border crisis, grave threats to our constitutional liberties, increased violence and lawlessness from the leftist groups Antifa and Black Lives Matter, a weakening dollar, the emboldening of our enemies worldwide, and even worse on the horizon. Biden's handlers are either catastrophically stupid and incompetent or actively working to weaken the United States. In either case, the result is the same.

This is the world Barack Obama has made. This is his legacy.

—GENERAL MIKE FLYNN, FORMER NATIONAL SECURITY ADVISOR
AND BEST-SELLING AUTHOR OF *THE FIELD OF FIGHT*

INTRODUCTION

by Daniel Greenfield

BARACK OBAMA'S PRESIDENCY WAS HISTORIC. Pundits said it, celebrities tweeted it, and the community organizer from Chicago was not shy about constantly bringing it up.

And it was true.

Over a decade after his inauguration, we are still living in his shadow. His history of economic decline, racial division, and terrorist appeasement is our present. The third term of his presidency under Biden makes him inescapable even long after leaving office. The Biden administration is extending his fundamental transformation of America. Its open borders, woke military, critical race theory, terrorist appeasement, and wealth redistribution are a continuation of Obama's war on our national sovereignty, on the middle class, on the family, and on free enterprise. From a new administration staffed with all his old people to the familiar economic misery that Americans thought they had left behind, it is as if the Obama administration never ended. And, as the nation endures a third term of Obama, many wonder if it will ever end.

His legacy of defeat abroad and division at home is all around us. From race riots to defeat in Afghanistan, and from the war on the middle class to massive power grabs, we are not only still living out his history, but it's clear that we will go on living there until we break free. Obama made history, but not the way that the mainstream media would have it. The truly historic elements of his presidency were not his accident of birth and choice of racial identification, that a political establishment obsessed with identity politics told Americans would serve as a national atonement for racism. Now that his third term is taking place under an old, white male figurehead, it is clearer than ever that identity is not history. The true legacy of Obama and Biden is in the impact of their destructive radicalism on the country, not which box they checked on their census forms. The community organizer from Chicago did not heal our racial wounds, he presided over a historically divisive era that reversed generations of progress in race relations.

But Obama did not just divide Americans by race, "Punish your enemies," he said. He divided us by gender, "You know, there's a reason we haven't had a woman president before," and by faith, "They get bitter, they cling to guns or religion," by all the flavors of sexual identity, and by every sort of identity politics. He broke America, and the fractures of our time are the aftershocks of his destruction.

Obama powered a historic economic shift that took power away from workers and gave it to Big Tech, that took American jobs and shipped them to China, and that took jobs from black teenagers and gave them to illegal aliens. He oversaw a historic power slide away from America and to China, Russia, and the Islamic terrorists of the world laboring to build their caliphates. And under Biden, in Obama's third term, all of this is worse than ever. To understand the crisis of the Biden administration, we have to go back to its origins in the Obama administration. And that is exactly what *Barack Obama's True Legacy* does.

Barack Obama's True Legacy grapples with the true history of a man who has produced multiple autobiographies, along with an unending stream of articles and interviews, without actually telling us his true goals and the true history that is driving him. That's why *Barack Obama's True Legacy* meticulously traces his ideological origins with John Drew's *Obama: The Young Communist I Knew* and that of his signature policy with Trevor Loudon's *The Marxist Origins and Goals of Obamacare*.

Barack Obama's True Legacy draws on experts and researchers who lay out and break down the insidious means by which Obama's ideological affinity for radicals and contempt for America led him to betray our national security and Christians and Jews, while making allies of Islamic terrorists. The book you hold in your hands delves into the Islamic alliances that created a historical realignment with America's worst enemies while betraying our national security in Stephen Coughlin's *Muslim Brotherhood's Penetration of U.S. Under Obama,* how Obama abandoned persecuted Christians in the Muslim world in Raymond Ibrahim's *How Obama Enabled Persecution of Christians,* and how he abandoned and betrayed Israel and Jews in Daniel Greenfield's *Obama's Betrayal of Israel* and *How Obama Funded the Murder of Israelis.*

In *Benghazi Betrayal and the Brotherhood Link,* Claire Lopez reveals the ideological agenda behind the infamous abandonment of our people in Libya. Jeff Nyquist's *Obama's Russian Collusion* tells the story of who was really colluding with Russia, and in three stunning essays, Robert Spencer expertly chronicles Obama's treasonous collusion with the forces of the Jihad in *Obama's Enabling of Jihad and Stealth Jihad, Obama's Enabling of ISIS,* and *The Iran Deal.*

Turning to the war on our border, Trevor Loudon's *Obama's Illegal Marxist Immigrant Amnesty Movement* and Matthew Vadum's *Obama's Damage to Border Security* expose Obama's role in the historic invasion of America. Joseph Klein's *ObamaGate: The Coup Attempt Against President*

Trump zeroes in on the historically unprecedented abuse of national security by Obama, while Daniel Greenfield's *Obama's Enabling of Racial Strife and Domestic Terror* digs into his role in the racist movements and race riots that tore apart America's body and soul.

In *An Ex-President's Post-Presidential War on America* and *Why Obama Should Have Been Impeached and Removed from Office,* Joseph Klein sums up Obama's post-election plots and his abuses in office. And finally, Dov Lipman, a member of Israel's Knesset, takes on *Obama's Revisionist "Promised Land,"* the dishonest manipulations of Israel's story and its ideological poison.

These experts, researchers, thinkers, journalists, scholars, and leaders have assembled a compelling history of Barack Obama's true impact on America, on Israel, and on the world.

That impact is not past tense. It is present tense.

Every one of Biden's executive orders, every illegal alien who crosses the border, every humiliating defeat on the world stage, every assault on the middle class, and every betrayal of our allies is a reminder that we are still living through the Obama nightmare.

Obama's presidency was historic. This is its true history.

Daniel Greenfield is a Shillman Journalism Fellow at the David Horowitz Freedom Center, and he is an investigative journalist and writer, focusing on the radical Left and Islamic terrorism.

1

OBAMA: THE YOUNG COMMUNIST I KNEW

by John Drew

EACH POLITICAL PARTY has all the incentive it needs to embrace and treasure the least savory elements of its political coalition, while at the same time doing whatever it takes to hide them from public view. At the political conventions, teams of political consultants carefully suppress the visibility of their most obnoxious supporters out of fear of offending sensitive swing voters or energizing enraged political opponents. For the Democrats, the drunk uncle expunged from the family photos has long been Bill Ayers, the co-founder of the Weather Underground, a Communist revolutionary group that bombed police stations, the United States Capitol, and the Pentagon during the 1960s and 1970s.

1

As an ex-Communist myself, I can report that as a younger man, I shared ideas, policies, outlook, and influences with Bill Ayers. What is most relevant about my story, however, is that I also shared those things with the young Barack Obama too. Today, my story remains helpful in understanding both Joe Biden and the Democrat party, if only because Barack Obama did more than anyone else to help Joe Biden break his presidential losing streak when Obama picked Biden as his running mate in 2008.

My first meeting with young Barack Obama raised strong feelings and left me with a positive first impression. At the time, I felt I had persuaded a young man preparing himself for a communist-style revolution to appreciate the more practical alternative of conventional politics as a channel for his socialist views. Long before I realized Obama had grown into a spectacular political career, I have treasured this memory as an early example of my own intellectual growth and an early sign of my modest promise as a teacher and a scholar.

I met Obama in December of 1980, a couple of days after Christmas, in Portola Valley—a small town near Stanford University in Palo Alto, California. I was a twenty-three-year-old, second-year graduate student in Cornell's Government Department. I had flown to California to visit a twenty-two-year-old girlfriend, Caroline Boss (now Caroline Grauman-Boss). Boss was a senior at Occidental College. She had gotten to know Obama while they were in an international relations class in the spring of 1980, co-taught by professors Larry Caldwell and Carlos Alan Egan.

I had been an angry Marxist revolutionary for almost my entire undergraduate career at Occidental College. During my hyperactive sophomore year, in the fall of 1976, I founded the Marxist-Socialist group on campus and named it the Political Awareness Fellowship. As I recall, I developed this innocuous sounding name because there were so few students on campus as radical as me, and I was fearful of turning off moderate students who might be willing to learn more about Marxist theory. On my watch, our group grew to a dozen student activists and managed to attract crowds of eighty or more to our events. The most successful of these was a campaign to raise awareness of the plight of homosexuals who were beaten by Los Angeles City police officers along the Hollywood strip. In the spring of 1977, I promoted this event with a large banner in the Occidental College quad reading: "Anita Byrant: Hitler in Drag?" During my junior year, I left Occidental College with the mission to study Marxist economics at England's University of Sussex in the fall of 1977.

By the time I returned to Occidental in the fall of 1978 for my senior year, the Political Awareness Fellowship had morphed into something much bigger, an organization with strong leadership, its own office space, and a new name. The group's president was Gary Chapman, an older student who had served as a Green Beret in Viet Nam. Chapman was a colorful figure who shared stories from his military career, including how he was required to take apart and reassemble his rifle in the dark. Under Chapman's leadership, the group had changed its name to the Democratic Socialist Alliance (DSA). As I recall, he told me "the old name wasn't letting people know what we stood for." I thought he was right. The DSA met weekly and brought in speakers about once a month. Events were advertised by big signs on the campus quad. During my time at Occidental, the group searched for ways to embarrass the administration, help students to see the evil of the US capitalist system, and mobilize people in preparation for the coming revolution.

In the spring of 1979, Chapman and I joined forces with other students on campus to found an anti-apartheid coalition, called The Student Committee Against Apartheid, which included the leadership of the DSA as well as several other groups. Although the coalition included liberals as well as radicals, I think it is fair to say the most significant intellectual and organizational leadership came from students in the DSA. One of the ironies of our effort is that the white students took the lead in organizing these protests while African American students seemed strangely passive and uninvolved in fighting the South African regime.

My romance with Boss began in the spring of 1979. Boss had joined the DSA the year before and had participated in the anti-apartheid events I helped organize that year. Like me, she was white, a committed Marxist, and preparing herself for the approaching revolution. That year, I completed my senior honors thesis on Marxist economics, joined Phi Beta Kappa, and graduated *magna cum laude* in political science. Boss and I danced together after I accepted my Occidental degree in June of 1979. As I accepted my diploma, I was wearing a red armband that signified my solidarity with my Marxist brethren around the world and my commitment to the anti-apartheid movement. From there, I lived with Boss—off and on—for slightly over two years between the spring of 1979 and the spring of 1981. Although I loved her with all my heart, it was an open relationship with boundaries as porous as a whiffle ball. In fact, too porous. I remember feeling hurt when she disclosed she was being intimate with both me and Chapman. For whatever reason, my hostility was ignited by his disrespect rather than her licentious. Years later, when presidential historian David Garrow informed me of Chapman's premature death, it took everything I had to repress any visible sign of my undeniable elation.

As I later learned, Boss had intense and memorable relationships with other young men at Occidental College, including the young Barack Obama. For example, I now know that elements of my girl-friend's story played a starring role in Obama's first book, *Dreams from My Father*. This is the insight I got from David Maraniss's book, *Barack Obama: The Story* (2012) which reveals Boss was one of the inspirations for the composite character "Regina." True, Regina appears in *Dreams* as "a big, dark woman," but why deny Obama a little poetic license?

One of the common traits I see in Joe Biden and Barack Obama is a surprising level of comfort in living a life of lies, plagiarism, and intellectual laziness. Similar to the manner in which Joe Biden crafted a backstory based on the ancestral musings of the Welsh Labor Party politician Neil Kinnock, we learn that Obama created Regina out of the European adventures of a young black female student at Occidental named Sarah Etta-Harris, the Chicago family stories of Michelle Robinson, the president's future wife, and the anti-apartheid activism of Caroline Boss. Significantly, Maraniss reported that the name Regina was also the name of Boss's real-life grandmother, a Swiss woman who worked as a maid, scrubbing floors and doing laundry for the banking community in the small Swiss town of Interlaken. In *Dreams*, Regina is such a central figure in young Obama's life that, along with Obama's communist mentor, Frank Marshall Davis, she is remembered as one of the key reasons why young Obama made the life-changing choice to become a community organizer.

In some ways, I was not surprised. When I first read *Dreams* in 2008, I remember thinking the character of Regina reminded me a lot of Boss, particularly what I remembered of her positive, soft, supportive nature. Obama introduces composite Regina by writing: "I had seen her around before, usually sitting in the library with book in hand, a big, dark woman who wore stockings and dresses that looked homemade, along with tinted, oversized glasses and a scarf always covering her head" (*Dreams*, pp. 103–104). In contrast to this description, I can report the real Regina was a fun, scintillating, hyper-extraverted figure. In contrast to the seriousness of Michelle Obama, I would say the young Boss was more like that character played by Lisa Kurdow on *Friends*—the independent, quirky, nurturing Phoebe Buffay.

Like Phoebe, Boss was a slim girl with long blond hair she wore pinned back in a bun or twisted up in a ponytail. Her posture was terrible. When she stood up at her full 5′8″ height, however, she was somewhat taller than me—especially in her clogs. By the time Boss introduced me to young Obama, she had turned into a thin, almost anorexic girl. I remember she dressed like a hippie from the 1960s, complete with a woven ankle bracelet, blouses that reflected her Swiss heritage, and big colorful Indian print skirts. Boss did wear big sunglasses. She was also fond of wearing scarves round her neck. I cannot remember her ever wearing a scarf over her head. What I recall best about her clothing was that she had a habit of wearing shirts tucked inside bulky light-blue overalls. I clearly remember the real Regina also had a sensible, if somewhat guilty, appreciation for the superior fit of designer jeans from Gloria Vanderbilt.

In contrast to the composite Regina, Boss was a Marxist and a socialist, looking forward to a communist revolution in the United States. She believed this revolution would be the inevitable result of larger social forces working through the dialectic logic of Marx's scientific socialism. Boss served as the co-president of the Democrat Socialist Alliance (DSA) at Occidental College while Obama was a sophomore. We also know, from David Maraniss's book, that Boss was one of the main speakers at the anti-apartheid event at Occidental on February 18, 1981. In Maraniss's book, Obama's smooth participation in a skit where he plays the role of a soon-to-be-arrested South African activist offers a stark contrast to Boss's performance in which—reminiscent of Phoebe Buffay—she nervously flubs the introduction of the guest speaker, a visitor from South Africa.

In the end, however, I do not remember Boss so much as a campus Stalinist leader as I remember her as an uninhibited, affectionate girl with a permanent, mischievous smile. She loved people and animals. I remember when I met her, she owned two cats. Above all, I remember her as someone who pushed the boundaries of social norms. Boss, for example, appeared in her own Occidental magazine, *Tattooed Lady,* as a tasteful nude in a manner that still reminds me of Gwyneth Paltrow in the film *Great Expectations.* Consistent with my circle of radical friends at Occidental, Boss enjoyed mixing Marxist feminist politics with art, literature, film, and photography. Accordingly, I am not surprised Maraniss indicates Boss was the model scout who introduced young Obama to Lisa Jack, the student photographer who captured him posing, Choom Gang–style, with a cigarette on his lips and a straw hat on his head.

I remember that my Marxist girlfriend was bookish but struggled in school. As I recall, she often failed to turn in papers on time and piled up a string of incompletes that would stretch out her undergraduate academic career. As I recall, she would take about five years to finish the normal four-year course at Occidental. She ended up being something of a perpetual student. Although I lost track of her whereabouts in 1982, I learned later that she earned an MS in Political Philosophy from the London School of Economics and then an MPhil in Politics from Columbia University. Given her educational experiences, it is not hard for me to imagine that Boss's intense interest in politics and colorful social life might have made for good reading in a more truthful version of *Dreams*.

Although I was thrown off by Obama's statement that Regina was "a big, dark woman," I had noticed highly significant traces of Boss in the character Regina. For example, she and I had both enjoyed—practically lived in—Occidental's on-campus coffee shop, The Cooler. As I recall, The Cooler was the center of our lives because you could eat there when you could not get a meal in the student union and because we could smoke our Marlboro Light cigarettes as we read books and sipped coffee. Like the character Regina, Boss expressed an exceptional interest in my graduate school papers, my reading assignments, and my future ambitions. Her overwhelming confidence in my future as a great scholar and as a revolutionary political leader was a striking contrast to my own family's lack of support. In retrospect, Boss's interest in my academic studies was particularly noteworthy since subsequent girlfriends displayed only bemused indifference to my research. (In spite of them, I ended up teaching at Williams College and winning the William Anderson Award from the American Political Science Association by the late 1980s.) Boss, as I recall, was the only person in my life to applaud my sense of mystic destiny. In one of the many effusive cards and letters she sent me, she wrote: "Go for greatness!"

Like the Boss I remember, the character Regina is highly curious about Obama's reading and academic work. Regina speaks in such an overwhelmingly encouraging and uplifting fashion that she seemingly transforms the young Obama. Referring to his heart-to-heart with Regina, Obama later writes: "Strange how a single conversation can change you" (*Dreams*, p. 105). I can report that those vignettes featuring Regina are an accurate echo of the curious, enthusiastic, and intellectually vibrant Boss I knew between 1979 and 1981.

In understanding Boss's role in *Dreams from My Father*, however, I think it is important to point out she was not at all a spoiled rich kid. Although she had her own car and could afford her own apartment, she did part-time work as a house cleaner. For example, I remember Boss had a job cleaning the home of one of Occidental College's political science professors, Jane Jacquette. In *Dreams from My Father*, Barack Obama makes a big deal about Regina being angered at the thoughtless mess Obama and his friends left behind for the maids to clean in their Haines Hall dormitory. I would not be surprised to learn Boss might have lectured Obama on the humanity of their maids and on the importance of not making fun of people like them, her, or her Swiss grandmother.

To continue my story, Boss made plans to spend the summer of 1980 with me at Cornell in Ithaca, New York. Her decision to follow me back to Cornell initially struck me as impulsive, even a little reckless. I was surprised when I saw her make it work. She was determined to bring both her cats with her too. One, however, ended up dying in front of us before we flew out of Los Angeles. We ended up bringing the remaining cat, Maddie, with us.

I believe I had a job that summer as a teaching assistant, leading discussion groups and grading papers in a political philosophy course. I remember she took a color theory class. Above all, it was a powerfully emotional summer, marked by intense overwhelming intimacy. I remember we got awfully close to creating a baby. As I recall, I had a moment of clarity which backed us off that high-dive platform and perhaps sent an unmistakable signal that our relationship was going to be temporary and not permanent. After that, the relationship was never as carefree or as spontaneous. In fact, we started to get a little cruel toward each other. I remember I unwisely introduced her to an extremely beautiful girl I had taken to dinner earlier in the year. Perhaps in retaliation, she expressed interest in an extremely bright, boyish, conservative, undergraduate science major who we both got to know over the summer.

After the summer courses were done, Boss decided to drive back to Occidental College with her friend Susan Keselenko. Keselenko had also met Barack Obama in the spring of 1980 at that same international relations class. It turned out that Keselenko was allergic to cats. She could not drive across the country with Maddie in the car. Somewhat abruptly, Caroline demanded immediate payment of her half of our rental deposit and left her cat in my care. The expectation is that I would bring her cat back with me when I returned to California. By the end of the summer, I was not sure where we stood, and she wrote a friend back at Cornell that she was "confused about John." In passionate relationships, I think the man is usually the first one in and the last one out. I suspect this was true of my love affair with Boss.

When I arrived back in northern California, Maddie in tow, I was startled to see Boss had lost so much weight. I thought maybe the distance between us had done her some damage and that she was not taking good care of herself. I was pleasantly surprised, however, by her renewed affection and the intensity of our physical attraction. It was not long, however, before I learned that I was not the only young man invited to spend time with Boss over the 1980 holiday season. As I later learned from Obama biographers, Boss had also invited both Barack Obama and his roommate Hasan Chandoo to stop by her house in Portola Valley. They were close-enough friends with her that they had presented her with cake in the college library to celebrate her birthday earlier that month.

When I first saw Obama, I remember I was standing on the porch of Boss's parents' impressive home as a sleek, expensive-looking, yellow Fiat 128S pulled up the driveway. It was mid-day when the two young men emerged from the vehicle. They were well-dressed and looked like they were born to wealth and privilege. I was a little surprised to learn they were Boss's friends from Occidental College until she articulated the underlying political connection. "They're on our side," she said. The taller of the two was Obama, then only nineteen, who towered over his 5'5" companion, Mohammed Hasan Chandoo—a wealthy, twenty-one-year-old Pakistani student. Chandoo had a full, dark-black, neatly trimmed moustache, and was dressed in expensive clothes. Nevertheless, Obama was the more handsome of the two. At 6'2", Obama carried himself with the dignity and poise of a model. The diminutive Chandoo, in contrast, came across as more of a practical, businessman type. I have often been asked what I thought when I first saw Barack Obama. I have always told the truth. I thought he was gay. I thought this because the two seemed so close to each other emotionally and physically. When I hang out with my male friends, we usually maintain a reasonable distance from each other. Obama and Chandoo, however, did not do that. They were so tightly in each other's space that they appeared to be a romantic couple. The initial sight of them together was so unusual that Boss told me, "They're not gay."

Chandoo was vaguely familiar to me as a participant in the earlier anti-apartheid rallies on the Occidental College campus. Young Obama, on the other hand, was completely new to me. We were inside the Boss's living room by the time the introductions took place.

"This is Barack Obama," Boss said.

Since I was not much taller than Chandoo, I remember I looked up at Obama as we shook hands. I was completely mystified by the pronunciation of his name. He did not put up a fight over it, however.

"You can call me Barry," Obama said.

In retrospect, one of the most interesting aspects of my introduction to Barack Obama is that it included absolutely no information about his parents, their occupations, or even their physical locations. While Joe Biden eagerly asserted he was the first "in a thousand generations" to graduate from college in homage to Kinnock, Barack Obama's ancestors were an irrelevant mystery. Nevertheless, during the introduction, Boss and Chandoo were eager to let me know that Obama was a graduate of the prestigious Punahou Academy, an elite prep school in Honolulu. I vividly remember that Chandoo was intensely proud of Obama's ties to Punahou. This prestige, however, was wasted on me. I had never heard of the school and did not have a clue about what it meant to be one of its graduates. Obama seemed embarrassed by the fuss. Boss, I remember, wanted to make sure I understood that young Obama was not merely an attractive socialite dabbling in Marxist theory. "You've worked with us," she reminded him. "You've been at our DSA meetings. You've been active in the anti-apartheid movement."

In contrast to the way Obama portrays himself in *Dreams from My Father*, the real young Obama struck me as an average white guy college student. He talked like a white guy. It never occurred to me to think of young Obama as African American. After all, the African American students at Occidental College were largely uninvolved in radical campus politics. They were more likely to be active in the Gospel choir than in the Democrat Socialist Alliance. Instead, young Obama seemed more like a foreign prince visiting the United States. Above all, he did not have any of the hostility to whites that I sometimes noticed among black students at Occidental College.

After a while, all six of us—the four students and Boss's adoptive parents—drove in two cars to a local restaurant for lunch. The owner knew Boss's father. The food was delicious, the setting spectacularly "California casual," with tall redwood trees all around. At the restaurant, we six continued our talk. Chandoo was quiet, less forceful, and deferential to Obama. Obama was polite to Boss's parents, calm, and distinguished in his manner. Mr. Boss disapproved of his daughter's radical perspective and could barely disguise his contempt for me.

Despite the recent election of Ronald Reagan, the focus of our discussion was on El Salvador and Latin America. I remember I was especially angry about what was happening in El Salvador, particularly the recent rape and murder of four American nuns and a laywoman. We also discussed the recent assassination of John Lennon in New York City. After lunch, the entourage returned to the Boss's home in Portola Valley. Mr. Boss took an interest in the yellow Fiat 128S.

"That's an impressive car. Which one of you is the owner?" he asked.

"It's mine," said Chandoo, graciously adding: "Would you like to see it?"

While Chandoo and Mr. Boss gave Chandoo's yellow Fiat a once over, the rest of us engaged in small talk until Chandoo returned. Chandoo beamed smugly, having impressed Boss's father with his expensive car. Inside the house, Mrs. Boss prepared snacks for everyone. All four of us lit up after-dinner cigarettes in the dining room. Boss sat at the head of the table to my left. Obama sat directly across from me. Chandoo sat on the other side of the table on Obama's left. Naturally, our conversation gravitated toward the coming revolution. I expected that my undergraduate friends would be interested in hearing my latest take on contemporary Marxist thought. I was in for quite a shock.

My graduate studies that fall had tempered my earlier Marxism with a more realistic perspective. I thought a revolution was not in the cards anymore. There was no inevitability, in my mind, to the old idea that the proletariat would rise up and overthrow the ruling class. Now, the idea that we could entirely eliminate the profit motive from an advanced industrialized economy seemed like a childhood fantasy. The future, I now thought, would belong to nations with mixed economic systems— like those in Europe—where there was government planning of the economy, combined with a greater effort to produce a more equitable distribution of wealth. Above all, it made more sense to me to focus on elections rather than on preparing for a coming revolution.

Boss and Obama, however, had a starkly different view. They believed that the economic stresses of the Carter years meant revolution was still imminent. The election of Reagan was simply a minor setback in terms of the coming revolution. As I recall, Obama repeatedly used the phrase "When the revolution comes . . ." In my mind, I remember thinking that Obama was blindly sticking to the simple Marxist theory that had characterized my own views while I was an undergraduate at Occidental College. "There's going to be a revolution," Obama said. "We need to be organized and grow the movement." In Obama's view, our role must be to educate others so that we might usher in more quickly this inevitable revolution.

I know this may be implausible to some readers, but I distinctly remember Obama surprising me by bringing up Frantz Fanon and colonialism. He impressed me with his knowledge of these two topics, topics which were not among my strong points—or of overwhelming concern to me. Boss and Obama seemed to think their ideological purity was a persuasive argument in predicting that a coming revolution would end capitalism. While I felt I was doing them a favor by providing them with the latest research, I saw I was in danger of being cast as a reactionary who did not grasp the nuances of international Marxist theory.

Chandoo let Boss and Obama take the crux of the argument to me. Chandoo, in fact, seemed chagrined by the level of disagreement in the group. I cannot remember him making any significant comments during this discussion.

Drawing on the history of Western Europe, I responded it was unrealistic to think the working class would ever overthrow the capitalist system. As I recall, Obama reacted harshly to my critique, saying: "That's crazy!"

Since Boss and Obama had injected theory into our debate, I reacted by going historical. As best I can recreate the argument, I responded by critiquing their perspective with the fresh insight I had gained from my recent reading of Barrington Moore's book, *Social Origins of Dictatorship and Democracy* (1966).[1] Moore had argued that a Russian- or Chinese-style revolution—leading to communism—was only possible in an agrarian society with a weak or nonexistent middle-class or bourgeoisie.

Since I was a Marxist myself at the time, and had studied variations in Marxist theory, I can state that everything I heard Obama argue that evening was consistent with Marxist philosophy, including the ideas that class struggle was leading to an inevitable revolution and that an elite group of revolutionaries was needed to lead the effort. If he had not been a true Marxist-Leninist, I would have noticed and remembered. I can still, with some degree of ideological precision, identify which students at Occidental College were radicals (or perhaps enemies of the Constitution) and which ones were not. I can do the same thing for the Occidental College professors at that time. By the time the debate came to an end, Obama—although not Boss—was making peace, agreeing with the facts I had laid out, and demonstrating an apparent agreement with my more realistic perspective. Had I really persuaded him, or was he just making nice to smooth things over with a new friend? With the advantage of objectivity, David Garrow interviewed all the participants in that evening's debate and concluded that Obama had "shifted to downplay their degree of disagreement, conceding that there was validity to some of Drew's points."

My memory, however, is much more dramatic because as I see it, there was only one point at stake—revolution or no revolution. As I recall the scene, I remember Obama surrendering to my argument, including signaling to the somewhat bewildered Chandoo—through his voice and body language—that the argument had concluded and had been decided in my favor. Soon, Chandoo and Obama left for another appointment, either in Palo Alto or San Francisco. In retrospect, Obama had proved to me that he was indeed, as Boss had promised, "on our side." At the time, I had the impression that I might have been one of the first to directly challenge Obama's Marxist-Leninist mindset and to successfully introduce him to a more practical view that saw politics, rather than revolution, as the preferred route to socialism.

I remember that Obama was friendly to me on at least six more occasions over the next several months. For example, Boss and I visited the apartment he shared with Chandoo. I spoke with him again on campus in the student union. I saw him on campus in The Cooler—the school's coffee and sandwich shop. I also spoke with him at a large outdoor party at his apartment complex. As best I can recall, I also hung out with him at a special event featuring the social activist comedian Dick Gregory. I certainly considered him a friend, a confidant, and a political ally in the larger struggle against poverty and oppressive social systems.

Whatever progress I made with Obama that evening, the price of our debate was an ideological wedge between me and Boss and a further decline in our relationship that would officially end in January 1981. As I recall, the split was painful enough to cause us to temporarily adopt the roles of imaginary divorce lawyers who combed through our conflicting feelings and amicably laid out the details of what became our eventual, imperfect separation. I knew the relationship was unsustainable, despite my intense love for her, because I placed the highest possible priority on my academic success. I remember both of us tearfully saying goodbye at Los Angeles International Airport. I remember she looked crushed, absolutely heart-broken. I left with the impression that I would probably never see or hear from her again.

Nevertheless, she surprised me one evening by giving me a phone call and asking me to listen to a new song, Grover Washington Jr.'s "The Two of Us." I remember thinking she sounded tired or drunk or high during the call. Later, when I was back in California to spend time with my family in May of 1981, she called out of the blue again. She asked me to join her at Occidental for the purpose of helping her finish her term papers. Without this assistance, she feared she would not be allowed to graduate with her class. Although I ended up living with her again for a few weeks prior to her graduation, I never implemented the anticipated academic rescue mission. Later, I found she had gotten an extension on her term paper deadlines. She would be allowed to graduate with her class. Instead of writing papers, we resumed our prior intimate relationship sans our prior romantic commitment. I remember her scolding me for buying her a rose to cheer her up, saying, "It's just all wrong."

At another party at another house closer to Oxy and nearer to Boss's graduation, I remember asking Barack Obama why she seemed so distant and frustrated in June 1981. I sincerely assumed she had developed a drug or emotional problem. I made a mistake of asking the question while we were chatting with his friends. I remember he surprised me again with a flash of anger and irritation. He said, enigmatically, that "Caroline is the sort of girl who needs a lot of attention."

After it was clear that Boss and I were through, I engaged in some unseemly revenge flirting. I remember a trip to Disneyland where I flaunted my new freedom by entertaining a group of younger Oxy coeds. I remember I turned around and noticed Boss and Tom Grauman—her future husband—playfully whispering behind my back. One of the new girls I found attractive was a sophomore from New York City, named Alex McNear. I traded addresses and phone numbers with her and left for an internship in Washington, DC, with the expectation that she and I would meet again in New York. What I did not know is that both Obama and Grauman had been interested in McNear. What I could not have known was that a year later, she and Obama would begin what appears to be his first, serious intimate relationship.

I recalled my interest in McNear because David Garrow wrote that he was in possession of a copy of a letter I wrote to her. According to Garrow, she kept almost everything from her college days. As I recall, I contacted her through social media, and she informed me that the letter was real and that it had been "innocent." Later, Garrow graciously sent me a copy. It included my apology to McNear for not stopping off in New York to visit her and some details regarding my summer internship in Washington, DC, with the leftist economist Gar Alperwitz at The National Center for Economic Alternatives. Ironically, McNear's uncanny commitment to archiving old correspondence was not matched with an equally intense commitment to full disclosure. She artfully kept from Garrow a startling portion of a letter in which the young Obama discusses his sexual interest in other men. He wrote: "You see, I make love to men daily, but in the imagination. My mind is androgynous to a great extent, and I hope to make it more so." While McNear's redaction of Obama's letter kept this inflammatory content out of the hardcover edition of Garrow's 2017 book, *Rising Star,* it nevertheless helps validate my own first impressions of Obama's sexual orientation.

As I recall the awful beauty and often cringe-worth realities of Occidental College in the early 1980s, I ask myself why would Obama delete someone who was so memorable and important to his life as

Caroline Boss from his autobiography and replace her with a big, dark composite character from Chicago?

As a political scientist, I think the best theory is that my girlfriend's story would not have scored him any points among his anticipated black constituents in Chicago. Acknowledging the influence of a white, Swiss-American girl would have called attention to Obama's politically incorrect attachments to a series of other wealthy white females including Alexandra McNear and later Genevieve Cook, his girlfriend at Columbia prior to his arrival in Chicago as a community organizer. Ultimately, I think the story of the real, white Regina would confront black readers with the uncomfortable, politically incorrect realities of the real young Obama, particularly his indifference to developing intimate relationships with black girls, prior to meeting Michelle.

As a recurring character in the story of young Obama, I was close enough to him and his friends to observe that he was nothing like the lifelong, pragmatic centrist that he was pretending to be in the 2008 presidential campaign. The young Obama I knew expressed a profound commitment to bringing about a socialist economic system in the US— an economic system completely divorced from the profit motive. This would occur in his lifetime through a potentially violent, communist-style revolution. In this context, I see my report on young Obama and his social milieu as a small, but highly significant data point, a data point which suggests a profound continuity in his anti-American views.

While my report on the ideological beliefs of the young Obama gravely contradicts the self-portrait he carefully crafted for public consumption, its greatest significance may lie in reminding voters of uncomfortable truths about the dangerous and unpleasant aspects of the Democrat party. It may, for example, help us better understand Joe Biden's own ties to radical Communists and his surprising comfort with the communist party elites in China. In this context, all my report can do is toss more increasingly pricy gasoline on the fire. After all, the Barack Obama I met in the Portola Valley in 1980 was a Marxist ideologue who would have been quite comfortable in the company of communist party members like Frank Marshall Davis, Marxist revolutionary students like Caroline Boss, committed socialist politicians like Illinois State Senator Alice Palmer, or—worst of all—retired domestic terrorists like Bill Ayers.

John C. Drew, PhD, is an award-winning political scientist featured in the documentary film, The Enemies Within *(2016). He is an author, trainer, and consultant in the field of grant-writing and program evaluation. He has raised over $54 million for charities and higher education.*

2

THE MARXIST ORIGINS AND GOALS
OF OBAMACARE

by Trevor Loudon

LOOKING BACK, President Barack Obama's legacy rests more than anything else on his signature Patient Protection and Affordable Care Act, widely known as "Obamacare"—and it wasn't even his idea. One recalls Obama's unforgettable line: "you didn't build that"—meaning that businesspeople owed their success to the social infrastructure built by the community as a collective whole.[1] Well, Obama didn't "build" Obamacare either. He was merely a vehicle for changes planned decades earlier. While its critics often derided Obamacare as a step toward "socialism," many on the Left have consistently ridiculed that idea. They were either badly mistaken or lying. Obamacare was a "designed to fail" step on the road to fully government-run healthcare. It pushed the boundaries of what was politically possible at the time and laid the groundwork for a fully socialized system in the future.

The move toward socialized healthcare under Obama has yet to be fully resolved. As Obamacare has proven hugely costly and inefficient, the Left has mounted a predictable campaign to push for fully government-controlled healthcare and the ending of private health insurance. They call it "Medicare for All." When Congresswoman Pramila Jayapal (D-WA) announced the launch of H.R.1384, "Medicare for All," on the Capitol steps on February 27, 2019, it was in fact a major step toward government healthcare and a socialist America. Jayapal was surrounded by more than 100 supporters, many from groups, such as National Nurses United, the Center for Popular Democracy, Our Revolution, Coalition of Labor Union Women, and the Labor Campaign for Single Payer.[2] All of the organizations represented or were at least heavily influenced by the Democratic Socialists of America (DSA). This overtly Marxist organization can quite rightly claim credit for both inspiring Obamacare and instigating the socialist Medicare for All movement, now building steam across the United States.

For decades, even most Democratic representatives shied away from any mention of government-run healthcare. But now, more than 100 Democratic congressmembers have signed on to a Medicare for All bill that would eventually eliminate the private health insurance industry. This would give the federal government near total control over every citizen's (and non-citizen's) healthcare.

What happened to cause such a massive shift?

MEET QUENTIN YOUNG

The roots of Medicare for All can be traced back to the 1930s in South Side Chicago, when a young Hyde Park High School student named Quentin Young first joined the Young Communist League.[3] Young was such a dedicated activist that he soon worked at the national level. In 1938, he was listed as a member of the National Executive Committee of the communist-dominated American Student Union.[4] After World War II, Young graduated from Northwestern Medical School and served his residency at Cook County Hospital in Chicago. Young joined the American Medical Association and served as chairman of the Department of Internal Medicine at Cook County, where he helped establish the Department of Occupational Medicine. Later, Young became a clinical professor of Preventive Medicine and Community Health at the University of Illinois Medical Center and senior attending physician at Michael Reese Hospital. In 1997, Young was inducted as a master of the American College of Physicians, and in 1998, he served as president of the American Public Health Association.[5]

Parallel to his solid medical career, Young remained close to the Communist Party for decades. In 1968, he refused to answer when the House Un-American Activities Committee accused him of membership in the Bethune Club, a Communist Party group for medical practitioners at Cook County Hospital.[6] Around the same time Young also served as president of the Medical Committee for Human Rights, one of the first American socialized-medicine advocacy groups in the modern era.[7] Young also helped to establish health clinics for the Marxist Black Panther Party and their equally militant allies in the mainly Puerto Rican activist group, the Young Lords.[8]

In 1970, Young served on the board of the communist-controlled Chicago Committee to Defend the Bill of Rights, alongside his old American Student Union friend, Milt Cohen, and several other well-known Communist Party USA members including Ben Green, Ernest DeMaio, Jesse Prosten, and Jack Spiegel.[9]

ENTER THE DEMOCRATIC SOCIALISTS OF AMERICA

In the early 1980s, Young, like many communists and socialists, migrated to the newly-formed DSA, which is now this country's largest Marxist organization. DSA would remain Young's political home until his death in March 2016.[10] In 1987, Young co-founded Physicians for a National Health Program (PNHP), which now has more than 17,000 members across the United States.[11] Under Young's long-term leadership, the heavily DSA-infiltrated PNHP became the major driving force behind the campaign for "single-payer" or socialized medicine in the United States. According to PNHP's website:

> Our members and physician activists work toward a single-payer national health program in their communities. PNHP performs ground-breaking research on the health crisis and the need for fundamental reform, coordinates speakers and forums, participates in town hall meetings and debates, contributes scholarly articles to peer-reviewed medical journals, and appears regularly on national television and news programs advocating for a single-payer system.
>
> PNHP is the only national physician organization in the United States dedicated exclusively to implementing a single-payer national health program.[12]

PHNP was only part of the DSA campaign for socialized healthcare. Los Angeles physician Steve Tarzynski, then a member of the DSA National Political Committee and chair of the DSA National Health Care Task Force, wrote in the January/February 1994 edition of the DSA magazine *Democratic Left*:

> We've met some of the modest goals that the national leadership set when DSA decided to make support for a single-payer Canadian-style health care system our major issue.
>
> DSA members have served on the Clinton Health Care Task Force and in the leadership and rank and file of national and state single-payer coalitions. Perhaps most importantly, in 1991, we organized a 22-city national tour of over forty Canadian health experts (from our sibling party, the New Democrats) that helped to galvanize the single-payer movement into action. No other organization was in a position to carry out such a major tour. We have done a good job as the socialist current within the single-payer movement, but still have

significant opportunities to improve DSA locals' level of activism and our recruitment of activists into DSA through this issue.

The most delicate aspect of our work is how we balance our efforts in improving the Clinton proposal and pushing for single-payer. This is not a new dilemma for the left. The tension between reform and revolution has existed within every socialist movement in Western industrialized democracies. It will always be with us. The solution lies in putting into practice Michael Harrington's notion of "visionary gradualism."[13]

Hillary Clinton's health reforms eventually failed, but the DSA refused to give up. The comrades pushed more initiatives through allies in Congress, such as Representative John Conyers (D-MI) and Senators Bernie Sanders (I-VT) and Ted Kennedy (D-MA).

According to the summer 2009 edition of *Democratic Left:*

DSA reaffirms its support for single-payer health insurance as the most just, cost-effective and rational method for creating a universal health care system in the United States.

In the House of Representatives, John Conyers has introduced H.R.676, the Expanded and Improved Medicare for All Act. This bill has 77 co-sponsors. In the Senate, Bernie Sanders has introduced S.703, the American Health Security Act of 2009. His bill has not yet attracted co-sponsors.

These two pieces of legislation take different approaches to universal health insurance, but both take for-profit insurance companies out of the picture.

DSA asks our locals to contact their senators and representatives and encourage them to co-sponsor these bills if they have not already done so.[14]

During Obama's first campaign for the presidency, DSA worked hard to corral every union, religious organization, medical pressure group, political lobby group, and congressmember within their sphere of influence behind the push for single-payer.

In 2007 Michael Lighty, a former DSA National Director, and then Director of Public Policy for the California Nurses Association, wrote in DSA's *Democratic Left*:

There's a growing movement for single-payer universal healthcare. The movement is led by activists in Healthcare-Now!, doctors in the Physicians for a National Health Program, nurses in the California Nurses Association, leaders in labor unions such as United Steelworkers of America and Communication Workers of America, activists in the Progressive Democrats of America, and Congressman John Conyers, with the support for HR 676 by 300 union locals, 75 Central Labor Councils, and 25 state Federations of Labor, and hundreds of clergy and faith-based organizations, as well as civil rights, women's and healthcare advocacy groups in the Leadership Conference for Guaranteed Healthcare.

The policy proposals developed by Beltway think tanks and the principles for reform adopted by the AFL-CIO confer support for single-payer while allowing for private insurance-based approaches as well. Other bills in Congress, notably sponsored by Ted Kennedy and John Dingell and "Americare" introduced by Pete Stark, seek to incrementally establish a single-payer system.[15]

Meanwhile, Young used his personal charm and connections to further the socialized healthcare cause.

QUENTIN YOUNG AND THE YOUNG OBAMA

Fortuitously, Young just happened to be a longtime friend and political mentor to Obama.

Obama was the patient of Young's practice partner, Dr. David Scheiner, for twenty years.[16] Young was even at the infamous meeting in the Hyde Park home of former Weather Underground terrorists Bill Ayers and Bernardine Dohrn, where Obama famously launched his political career.

According to Politico:

"I can remember being one of a small group of people who came to Bill Ayers' house to learn that Alice Palmer was stepping down from the senate and running for Congress," said Dr. Quentin Young, a prominent Chicago physician and advocate for single-payer health care, of the informal gathering at the home of Ayers and his wife, Dohrn. "[Palmer] identified [Obama] as her successor."

Obama and Palmer "were both there" he said.[17]

On March 5, 2000, Obama received the endorsement of former congressman, White House counsel and DSA supporter Abner Mikva, former Chicago alderman, former Socialist Party USA member Leon Despres, and Young, an "advocate for universal health" care in his unsuccessful bid to unseat incumbent US Rep. Bobby Rush.[18]

Young is happy to claim credit for introducing the future president to the concept of socialized healthcare. From his March 2009 interview with *Democracy Now!* host Amy Goodman:

Goodman: You've been a longtime friend of Barack Obama.

Young: Yeah.

Goodman: "How has he changed over the years?

Young: Well, Barack Obama, as we know, was a community organizer, a very lofty calling, in my book, and he made the decision, when the opportunity came, that he could get more done politically, and he accepted the nomination for the seat in the state Senate. It's not that long ago, really. It's about six, eight years ago.

Barack Obama, in those early days—influenced, I hope, by me and others—categorically said single payer was the best way, and he would inaugurate it if he could get the support, meaning majorities in both houses, which he's got, and the presidency, which he's got. And he said that on more than one occasion, and it represented the very high-grade intelligence we all know Barack has.[19]

Obamacare was certainly not single-payer. It was an incremental, halfway measure that satisfied few on the left and drove health insurance costs through the roof. According to the website Corporate Crime Reporter, Young was disappointed with what his protégé managed to achieve:

> "I knew him before he was political," Young says of Obama. "I supported him when he ran for state Senate. When he was a state senator, he did say that he supported single payer. Now, he hedges. Now he says, if we were starting from scratch, he would support single payer."
>
> "Barack's a smart man," Young says. "He probably calculated the political cost for being for single payer—the shower of opposition from the big boys—the drug companies and the health insurance companies. And so, like the rest of them, he fashioned a hodge podge of a health insurance plan."
>
> "And the problem with the hodge podge is that it keeps the insurance companies in the mix," Young said. "And the insurance companies cannot be part of the solution because they are part of the problem. And so, in terms of getting single payer passed, Obama is now part of the problem."[20]

Bruce Dixon of Black Agenda Report was also disappointed with Obama's back-down on fully socialized healthcare:

> Back in the late 1990s, when he was an Illinois State Senator representing a mostly black district on the south side of Chicago, Obama took pains to consistently identify himself publicly with his neighbor Dr. Quentin Young.

He signed on as co-sponsor of the Bernardin Amendment, named after Chicago's late Catholic Archbishop, who championed the public policy idea that medical care was a human right, not a commodity. At that time, when it was to his political advantage, Obama didn't mind at all being perceived as an advocate of single payer. During his days in the Illinois State Senate, Obama was an advocate of universal medical coverage as a human right. But as Senator and presidential candidate, Obama has devolved into the timid and calculating creature we see today.[21]

THE JOHN MCDONOUGH CONNECTION

Young was not the only leading DSA comrade to play a role in the implementation of Obamacare. John McDonough is a professor of public health practice at the Harvard School of Public Health and director of the new HSPH Center for Public Health Leadership.[22] For many years, he had also been a leader of the Boston Democratic Socialist Organizing Committee, the forerunner of DSA.[23]

Between 2003 and 2008, he served as executive director of Health Care for All, Massachusetts's leading consumer health advocacy organization, where he played a key role in passage and implementation of the 2006 Massachusetts health reform law, otherwise known as "Romneycare." He was also an "architect" of Obamacare. [24]

In McDonough's words: "I helped craft and pass Massachusetts health reform in 2006 and the Affordable Healthcare Act in 2010."[25]

So, Young inspired Obamacare, and McDonough helped design it. Both were members of a Marxist organization of less than 10,000 members nationwide. When it comes to revolution, numbers are of minor importance. It's influence and access that makes the difference.

PLANNED TO FAIL?

There is no doubt that the single-payer movement wants a socialist America. In 2005, Young and several PHNP activists spent ten days in Cuba, studying the communist-run nation's socialized healthcare system. The delegation met with health ministry officials and visited the range of healthcare facilities from the community and family clinics to the largest hospitals. They also met with medical students from the US attending the Latin American School of Medicine in Havana, many of them the sons and daughters of American communists.[26] However, Young and others on the left have expressed concern at the mishmash that is Obamacare. It is far from the single-payer, completely government-controlled system that they envisaged.

Obamacare is limping along, just popular enough to prevent the Republicans from abolishing it but also beset with spiraling cost increases and big coverage gaps. Obamacare seems likely to eventually collapse under its own weight. But was that, perhaps, the plan all along? Gerald Friedman is a Massachusetts labor economist, and as a Boston DSA member, a longtime comrade of Obamacare "architect" McDonough.[27] Writing in DSA's *Democratic Left* in October 2013, Friedman explained that when Obamacare inevitably failed, fully socialized healthcare would become the next option:

> After a century of struggle, the ACA [Affordable Care Act] commits the United States to providing universal access to health care. This is a great achievement, one to be treasured and nurtured.
>
> Now the real fight begins, to turn this commitment into a reality that the ACA itself cannot produce. Barack Obama was right the first time: only a single-payer program can provide universal coverage, and only a single-payer program can control costs. The ACA may be the last bad idea that Americans try; after it fails, we will finally do the right thing: single-payer health insurance.[28]

Friedman was even more explicit in an address to a PNHP branch in Seattle on May 4, 2013. Friedman first assured the audience that he was a big fan of the president: "The other day I showed up in my Obama shirt . . . I love the man . . . I admit it. Half my friends have jobs in the administration and council of economic advisors." Then he went on tell the audience what he really loved about Obamacare:

There's a lot I like in the law. The thing I most like about it is that it makes promises it can't realize . . . so in a couple of years you're going to have an opportunity to really do something.

They're going to give those exchanges a chance. They're going to try this thing and then it's going to fail. Because it can't succeed. The White House doesn't even say it will succeed . . .

It commits the United States to universal coverage, but the White House admits that it will not cover everybody.

There will be 20 million people left out and what's worse the uninsured will go up. The number of uninsured will rise, starting after 2017.

So what happens then? "And in 10 years we have to be ready with a single-payer plan."[29]

Which is exactly why, as healthcare costs skyrocket, DSA and many Democratic representatives are now promoting Medicare for All—a single-payer plan.

WILL OBAMACARE DESTROY AMERICAN FREEDOM?

A few thousand DSA Marxists, working through the unions, the Democratic Party, and with former President Obama have almost succeeded in destroying the world's greatest healthcare system. Now they stand ready, as soon as they can regain control of the Senate and the White House, to impose fully socialized, Cuban-style healthcare on every American. That's where the United States is now. The DSA and its friends in Congress have so butchered the finest health system in the world and have driven affordable care beyond the reach of millions of Americans that government-run healthcare now looks like a viable option to many. If Obamacare is not repealed and the country returned to more market-driven healthcare soon, socialized medicine will inevitably prevail. Under Obama, the Democrats proved their willingness to weaponize the Justice Department, the FBI, and the IRS against their opponents.

To those who argue that if Americans don't like single-payer then they should protest and demand it be abolished, I say this: who among you will stand against a government that has the power to deny your bowel cancer operation, your spouse's hip replacement, or your grand-daughter's lifesaving bone marrow transplant? Socialized healthcare is the single best way to usher in complete control of the population. According to National Organization of Women founding-activist-turned-Conservative Mallory Millett, "The very first thing that anybody does when they want to Marxify a nation is universal healthcare. Because from that moment on, everybody in that nation belongs to the state."[30]

While President Donald J. Trump worked to repeal some elements of Obamacare, much more needs to be done. President Biden has shown no inclination to do this. In fact, it's probably fair to say that Biden's heavy-handed Covid vaccine mandates have only been made possible because of the much greater state involvement in the health sector since the advent of Obamacare. If Obama's legacy is not completely reversed, and genuine free-market reforms implemented in its place, socialized healthcare will be institutionalized—and that will be the end of the great American experiment.

Trevor Loudon is an author, filmmaker, and public speaker from Christchurch, New Zealand. For more than thirty years, he has researched radical left, Marxist, and terrorist movements and their covert influence on mainstream politics. His latest book is White House Reds.

3

MUSLIM BROTHERHOOD'S PENETRATION OF THE US UNDER OBAMA

by Stephen C. Coughlin

If it is possible, the practice of Countering Violent Extremism (CVE) is even more of a national security disaster than the theory. This is probably best documented by Stephen Coughlin in a recent and essential book: Catastrophic Failure: Blindfolding America in the Face of Jihad. *Apart from being an exceptional lawyer, Coughlin is a trained military intelligence officer who has studied sharia supremacism closely.* Catastrophic Failure *is about how the United States government has systematically stifled the study of this doctrine since before 9/11. CVE is the paragon illustration of how the Obama administration has exacerbated this catastrophic failure that is referred to a "willful blindness" in my memoir. As Coughlin demonstrates, "CVE is no secret. For example, the Department of Homeland Security's Office for Civil Rights and Civil Liberties—which is every bit as radical as the infamous Civil Rights Division in the Obama Justice Department was—has worked with the National Counterterrorism Center to develop government agency training programs that "bring together best [CVE] practices."*

ANDREW C. MCCARTHY
Testimony, Senate Judiciary Committee Subcommittee on Oversight, Agency Action, Federal Rights and Federal Courts, June 28, 2016:

> So, I can understand what the FBI sometimes believes when I said there are cases they got wrong, dead wrong. Many times, and that's owing to civil rights groups like CAIR and the MLFA and others who were able to stop Islamophobes giving lectures and workshops and training to our FBI agents. That's wrong, and we've been able to stop them and tell the leadership. And I have to thank the leadership of the FBI because they did stop and cancel those training once we told them that those are Islamophobes, you cannot have them train FBI agents who are going to investigate us.

OUSSAMA JAMMAL
Secretary General, US Council of Muslim Organizations (USCMO)
Director, Muslim American Society (MAS)—Public Affairs and Civic Engagement
President, The Mosque Foundation
Speech at "FBI Inventing Terrorists Through Entrapment" Forum
MAS ICNA Convention, Chicago, December 28, 2019

> "Show me the man and I'll find you the crime."

LAVRENTIY BERIA
Marshall of the Soviet Union
(and Stalin's Henchman)

Living the purge—not loving it.[1]

INTRODUCTION

From October 2011 to July 2012, the Obama administration undertook a purge of counterterrorism professionals. "Wait! Purge? What purge?" you ask. Well, the purge that transitioned the counterterror effort from fact-based threat analysis to the enforcement of Muslim Brotherhood–inspired narratives. The purge supported the administration's effort to transition America's national security focus from threats in support of the counterterror effort to that of enforcing the mindlessly seditious *Countering Violent Extremism* (*CVE*) memes. It certainly happened. When asked at a House Judiciary Committee hearing, then-FBI Director Robert Mueller testified that there was a purge but that it wasn't that big.[2] He is the same Mueller who ran the "special" investigation on Russian collusion that was designed to undermine the Trump administration.

The purge foreshadowed the extralegal active-measures[3] campaign run by the same deep state[4] actors and "progressive" media that orchestrated Russia-Gate in the Trump administration and continues today under the Biden administration with the *faux* January 6 Uprising narrative. Taking stock of the prominent roles senior national security leaders played, including former CIA Director John Brennan in *Crossfire Hurricane*,[5] it is clear that "we, the purged," never had a chance. It was a successful mass line attack that sought the destruction of professional counterterror professionals for doing their jobs. It made a mockery of their constitutional protections. Skeptical? Let's take a look.

THE CVE DERACINATES INTELLIGENCE

The purge imposed the *CVE*. While this paper will not get into the details of the *CVE*, a few aspects are on point to the purge.[6] The term for separating something from its native environment is "deracination."[7] What is worse: that the counterterror community allowed the *CVE* to deracinate the counterterror mission from its essential national security purpose, or that nobody in that community seems aware that it did? As with all national security activities, true counterterror efforts are based on identifying, recognizing, and analyzing people, places, things, doctrines, and ideologies. The *CVE* deracinates the counterterror collection effort from reality-based analysis while tying that effort to complexity narratives designed to transition analysts from a reality-based to a pseudoreality-based orientation. The *CVE* has not lost its relevance over time. In June 2021, the Biden administration's *National Strategy for Countering Domestic Terrorism* is steeped in the language of *CVE*, using the term "violent extremist" twenty-three times while not mentioning ISIS or jihad (or Antifa) once.[8]

THE PURGE

The purge was launched when Farhana Khera posted her October 19, 2011, *Letter to John Brennan* ("*Khera Letter*") demanding a "review of trainers and training materials," a "purge" of those materials, and "mandatory re-training."[9] At the time, Khera was president and executive director of *Muslim Advocates,* while Brennan was the assistant to the president (Obama) for Homeland Security and Counterterrorism—assistant national security advisor. While *Muslim Advocates'* tagline, "Freedom and Justice for All,"[10] evokes "Liberty and Justice for All" among the unsuspecting, it is a Muslim Brotherhood designation.[11] Of course, the *Muslim Advocates'* tagline is *Milestones*-esque in resonating Sayyid Qutb's "freedom from the laws of man, justice according to shariah."[12]

Khera's letter was signed by the same organizations that a federal court successfully identified as Muslim Brotherhood just a few years earlier,[13] most notably through a document entered into evidence, popularly known as the "Explanatory Memorandum,"[14] that included the Islamic Society of North America (ISNA), the Muslim Students Association (MSA), the Council on American-Islamic Relations (CAIR), and the Islamic Circle of North America (ICNA). Brennan's response to Khera was light speed as government action letters go. In his response, Brennan agreed with Khera. He committed that the "White House [would] immediately create an interagency task force to address the problem."[15] Thus began the systematic purge of personnel and products that the Muslim Brotherhood deemed "biased, false, and highly offensive."[16] These charges lead to the suspension of professional counterterror analysis and its replacement by *faux CVE* narratives. The "purged" were never allowed to defend themselves or their work product—no due process. They were not even allowed to know who their accusers were, not to mention being able to confront them.[17] With Brennan's concurrence, careers and professional reputations were targeted for attack and left in ruins.

This paper will discuss the Muslim Brotherhood's influence in the Pentagon in light of my purge experience during the Obama administration. Recognizing the Muslim Brotherhood's preference for destroying America through "civilizational jihad by [our] hands,"[18] that is, by getting Americans to undermine our national security on their behalf, it should come as no surprise that most of my experiences came at the hands of deep-state actors and committed "progressives" operating through a united front.[19] This paper will focus on two clusters—they are not exhaustive:

1. Pre-Purge activity leading to the development of the *CVE* as the replacement narrative to *bona fide* counterterror efforts in tandem with escalating media support; and

2. The execution of the purge.

1. PRE-PURGE ACTIVITY

Pre-purge activity refers to the development and preparation of the *CVE* in anticipation of the purge and those efforts that logically precede the purge while simultaneously also running concurrently with it.

Pre-purge activity can be traced to a January 2010 exchange of e-mails that a *Judicial Watch FOIA* made public. In these e-mails, Kareem Shora provided the attendance list for a January 28, 2010, Homeland Security Advisory Council (HSAC) meeting. Mr. Shora was the Senior Policy

Advisor, US Department of Homeland Security (DHS), Office of Civil Rights and Civil Liberties (CRCL). Fashioning *CVE* narratives was the focus of these meetings. Individuals from the Muslim Brotherhood and associated Islamic movement organizations were overrepresented in these meetings.[20] Khera was on the HSAC advisor list. The January 2010 meeting was followed in May 2010 with a "*Countering Violent Extremism (CVE) Working Group*" meeting of the HSAC in which, again, the Muslim Brotherhood and associated Islamic movement organizations were well represented.[21] Looking back, an Islamic movement presence at DHS seems to have been institutionalized. Less than a month after President Biden took office, on February 11, 2021, the US Council of Muslim Organizations (USCMO)[22] co-sponsored a DHS/FEMA Nonprofit Security Grant Program (NSGP) Information event[23] with Secure Community Network,[24] an organization run by Michael Masters, former vice president of *The Soufan Group*.[25]

DHS CRCL has been at the center of the *CVE* effort from the beginning. As the *CVE* approached readiness later in 2010, the low-level complaints of biased "extremism" in training programs raised by organizations like the Muslim Public Affairs Council (MPAC)[26] began giving way to pre-operational narratives in advance of their release. On July 15, 2011, Secretary of State Hillary Clinton met with the General Secretary of the Organization of Islamic Cooperation (the OIC) in Istanbul, Turkey. At that meeting, Secretary Clinton committed to curbing the speech of American citizens through "old fashioned techniques of peer pressure and shaming so that people don't feel that they have the support to do what we abhor" should those Americans exercise their First Amendment right.[27] In other words, the secretary of state committed to suppressing the free speech rights of American citizens on behalf of a foreign supra-state actor.

Clinton's commitment was followed by a coordinated information campaign that interlaced "*exposés*" on "bigoted" counterterror trainers from "progressive" news outlets alongside *CAIR* press releases demanding that action be taken based on those "exposés." This began with a July 18, 2011, *NPR* article by Dina Temple-Raston titled "Terrorism Training Casts Pall over Muslim Employee"[28] that was immediately followed by a CAIR demand that the CIA drop a trainer from its upcoming conference.[29] As Temple-Raston concluded:

> Omari filed suit last week against the Ohio Department of Public Safety and several individuals for wrongful dismissal. He said he'd love to get his job back. And the trainers who came to the Columbus police department? One of them is scheduled to hold another training session in August at the CIA. [30]

I was the trainer who *CAIR* wanted dropped. Omari attended the Spring 2010 *Countering Violent Extremism (CVE) Working Group* meeting mentioned above.[31] For the record, the court threw Omari's suit out. On July 22, 2011, I received an e-mail from the CIA announcing the cancellation of the August 10–12 "Conference on Homegrown Radical Extremism," along with the suspension of the mission until DHS released its new "National Strategy for Counterterrorism," which, of course, was the *CVE*.[32] By design, DHS CRCL, a non-counterterror, non-law enforcement, non-intelligence organ, assumed control of the counterterror mission through control and enforcement of the *CVE* narrative. Using a process that follows mass line concepts, DHS CRCL powered down on those counterterror and counterintelligence personnel who refused to conform to such narratives.

The "progressive '*exposé*'/CAIR demand" formula continued with *WIRED Magazine's Spencer Ackerman* taking the lead in the production of exposés. For reasons that will become obvious, Ackerman's background is disturbing. As J.E. Dyer pointed out, Ackerman was a member of the *JounoList*,[33] a group that crossed the line from biased reporting to that of coordinating and disseminating disinformation. Before that, *The New Republic* was forced to fire Ackerman in 2006.[34] Ackerman's profile resonates with the rising violent neo-Marxist Left. From a 2010 *Politico* article:

At another point, Ackerman acknowledged that, while he didn't like having to toe a partisan line, "what I like less is being governed by racists and warmongers and criminals. . . . In other words, find a right winger's [sic] and smash it through a plate-glass window. Take a snapshot of the bleeding mess and send it out in a Christmas card to let the right know that it needs to live in a state of constant fear. Obviously, I mean this rhetorically."[35]

Because *WIRED Magazine* was aware of Ackermann's ideologically compromised reporting when it hired him, it gets no pass.[36] While specific aspects of Ackerman's reporting will be addressed later, a few examples of how his products interoperated with Islamic Movement demands is in order:

- The September 18, 2011, article, "M. Elibiary—FBI Training, the Ackerman Expose & American Muslim Community Concerns," Mohamed Elibiary article in *Muslim Matters*[37] was followed on September 20, 2011, by Ackerman's "Video: FBI Trainer Says Forget 'Irrelevant' al-Qaeda, Target Islam" in *WIRED Magazine.*[38]

- Ackerman's April 24, 2012, article "Exclusive: Senior U.S. General Orders Top-to-Bottom Review of Military's Islam Training, Spencer Ackerman" in *WIRED* Magazine[39] was followed the next day by the CAIR demand, "CAIR Commends Pentagon for Dropping Islamophobic Course."[40]

- Ackerman's attack on the Joint Forces Staff College, in the May 2012, *WIRED Magazine* article, "U.S. Military Taught Officers: Use 'Hiroshima' Tactics for 'Total War' on Islam,"[41] was followed by CAIR's demand that "CAIR Asks Pentagon to Dismiss Officer Who Taught 'Total War' on Islam." [42]

DHS unveiled the *CVE* in October 2011 with the release of the October 7, 2011, "Countering Violent Extremism (CVE) Training Guidance & Best Practices"[43] along with the imprecisely dated "Countering Violent Extremism (CVE) Training—Do's and Don'ts."[44] From the beginning, the purpose of the *CVE* was to suppress and replace professional national security analysis with false narratives designed to enforce Islamophobia speech codes, which, as noted, remain to this day. CAIR bragged about its role in the purge in an October 2017 press release when stating that the *"Do's and Don'ts"* was implemented to "prohibit the federal use of funding of Islamophobic trainers."[45] In other words, the Muslim Brotherhood-inspired *"Do's and Don'ts"* implemented by DHS was used to terminate careers based on Brotherhood claims of Islamophobia specifically designed to suppress counterterror analysis, not to mention protected speech.

It should be noted that the narrative arc of these events culminated shortly after the September 11, 2012, Benghazi attack that Secretary Clinton deliberately misrepresented. She did this to force conformance to a coordinated[46] Islamophobia/*CVE* campaign set to peak later that month. On September 25, 2012, President Obama declared to the UN General Assembly that "the future must not belong to those who slander the prophet of Islam."[47] This was later followed by his October 12, 2012, statement on *60 Minutes* that, "I was certain and continue to be pretty certain that . . . in a lot of these places, the one organizing principle has been Islam, the one part of society that hasn't been completely controlled by the government."[48] Obama's General Assembly statement asserted the Islamophobia standard while the *CVE* disallowed national security assessments based on Islam's "one organizing principle."

2. EXECUTING THE PURGE, FROM THE WHITE HOUSE TO THE PENTAGON

I was named in the October 19, 2011, *Khera Letter.*[49]

In January 2011, Stephen Coughlin, a former consultant on Islamic law for the Joint Chiefs of Staff who criticized ex-President George W. Bush's assurances that the U.S. is not at war with Islam for having a 'chilling effect' on intelligence analysis, gave a presentation to the FBI's D.C. field office, during which, according to attendees, he claimed that Islamic law was incompatible with the U.S. Constitution and that there is no such thing as a loyal American Muslim.[7]

Footnote 7 referred to a Spencer Ackerman article in *WIRED Magazine*:

Spencer Ackerman, New Evidence of Anti-Islam Bias Underscores Deep Challenges for FBI's Reform Pledge, *WIRED MAGAZINE*, Sept. 23, 2011, available at http://www.wired.com/dangerroom/2011/09/ fbi-islam-domination/all/1. (as cited in the *Khera Letter*)

Of the thirteen times that Khera footnoted a source for her accusations, all of them stated as facts, twelve of them were attributed to Spencer Ackerman.[50] This means the entire Khera/Brennan exchange was based on the scribblings of Ackerman, a known left-wing agitator. At one point, Ackerman was forced to disclose that his wife worked for the ACLU.[51] Coordinated with the Khera Letter, the ACLU wrote its own *ACLU Letter to FBI Director Robert Mueller* on October 4, 2011, that was co-signed by MPAC, Khera's *Muslim Advocates,* ISNA, MAS, and CAIR.[52] As with Khera's, the ACLU Letter, also relied on Ackerman, citing him four times.[53] From the beginning, the Islamic Movement and the Left synchronized their efforts along common attack vectors to neutralize America's national security counterterror capabilities.

The *Khera Letter* relied on Ackerman to say that I "criticized ex-President George W. Bush's assurances that the U.S. is not at war with Islam for having a 'chilling effect' on intelligence analysis, [at] a presentation to the FBI's D.C. field office."[7] As actually stated in Ackerman's FBI "*exposé*":

Coughlin's 2007 master's thesis at the *National Defense Intelligence College* claimed that President George W. Bush's reassurance that the U.S. was not at war with Islam had "a chilling effect on those tasked to define the enemy's doctrine by effectively placing a policy bar on the unconstrained analysis of Islamic doctrine as a basis for this threat.[54]

For the record, this is what the thesis actually stated:

Following the catastrophic events of 9–11 when 19 Muslim men attacked U.S. targets for reasons associated with *jihad* in furtherance of Islamic goals, President George Bush made broad statements that held Islam harmless:

> The terrorists are traitors to their own faith, trying, in effect, to hijack Islam itself. The enemy of America is not our many Muslim friends; it is not our many Arab friends. Our enemy is a radical network of terrorists and every government that supports them.

> While there is little doubt that the President made these comments to allay fears in the Muslim community while staring-down thoughts of vigilante justice in some circles, his statements exerted a chilling effect on those tasked to define the enemy's doctrine by effectively placing a policy bar on the unconstrained analysis of Islamic doctrine as a basis for this threat.[55]

This assessment is as valid today as it was then. Brennan's commitment to Khera was no empty gesture. The purge began days before Khera wrote the October 19 letter. Based on "recent media attention on the Federal Bureau of Investigation's Countering Violent Extremism (CVE) training and DoD lectures," Assistant Secretary of Defense (ASD) José Mayorga sent a *Memorandum for the Director*, Joint Staff to "Request for Joint Staff Coordination" dated October 14, 2011.[56]

The *Memorandum* was based exclusively on one Ackerman article.[57] The article in question, "Justice Department Official: Muslim 'Juries' Threaten 'Our Values',"[58] was among those named in the *Khera Letter*.[59] In the staff coordination, Mayorga demanded the suppression of counterterror analysis through the forced imposition of *CVE* narratives. In the *Memorandum*, ASD Mayorga placed particular emphasis on those national security functions relating to vigilance:

> The intent is to determine the criteria used to establish professional qualifications for teachers and lecturers providing instruction on countering violent Islamic extremism; with particular focus on **M**ilitary **I**nformation **S**upport **O**perations, **I**nformation **O**perations, and **M**ilitary **I**ntelligence curriculum.[60]

Military **I**nformation **S**upport **O**perations is better known as Psyops and Civil Affairs. MISO, IO, and MI are the ever-vigilant "eyes out" and "ears always listening" components of our intelligence collection effort. What does it mean that an ASD would deliberately suppress fact-based, threat-focused intelligence analysis in favor of *CVE* narratives that deliberately warp the collection effort by forcing missions to support hostile narratives? These narratives enforce Islamic speech codes on American citizens tasked with national security by virtue of their implementation. Just as concerning, they were undertaken at the bidding of resident Islamic movement actors committed to "'sabotaging' [America's] house by [our] hands and the hands of the believers so that [America] is eliminated?"[61]

ASD Mayorga's *Memorandum* was the cover sheet to an Office of the Secretary of Defense Staff Action Control and Coordination (*OSD SACCP*) tasking[62] that the Joint Staff acknowledged on October 25, 2011, with a Joint Staff Action Process tasking (JS *JSAP*).[63] Running through the White House, the entire Pentagon purge was based on uncorroborated claims by Ackerman that Khera promoted. This was an op. The Ackerman article, included as TAB A, "Justice Department

Officials," drew from the same information provided in the previous week's article, "New Evidence of Anti-Muslim Bias," dated September 23.[64] Because both pieces were identified in the *Khera Letter,* and both drew from the same *YouTube* example "America at the Crossroads—2010,"[65] a comparison of what was briefed in the recording to what Ackerman implied demonstrates the lack of substance or integrity in Ackerman's reporting.

From an information campaign/mass line perspective, it is essential to recognize that the misrepresentations were obvious. The purpose of mass line attacks is intimidation designed to demobilize the efforts they target, not education. If those in the purge-chain were truly interested in the truth, a simple sampling of Ackerman's evidence would have revealed his malice. A series of examples of Ackerman's allegations can be resolved by simply referencing the video presentation that *he provided* in support of his claims.

- Ackerman engages in narratives ripe with innuendo, for example, that I engage in broad categorical statements concerning "all Muslims." Yet, the frozen image[66] of "America at the Crossroads—2010" captured by the "New Evidence" article shows the slide (3:43–4:58) that states:
  - » (I'm) Not asking you to believe (in) this presentation—Rather just pointing (out) that this is an issue of fact that can be resolved by direct analysis of peer-reviewed and authoritatively approved English language translations of authoritative treatments on Islamic law!

    There is a matter of the professional duty to know!
    - * What is clear—even if this understanding of Islamic law is in error, it is still in error in EXACTLY the way the enemy in the WOT got it wrong and, hence, is still an accurate reflection of the enemy's stated threat doctrine.
      - » How about a return to fact-driven analysis!

    "My job as an intelligence analyst was never to know "True

Islam," it was to define the doctrine the enemy fights in furtherance of."

- Ackerman suggests that my briefings are based on "opinions" that are, at best, only tangentially related to reality in a tone that suggests a conspiracy theory bent. Hence, for Ackerman:

  » I "claim" Muslim Nations have a "Ten Year Plan" as if the idea was conjured from online conspiracy theory forums when, in fact, the "Ten Year Plan" was a formally stated initiative of the OIC. The "America at the Crossroads—2010" presentation shows that I briefed directly from OIC documents.[67]

    * From 22:14 to 22:52, the concept of slander in Islamic law is explained using Islamic law to set up the seriousness of the OICs "Ten Year Plan";

    * From 22:53 to 25:08, the OIC's Ten Year Plan is explained using the OIC's own document on the Ten Year Plan, which is plainly visible.

- That I engage in obscurantist flights when discussing abrogation:[68]

  » From 7:20 to 8:25, the concept of abrogation was explained by direct reference to sanctioned texts of Islamic law;

  » From 8:26 to 10:32, the briefing transitions to the Muslim Brotherhood's reliance on abrogation as the engine of their doctrine, relying heavily on Sayyid Qutb's *Milestone*s to make the point;

  » Then from 10:33 to 19:1, the briefing provides direct reference to the Quran, hadith, and shari'ah authority for abrogation and then demonstrates how Major Hasan, the Fort Hood shooter, appealed directly to the doctrine of abrogation for his authority to engage in his mass-shooting terrorism at Fort Hood. Regarding Major Hasan and Fort Hood, *people died because our national security leaders embargoed our understanding of the Islamic doctrine of abrogation that the Muslim Brotherhood demanded to be banned, which the White House sought to enforce.*[69]

* Ackerman would have the reader scoff at analyzing "obscure" doctrines like the "Rule of Abrogation." Even though people die because we don't understand such concepts, they inform the strategy and decision-making of the Islamic Movement from the Muslim Brotherhood to Al Qaeda. It was never obscure to Major Hasan, Anwar al-Awlaki, Ayman Zawahiri, or Sayyid Qutb.

Major Hasan made a *PowerPoint* briefing of his declaration of jihad that he presented to national security personnel many times. So close was my presentation to Hasan's, I superimposed his slides over identical slides in my briefing to show the word-for-word exactness. Those slides were included in the "America at the Crossroads—2010" briefing Akerman posted. I briefed these slides to William Webster, head of the *Webster Commission,* along with other factual findings. Not one of those findings made it into the 2012 *Final Report of the Webster Commission.*[70] Instead, America got an institutionalized refusal to acknowledge Hasan's stated reasons for engaging in jihad, replacing his truth with the *CVE* inspired *"workplace violence"* report that came out in January 2010.[71]

• With comments like, "But not everyone was comfortable with the presentation. Some walked out in boredom or disgust, according to the source. Others made fun of it," Ackerman suggests a seething dissent, a sense of offense, a rancorous divide among professional staffs concerning my briefings. Yet, while the briefings were often long and tediously fact-laden, they were also popular, never mocked, and met with minimal dissent. There were no dissenting voices at that FBI briefing. There were no "walkouts." Because the purge narratives were often associated with supporting narratives suggesting the need for intervention to avoid dissent among the ranks, it should be pointed that, in 2012, the *GAO* looked into the *CVE* "dissent" narrative and discovered that, to no one's surprise, there was virtually no dissent or offense taken, in fact, less than one half of 1%.[72]

- Whenever Ackerman needed a dissenting voice, and he found as many as his narratives required, he never seemed able to associate them with a name. Not so, however, for those who came to my support. In "Justice Department Official," Ackerman targeted my briefings at the FA-30 Information Operations Course at Fort Leavenworth, Kansas. In the article, Col Mike Dominique spoke favorably of my efforts:
  - » "What Mr. Coughlin brings is a certain level of expertise on these extremist groups. He brings a perspective to the audience."
    While LTC Steve Leonard at the Combined Arms Center noted that I "do not cross a line into anti-Islam sentiment," adding:
  - » "He helps the students develop a mental model of extremist groups and the process they use to influence moderate Muslims. . . . He explains how extremists use the Quran and Sharia law to build a jihadist narrative that creates significant influence within a moderate population."[73]

Supporting me came at a price. When reading of the support I received from Ft. Leavenworth, I heard that individuals were singled out and sanctioned. For his support, I heard that the White House let Col Dominique know that they were not satisfied with his response. One of the people involved in Col Dominique's beat-down went so far as to tell him that my briefings violated the White House's Policy on Islamophobia.

SUMMATION

This chapter ends as it began. Brennan was the conduit to execute Khera's demands, and her demands were met. With an eye toward *Crossfire Hurricane* and *Russia Gate,* in the Trump administration, Brennan used the immense powers of his office to orchestrate hostile extralegal information campaigns directed against American citizens and institutions. Progressive media, especially Spencer Ackerman and *WIRED Magazine,* published accusations that positioned *CAIR* to make demands that escalated its effects when targeting specific institutions with each turn in the narrative. It was a hostile, active measures, information campaign. It was directed against Americans. It was a purge.

The target audience of the *WIRED Magazine* and *CAIR* attacks was not the reading public but rather the associated leaderships of the targeted organizations. The colonels at the FA-30 Information Operations class caught the ire of the White House for coming to my support. The Ackerman narratives were based on false light innuendo and ridicule. My briefing schedule was not publicly available. Yet, from the CIA conference to the FBI Washington Field Office, to the FA-30 (Information Operations) course at Fort Leavenworth, to the Joint Staff raid on the Joint Forces Staff College, I was stalked by those positioned to be able to do so from the inside.

There was no due process for those targeted by this campaign. The accused were never allowed to defend themselves or their work product. This was the "peer pressure and shaming" Secretary Clinton committed to the OIC, a foreign supra-state actor when promising to direct the government apparatus into silencing American citizens engaged in disfavored speech. Taking stock of the scale of the seditious activities coming to light from investigations into *Crossfire Hurricane,* it becomes clear that those targeted for the purge in 2011 never had a chance.

Targeted by the Muslim Brotherhood, orchestrated by Brennan from the White House, and executed by ASD Mayorga, the eyes and ears of the Pentagon were blinded to the counterterror threat posed by the Islamic Movement. As the Biden administration's June 2021 *National*

Strategy for Countering Domestic Terrorism indicates, they remain so to this day. The *CVE* survived the Trump administration intact, operationally capable, and institutionally ready upon Biden's taking office. It replaced the genuine counterterror and counterintelligence missions. The Muslim Brotherhood is still in control. In December 2019, the Secretary-General of the USCMO, Oussama Jammal, reaffirmed the mission that groups like the *USCMO* and *CAIR* continue to play in controlling the counter-terror mission through control of counterterror narratives:[74]

We are here to protect the entire community . . . We will not allow anyone to mess with our community, with our safety, the safety of our mosque, our school, our community. *[Replace "community" with the term "Ummah."]*

How many of you receive *CAIR* E-Mails . . . Did you notice that when somebody is doing something against the community, what's the first thing that CAIR says? *"We demand the FBI to investigate this or that, or this case or that case.* Right? . . . So, when there's something, who are we going to call? . . . We have a way to, and thanks to orga-nizations like this, who are trying to take and expose all the wrong *"don'ts"* that have been done before. And they have [been] successful, in many cases. And the point is, even our civil rights groups, when they see something, they said, "we asked the FBI to investigate, we asked the FBI to go after this group or that group or so on and so forth." So, we are not talking out of the town.

We are not done. They know we are no longer done. But it is the fight that we have to take every single day, and that's why we're becoming resilient now. *We now understand the system.*

Stephen Coughlin is the founder Unconstrained Analytics, Inc, the author of numerous works, including Catastrophic Failure: Blindfolding America in the Face of Jihad, Defeating the Islamic Movement Inside the United States: A Strategic Plan, Re-Remembering the Mis-Remembered Left: The Left's Strategy and Tactics to Transform America, *and* Warning on Racism. *A decorated Intelligence officer, Major Coughlin (Ret) served on the Joint Chiefs of Staff Intelligence Directorate, the US Central Command Intelligence Directorate, and more through the War on Terror. He also serves as an adjunct professor at Regent University.*

4

HOW OBAMA ENABLED THE PERSECUTION OF CHRISTIANS

by Raymond Ibrahim

ONE OF THE WORST, though overlooked, aspects of US President Joe Biden's shameful withdrawal from Afghanistan—if not outright capitulation to the jihadist group, the Taliban—is not only that he threw Christian minorities in that nation under the bus but that he intentionally prevented their rescue. As Glenn Beck explained to Tucker Carlson on August 26, 2021, he and his charity, the Nazarene Fund, had hired charter planes to rescue Christian minorities from the wrath of the Taliban, only to be blocked by the Biden State Department:

We believe that our State Department is directly responsible [for preventing the rescue of some 500 Christians] . . . The State Department has blocked us every step of the way. The State Department and the White House have been the biggest problem. Everyone else, everyone else, has been working together, putting aside differences and trying to get these people to safety. The State Department and the White House have blocked us every single step of the way. In fact, an ambassador was called in Macedonia last night and told not to accept any of these people, as we were trying to get them off of the tarmac here, to keep the airport flowing, and getting these Christians out. We haven't really been able to move anybody for about 12 hours. Our mission is now changing greatly. We have to send people into even greater danger to try to smuggle these Christians out, who are marked not just for death, but to be set on fire alive because they're converted Christians.[1]

Beck, it should be noted, was not exaggerating. According to one recent report, "Taliban militants are even pulling people off public transport and killing them on the spot if they're Christians."[2] Similarly, any Afghan caught with a Bible app on their phone is executed. "How we survive daily only God knows," a Christian Afghani said earlier this year on condition of anonymity. "But we are tired of all the death around us."[3] At one point in his interview with Carlson, Beck mentioned two nations that were being cooperative in helping him rescue Christians—though he was anxious to add, "I don't even want to say who they are because I'm afraid our State Department will call them and threaten them!"[4]

"I don't know why we have open borders and closed airports," Beck concluded his interview. While it is easy for all sorts of illegals to cross over the porous US/Mexico border, "one group of people"—he said referring to persecuted Christians—is not even allowed to enter airports and are abandoned to be "raped, exploited and crucified or set on fire by terrorists," said Beck, before adding, "There seems to be a pattern with the Biden administration." In fact, this is a pattern begun by the

Obama administration. Biden—who it bears recalling was for eight years Obama's vice president—is merely continuing it. After all, in word and deed, implicitly and explicitly, passively and actively, Barack H. Obama and his administration discriminated against and enabled the horrific persecution of Christians at the hands of Muslims throughout his eight year tenure. A few examples categorized by theme follow:

ISLAMIST SUPPORT EQUALS CHRISTIAN PERSECUTION: A SYMBIOTIC RELATIONSHIP

The Obama administration's well-known support for Islamists in the context of the so-called Arab Spring—whether the Muslim Brotherhood in Egypt or Islamic terrorists in the guise of "rebel freedom fighters" in Libya, Syria, and Yemen—always and naturally translated into an increase in the persecution of Christians in those nations. For example, the Obama administration armed/supported the "freedom fighters" who overran Libya and killed Gaddafi, even though it was common knowledge that many of them were connected to al-Qaeda, the Islamic State (ISIS), and other jihadi organizations. In March 2011, Obama justified US aid by invoking "our responsibilities to our fellow human beings," and how not assisting them "would have been a betrayal of who we are."[5] Soon after their empowerment, some of these "fellow human beings" decided to repay the US by attacking its consulate in Benghazi—on the anniversary of September 11, no less. This resulted in the murder of American ambassador Christopher Stevens (who was possibly sodomized beforehand).[6]

Lesser known, however, was that Libya's small Christian community, which consisted mostly of Coptic Christian laborers from neighboring Egypt, was also savagely targeted. Early telltale signs included attacks on the very few churches there, the abuse of nuns that had served the sick and needy for decades, and the arrest and torture of foreign Christians possessing Bibles (one died from his torture).[7] On several occasions, Coptic Christians were abducted and slaughtered.[8] The most notorious instance—a video recording of the Islamic State slaughtering twenty

Coptic and one Ghanaian Christians by the Libyan seashore—appeared in February 2015. Two months later ISIS released another video of their jihadis butchering over thirty Christians from Ethiopia.[9]

The same pattern was on display in Syria, following uprisings against President Bashar Assad in 2011. The Obama administration supported and armed what were then presented to the American public as "freedom fighters" and "rebels" but who in reality were Islamic terrorists. By so doing, the Obama administration essentially also supported the unprecedented terrorization, slaughter, rape, and sexual enslavement of Christians and other minorities in modern Syria. This proxy "jihad" on Syria was also presented to Americans as a war to safeguard the "human rights" and "freedoms" of the Syrian people. Years later, the full extent of the US-sponsored rebels' atrocities—including the torture, rape, and massacre of an entire Christian village (that no "mainstream media" reported) in 2013—still remain unknown.[10]

Egypt offers another example. Once unrest began there in early 2011, the Obama administration instantly turned its back on then-President Hosni Mubarak, America's most stable and secular Arab ally for thirty years. Next, it openly supported the Muslim Brotherhood—one of the world's oldest Islamist organizations. Although "radical" in its origins and early history—its chief theoretician, Sayyid Qutb, issued a 1980 fatwa calling for the destruction of all Coptic churches in Egypt—the Brotherhood eventually learned to play politics and put on a front.[11] Nonetheless, once the Brotherhood's Muhammad Morsi became president in June 2012, the persecution of Egypt's Christians was virtually legalized; unprecedented numbers of Copts—men, women, and children—were arrested, often receiving more than double the maximum prison sentence under the accusation that they had "blasphemed" against Islam and/or its prophet.[12] It was also under Brotherhood rule that another unprecedented scandal occurred: the St. Mark Cathedral—one of Coptic Christianity's most sacred sites and home to the Coptic pope himself—was besieged in broad daylight by Islamic rioters, even as security forces stood and watched.[13]

The Obama administration's only response was to urge the Coptic Pope to dissuade the Christian Copts from joining millions of other Egyptians in the July 2013 protests that eventually overthrew the Morsi government—proving yet again that the administration was more concerned about the wellbeing of the Muslim Brotherhood than the human rights of those they abuse.[14] Earlier, in 2011, in what became known as the "Maspero Massacre"—when the Egyptian military indiscriminately opened fire on and ran armored vehicles over dozens of unarmed Christians for protesting the destruction of their churches—all the White House would say is: "Now is a time for restraint on all sides," as if Egypt's beleaguered Christian minority needed to "restrain" itself against the Muslim nation's military.[15]

It's worth noting that, humanitarian concerns aside, the Muslim persecution of Christians is a litmus test on how "radical"—and thus anti-American and anti-Western—an Islamic society has become. In other words, the rise of Christian persecution in a Muslim nation is synonymous with the rise of Islamist jihadi power. Accordingly, the Islamist forces that Obama empowered in Libya, Syria, Egypt, and Yemen were not just hostile to Christians; they were and are fundamentally hostile to all non-Muslims, including secular Americans.

COVER UPS

Not only did Obama support Islamists, which significantly worsened the plight of Christians across the Middle East; he and his administration tried to cover up their shameful sponsorship. For example, according to a June 7, 2012 report:

> The U.S. State Department removed the sections covering religious freedom from the Country Reports on Human Rights that it released on May 24, three months past the statutory deadline Congress set for the release of these reports. The new human rights reports—purged of the sections that discuss the status of religious freedom in each of the countries covered—are also the human rights reports that include

the period that covered the Arab Spring and its aftermath. Thus, the reports do not provide in-depth coverage of what has happened to Christians and other religious minorities in predominantly Muslim countries in the Middle East that saw the rise of revolutionary movements in 2011 in which Islamist forces played an instrumental role. For the first time ever, the State Department simply eliminated the section of religious freedom in its reports covering 2011. [16]

Several US officials questioned the Obama administration's motives. Former US diplomat Thomas Farr said that he had "observed during the three-and-a-half years of the Obama administration that the issue of religious freedom has been distinctly downplayed." Leonard Leo, former chairman of the US Commission on International Religious Freedom, said "to have pulled religious freedom out of it [State Dept. report] means that fewer people will obtain information," so that "you don't have the whole picture."[17]

Obama was also notorious for never using American leverage on behalf of Christians. One obvious example occurred in March 28, 2014, when he met with (and earlier bowed to) King Abdullah of Saudi Arabia, where all religions except Islam are banned. Not once did Obama broach the topic of religious freedom, despite a letter from some seventy members of Congress urging him to "address specific human rights reforms" with Abdullah and other officials. As one human rights activist explained, it was "remarkable that the president could stay completely silent about religious freedom" despite congressional pressure "to publicly address the issue, as well as other human rights concerns, with King Abdullah." Obama aides eventually responded by saying that "Obama had not had time to raise concerns about the kingdom's human rights record."[18]

GENOCIDE DENIAL

In its effort to suppress what its support for Islamic terrorists had wrought among Christians and other non-Muslim minorities in the Muslim world, the Obama administration went so far as to ignore or deny what a variety of experts were confirming—that what religious minorities were experiencing in the aftermath of the so-called Arab Spring "fits the definition of ethnic cleansing," to quote the Simon-Skjodt Center for the Prevention of Genocide at the US Holocaust Memorial.[19] In March 2015, the UN Security Council held a meeting to discuss this genocide. Although "many high level delegations from UN member states addressed the Security Council meeting, some at the Foreign Minister level, the United States failed to send UN Ambassador Samantha Power (and Secretary Kerry was busy negotiating a nuclear deal with Iran) or a high ranking member of the State Department."[20] Over the following year, several other authorities—including the US Commission on International Religious Freedom, the European Parliament, and the Office of the United Nations High Commissioner for Human Rights—reaffirmed that Christians and other minorities were experiencing a genocide, particularly in those nations where the US president supported Islamists and other "freedom fighters" and "rebels," even as the Obama administration refused to acknowledge that word *genocide*, particularly in regards to Christians.[21]

Most notably, during a February 29, 2016 press briefing, White House spokesman Josh Earnest was earnestly asked: "Is the Islamic State carrying out a campaign of genocide against Syria's Christians?" He equivocated and turned the conversation to Yazidis. When pressed to answer specifically about Christians, he responded: "My understanding is the use of that word involves a very specific legal determination that has at this point not been reached."[22] In the following month, March 2016, the US House of Representatives unanimously (393 to 0) passed a resolution to pressure the Obama administration to declare that the Islamic State's actions against Christians, Yazidis, and others were indeed a "genocide, war crimes and crimes against humanity."[23] A few days later Secretary of State John Kerry finally conceded the point.

Obama's genocide denial manifested in more subtle ways. For instance, when still running for president, he stated his "firmly held conviction" that the Armenian Genocide—another instance when

Muslims (Turks) sought to eradicate Christians (Armenians)—"is not an allegation, a personal opinion, or a point of view, but rather a widely documented fact supported by an overwhelming body of historical evidence. The facts are undeniable. . . . [A]s President I will recognize the Armenian Genocide. . . . America deserves a leader who speaks truthfully about the Armenian Genocide and responds forcefully to all genocides. I intend to be that president."[24] Eight Armenian genocide anniversaries passed under Obama's tenure as president, and eight times he failed to stand by his word. When he refused to mention it on the one-hundredth anniversary of the genocide, the Armenian National Committee of America responded by saying, "The president's surrender represents a national disgrace. It is a betrayal of the truth, and it is a betrayal of trust." The Armenian Assembly of America added that "His failure to use the term genocide represents a major blow for human rights advocates."[25]

As seen, however, the president's actions are consistent in other ways. Put differently, it is no marvel that Obama denies the genocide of Christian minorities at the hands of Muslims from a century ago, when one considers that he denies the rampant Muslim persecution of Christians taking place under—and often because of—his own presidency.

IMMIGRATION

In November 2015, Obama lashed out against the idea of giving preference to Christian over Muslim refugees. He described the notion as "shameful," adding, "That's not American. That's not who we are. We don't have religious tests to our compassion."[26] The day after Obama's moralizing, statistics were revealed indicating that "the current [refugee] system overwhelmingly favors Muslim refugees. Of the 2,184 Syrian refugees admitted to the United States so far, only 53 are Christians while 2,098 are Muslim," noted the November 17, 2015 report.[27] The flagrant disparity only got worse with time. A May 2016 report indicated that from May 1 to May 23, 499 Syrian refugees were received into the US. *Zero* Christians were among them; 100 percent were Muslim.[28]

According to an October 5, 2016 report from the Pew Research Center, "A total of 38,901 Muslim refugees entered the U.S. in fiscal year 2016, making up almost half (46%) of the nearly 85,000 refugees [from all around the world, not just Syria] who entered the country in that period." The bias could not be clearer: although Muslims amount for less than a quarter of the world's population, they amounted for nearly half of all refugees coming from every corner of the world. "That means," Pew continues, "the U.S. has admitted the highest number of Muslim refugees of any year since data on self-reported religious affiliations first became publicly available in 2002."[29] Such discrepancies prompted a federal appellate court to file a Freedom of Information Act lawsuit against the Department of Homeland Security. In it, Judge Daniel Manion expressed his "concern about the apparent lack of Syrian Christians as a part of immigrants from that country. . . . Perhaps 10 percent of the population of Syria is Christian, and yet less than one-half of one percent of Syrian refugees admitted to the United States this year are Christian. . . . To date, there has not been a good explanation for this perplexing discrepancy."[30]

It bears mentioning that even under the assumption that religion should have no say in who is regarded a refugee, the simple demographics of Syria are enough to demonstrate the pro-Muslim, anti-Christian bias of the Obama administration: Christians accounted for 10 percent of Syria's total population—yet they accounted for less than 0.5 percent of all refugees admitted. In other words, even without "favoring" Christians, from an objective and ratio-based perspective, there should have been twenty times more Christians granted refugee status.

Aside from the obvious—or to use Obama's own word, "shameful"—pro-Muslim, anti-Christian bias evident in the Obama administration's refugee policy, there were a number of other troubling factors as well. For starters, the overwhelming majority of refugees admitted into the United States were not just Muslim, but Sunnis—the one Muslim sect that the Islamic State did not persecute or displace. After all, ISIS—not to mention most Islamic terrorist groups (Boko Haram, Al Qaeda, Al

Shabaab, Hamas, et al.)—are all Sunnis. Obama himself was arguably raised a Sunni. In this context, how were Sunnis "refugees"? Who were they fleeing? Sunni Muslims were not slaughtered, beheaded, enslaved, and raped because of their religion, whereas Christians and other minorities constantly were. Sunnis did not have their mosques bombed and burned whereas literally hundreds of churches in Syria, Egypt, and Libya were destroyed during the Obama-sponsored "Arab Spring." And yet, under Obama, approximately 98 percent of all refugees accepted into the US were Sunni (as seen, Christians were about .5 percent, whereas Shias, Yazidis, and so forth accounted for approximately 1.5 percent).

A look at refugee camps all throughout Western Europe further highlights the topsy-turvy nature of the Obama administration's approach. Local human rights agencies repeatedly asserted that Sunni Muslim–dominated refugee centers are hotbeds of radicalization. Christians were regularly harassed, pressured to convert, attacked, raped, and sometimes murdered there.[31] In one April 2015 case, before they could even reach Europe, Christian refugees were murdered by their Sunni Muslim counterparts. While shouting "Allahu Akbar," the Muslim majority aboard a ship sailing from Libya to Sicily drowned approximately fifty Christians in the Mediterranean.[32] Such was the quality of the Muslim "refugees" that Obama took in a disproportionate share of—at the sacrifice of their Christian victims, who truly deserved but were denied refuge in America.

JOBS AND VISAS

Obama's anti-Christian pro-Muslim bias was on display above and beyond the question of refugees. In 2016, WikiLeaks released a 2008 email concerning who should—and should not—fill top staff positions if Obama became president. The email was written by former New York Solicitor General Preeta D. Bansal to Michael Froman, a member of the twelve-person advisory board for the Obama campaign's transition team. The key passage reads:

In the candidates for top jobs, I excluded those with some Arab American background but who are not Muslim (e.g., George Mitchell). Many Lebanese Americans, for example, are Christian. In the last list (of outside boards/commissions), most who are listed appear to be Muslim American, except that a handful (where noted) may be Arab American but of uncertain religion (esp. Christian).[33]

In other words, Arabs from nations with large Christian populations (such as Lebanon) or those with obviously Christian names need not apply, for they fail Obama's and his team's "religious test." Similarly, in 2015, Sister Diana Momeka, an outspoken human rights activist, was to be a member of a delegation of religious leaders, including Shia and Yazidi, from Iraq to visit Washington, DC, in order to describe the situation of their people. The Obama State Department granted every member of the delegation a visa—except for the only Christian, Sister Diana, despite the fact that she had visited the US before, most recently in 2012.[34] When this became known, a number of religious and political leaders expressed their shock. According to Johnnie Moore, "Sister Momeka is a gift to the world and a humanitarian whose work reminded me—when I met her in Iraq—of Mother Teresa. It is incomprehensible to me that the State Department would not be inviting Momeka on an official visit to the United States, as opposed to barring her from entry."[35] Chris Seiple, president of the Institute for Global Engagement, observed: "In the same week that the State Dept says it will take the engagement of religious leaders seriously . . . it refuses a visa to a persecuted Christian nun who has fled ISIS, Sister Diana."[36] Former House Speaker Newt Gingrich said: "This is an administration which never seems to find a good enough excuse to help Christians, but always finds an excuse to apologize for terrorists . . . I hope that as it gets attention that Secretary [of State John] Kerry will reverse it. If he doesn't, Congress has to investigate, and the person who made this decision ought to be fired." The State Department responded to this outcry by quickly reversing its decision and approving of Sister Diana's visa.[37]

It is worth noting that the Obama administration's bias against and indifference for Mideast Christians mirrors the traditional bias Muslim governments have against Christians. This is understood in the context of active and passive persecution: Muslim criminals actively kidnap, rape, rob, and/or kill Christian minorities precisely because they know Muslim authorities will respond passively, mostly by looking the other way. Similarly, Muslim governments seldom if ever hire Christians to positions of authority. Thus, whether by discriminating against Christians and favoring Muslims for positions of authority, or whether by welcoming a disproportionately large number of Sunni Muslims, while barring the true victims of genocide, Christians—the Obama government's bias was representative of a tradition that Christian minorities have long been familiar with living in the Muslim world.

NIGERIA: A PARADIGMATIC CASE

In many respects, virtually all of the aforementioned anti-Christian pro-Muslim policies were on display in the Obama administration's dealings with Nigeria, a nation which is roughly half Muslim, half Christian, and which, then and now, hardly sees a week pass without Muslims—from Fulani herdsmen to Boko Haram—slaughtering Christians.

First, a 2011 ABC News report helps establish context:

> The current wave of [Muslim] riots was triggered by the Independent National Election Commission's (INEC) announcement on Monday [April 18, 2011] that the incumbent President, Dr. Goodluck Jonathan [a Christian], won in the initial round of ballot counts. That there were riots in the largely Muslim inhabited northern states where the defeat of the Muslim candidate Muhammadu Buhari was intolerable, was unsurprising. Northerners [Muslims] felt they were entitled to the presidency for the declared winner, President Jonathan, [who] assumed leadership after the Muslim president, Umaru Yar'Adua died in office last year and radical groups in the north [Boko Haram] had seen his [Jonathan's] ascent as a temporary matter to be corrected at

this year's election. Now they are angry despite experts and observers concurring that this is the fairest and most independent election in recent Nigerian history.[38]

Even so, Obama made clear whose side he was on. Dr. Goodluck Jonathan, Nigeria's former president (2010–2015), accuses the Obama administration of meddling with his nation's politics in order to replace him with Nigeria's current president, Muhammadu Buhari—whom many accuse of facilitating an unprecedented jihad and "genocide" against Christians.[39] According to Jonathan:

> On March 23, 2015, President Obama himself took the unusual step of releasing a video message directly to Nigerians all but telling them how to vote . . . In that video, Obama urged Nigerians to open the "next chapter" by their votes. Those who understood subliminal language deciphered that he was prodding the electorate to vote for the [Muslim-led] opposition to form a new government.[40]

As for the violence and bloodshed plaguing Nigeria—almost all of which was committed by Muslims against Christians—the Obama administration repeatedly insisted that it had absolutely nothing to do with religion. This despite the fact that Boko Haram—which was engaging in ISIS type atrocities, including slaughter, kidnap, rape, plunder, slavery, and torture before ISIS was even born—openly presented its terrorism as a jihad in the name of Islam. In one instance, Boko Haram even called on President Jonathan to "repent and forsake Christianity" and convert to Islam as the price for peace.[41] Despite all this, the Obama administration refused to designate Boko Haram as a foreign terrorist organization until November 2013—after years of increasing pressure from lawmakers, human rights activists, and lobbyists.[42] The willful denial was on display in other ways. After a Nigerian church was destroyed in an Easter Day, 2012, bombing that left nearly forty Christians dead—one of hundreds of church attacks, several fatal, over the years in Nigeria—Obama's Assistant Secretary of State for African Affairs, Johnnie Carson, said, "I want to take this opportunity to stress one key point and that is that religion is not driving extremist violence" in Nigeria.[43]

Instead, "inequality" and "poverty"—to quote Bill Clinton who well summarized the Obama administration's position—are "what's fueling all this stuff" (a reference to the jihadi massacre of then thousands of Christians).[44] Apparently to prove that it believed what it was saying, the Obama administration even agreed to allocate $600 million in a USAID initiative to ascertain the "true causes" of unrest and violence in Nigeria, which supposedly lay in the socio-economic, never the religious, realm.[45]

Also telling is that, although the Obama administration offered only generic regrets whenever Christians were slaughtered by the dozens—without acknowledging the religious identity of persecutor or victim—it loudly protested whenever Islamic terrorists were targeted. When, for instance, Nigerian forces under Jonathan's presidency killed thirty Boko Haram terrorists in a May 2013 offensive, US Secretary of State John Kerry issued a strongly worded statement to Jonathan, saying: "We are . . . deeply concerned by credible allegations that Nigerian security forces are committing gross human rights violations, which, in turn, only escalate the violence and fuel extremism."[46]

Nor was Sister Diana Momeka from Iraq the only Christian to be denied a visa. After the United States Institute for Peace (USIP) brought together the governors of Nigeria's mostly Muslim northern states for a conference in the US, the State Department blocked the visa of the region's only Christian governor, Jonah David Jang, an ordained minister, citing "administrative" problems. The USIP confirmed that all nineteen northern governors were invited, but the organization did not respond to requests for comments on why they would hold talks without the region's only Christian governor. Discussing that incident, Emmanuel Ogebe, a human rights lawyer from the US Nigeria Law Group based in Washington, DC, said "The U.S. insists that Muslims are the primary victims of Boko Haram. It also claims that

Christians discriminate against Muslims in Plateau, which is one of the few Christian majority states in the north. After [Jang, the Christian governor] told them [U.S. authorities] that they were ignoring the 12 Shariah states who institutionalized persecution . . . he suddenly developed visa problems . . . The question remains—why is the U.S. downplaying or denying the attacks against Christians?"[47]

CONCLUSION

The verdict is clear: under Barack Hussein Obama's tenure, Christian minorities throughout the Muslim world suffered unprecedented persecution in the modern era. However, not only did he knowingly empower those Muslims—Islamic jihadis/terrorists—most prone to terrorizing, raping, enslaving, and slaughtering Christians and other minorities; he habitually covered up and denied these atrocities—even when it reached the point of genocide; and, on the domestic front, he regularly discriminated against those same persecuted Christians—denying them immigration, visas, and so forth—while lavishing the same on their persecutors. In short, it was the Obama administration's discriminatory policies, "religious tests," and empowerment of Christian persecuting terrorists that—to use his own words when condemning the idea of prioritizing Christian refugees—were "shameful," "not who were are," and certainly "not American."

Raymond Ibrahim is a Shillman Journalism Fellow at the David Horowitz Freedom Center and a Judith Friedman Rosen Writing Fellow at the Middle East Forum. His latest book is Sword and Scimitar: Fourteen Centuries of War between Islam and the West.

5

OBAMA'S BETRAYAL OF ISRAEL

by Daniel Greenfield

THE ALLIANCE BETWEEN the United States and Israel is based on shared history, values, and threats. But what happens when there are no more shared values or shared threats? That's the story of the breakdown in relations between Obama, Biden, and Israel.

For eight years the mainstream media blamed the broken relationship between America and Israel on the mismatch between Obama and Israel's Benjamin Netanyahu. But now that Biden is in the White House and there is a new leader in Israel, it is painfully obvious that the issue was never one of personalities, but of values and worldviews. There have been mismatches between American and Israeli leaders before, but there has never been a divergence of values and worldviews as profound as the one that divided the two nations under Barack Obama and under his successor, Joseph Robinette Biden. The total divergence of worldviews is moral, cultural, and strategic. The fundamental disagreement was not limited to the sphere of policy, but spilled out into smear campaigns by the administration and its allies against Prime Minister Netanyahu, eavesdropping on Netanyahu, on pro-Israel activists, and even on members of Congress, and into administration rhetoric that even the ADL denounced as anti-Semitic.

By the end of the Obama administration, Israel had been betrayed at the United Nations, and forced to witness its closest ally illegally smuggling billions in payments to its worst enemies. And it watched as the anti-Israel activists were welcomed at the White House while supporters of Israel were harassed. Now, under Biden, Obama's old people pressure Israel to allow them to violate its sovereignty by opening a terrorist consulate in Jerusalem, warn the Jewish State that they will not tolerate Jews living in Jerusalem, and plot to send billions to Iran. History is repeating itself. This betrayal of Israel comes down to how Obama and Biden see America. Before Obama and Biden rejected and betrayed Israel, they rejected and betrayed America.

Previous administrations had viewed Islamic terrorists and the Iranian regime as threats. The Obama administration, however, saw them as victims of American foreign policy. Israel was an ally, but it was not interested in supporting allies to prop up American global influence that it believed represented an unjust and oppressive system. Obama believed that Israel, like America, and other allies in the region, was part of the problem.

The Bush administration had believed that the problem was terrorism, while the Obama administration was convinced that it was colonialism. Its betrayal of Israel was part of its answer to the question of why *they* hated us. The other part of the answer was the betrayal of our other allies and our soldiers. The final part of the answer was the Obama administration's embrace of Iran, of the Muslim Brotherhood, and other enemies. This is what happened in those eight years when the governments of America and Israel no longer shared values, a strategic vision or any common goals. And this was how it all fell apart.

THE JERUSALEM STRATEGY

"Jerusalem will remain the capital of Israel, and it must remain undivided," Barack Obama announced. It was June 4, 2008 and the senator from Illinois was trying to sell his candidacy to American Jews. In his address to AIPAC, he dismissed the "provocative e-mails" filled with "tall tales and dire warnings" that were "circulating throughout Jewish communities."[1] Jewish organizations rushed to praise Obama's new position only to have the rug pulled out from them. By the next day, Obama had retracted his support for Jerusalem. The next month, he dismissed it as "poor phrasing" and argued that what he meant is that Jerusalem wouldn't be divided by barbed wire.[2]

In 2010, when the Jerusalem municipality passed some houses in a Jerusalem neighborhood where Jews had lived for over a century through one stage of a multi-stage approval process, the White House went to war. Biden, who was visiting Israel, stood up Netanyahu for ninety minutes. Secretary Hillary Clinton spent two hours yelling at Netanyahu over the phone and called it, "an insult to the United States."[3] By 2012, Jerusalem had been purged from the DNC platform.[4] After protests from Jewish groups, it was put back in, and its restoration was met with loud boos by delegates at the convention.[5] In 2014, Secretary of State John Kerry urged a ban on non-Muslims praying on the Temple Mount in Jerusalem.[6] The Biden administration recently reasserted this prayer ban, ordering Israel to "preserve the historic status quo on the Haram al-Sharif/Temple Mount—in word and in practice." This "historic status quo" was imposed by the Muslim occupiers and bans Jews from praying at their own holiest site.[7]

The Trump peace plan had proposed that, "People of every faith should be permitted to pray on the Temple Mount/Haram al-Sharif, in a manner that is fully respectful to their religion, taking into account the times of each religion's prayers and holidays, as well as other religious factors." But Biden, like Obama and Hamas, rejected religious freedom in Jerusalem. The Jerusalem double cross by Obama was emblematic of his strategy of cloaking an ideological betrayal in a manufactured personality clash which shifted the blame from his administration to the Israelis.

Prime Minister Netanyahu and President Obama had taken office a few months apart. Both men were the products of prestigious Boston schools, MIT for Netanyahu and Harvard for Obama. But their backgrounds, worldviews, and life experiences were far apart. Netanyahu had taken a break from pursuing higher education to fight in an elite commando unit during a war that threatened the survival of the Jewish State, while Obama had taken a break to work as a community organizer in Chicago. To Obama and Netanyahu, Israel wasn't just a geopolitical issue, but a personal one. Netanyahu had been taught to love Israel by his conservative historian father. Obama identified with the volatile mixture of Islamism and third-world nationalism that he had encountered through his father's family. Netanyahu saw Zionism as a movement of national liberation. Obama saw Islamism that way. To the new Israeli PM, his country was a liberation movement. To the new occupant of the Oval Office, it was a relic of European colonialism. An outpost of white settlers impeding the Third World revolution that would sweep away the last relics of imperialism and usher in a new order in the region and the world.

Obama's closest friend with a strong perspective on Israel was Rashid Khalidi: a former PLO spokesman. These were not just policy differences. Obama and Netanyahu came to their respective offices with irreconcilable worldviews rooted in history, passion, and culture. There could be no common ground. And yet Obama was the candidate of a political party that represented the majority of American Jews. At events like the AIPAC conference, he was forced to mouth pro-Israel sentiments, even if he would swiftly disavow or undermine them. He had gathered around him advisers and aides who shared his worldview, men like Ben Rhodes and Robert Malley, but during the campaign, he was temporarily forced to banish Malley over a backlash from American Jews due to his backdoor contacts with Hamas.[8] The AIPAC and Malley imbroglios brought home to Obama the need to break with Israel, while retaining the political support of American Jews. And he did that by making the conflict about Netanyahu.

By making Netanyahu the public face of Israel, Obama and his associates spun the growing break with Israel as personal and political, but not national. Even as Obama cut a deal with Iran that allowed it to maintain its nuclear program, empowered the Muslim Brotherhood, and by extension, its affiliate Hamas, pressured Israel to free killers, and sold out Israel at the United Nations, his allies were able to depict these as not national issues, but a conflict between American progressives and Israeli rightists. Israel, they claimed, had gone far to the right. Netanyahu was their unlikely poster boy for radicalism. Jewish Democrats were given a choice between siding with Israeli "right-wing extremists" or with Obama. And the White House arsonists accused Netanyahu of making Israel into a partisan issue. The Obama administration wanted to engineer a break with Israel while blaming Israel for that break. Using the Jerusalem Strategy, the White House staged provocations and played the victim. Netanyahu, it insisted, had provoked Obama by authorizing construction in Jerusalem during Biden's visit, even though it was the Jerusalem municipality that had done it for reasons having nothing to do with Biden.

In the media narrative staged by fixers like Ben Rhodes, Netanyahu was always provoking, insulting, and undermining Obama, while Obama patiently tried to bear the ceaseless insults from Netanyahu. Obama hectored Netanyahu, and when the latter responded, another provocation had occurred. No matter how many concessions Israel made, Netanyahu was depicted as undermining Obama's agenda. Media mouthpieces began suggesting that Netanyahu's disagreements with Obama were even racial.

The campaign reached its climax with the debate over the Iran Deal. When Netanyahu arrived to argue against the blank check being given to Iran's nuclear program, this was not only depicted as an insult to Obama, but as a racist move. Obama's Congressional Black Caucus allies announced that were boycotting Netanyahu's speech to Congress and accused him of racism. "This is a real in-your-face slap at the president, and black folks know it," Rep. James Clyburn insisted, and suggested that Netanyahu, "wouldn't have done it to any other president."[9] Netanyahu and other Israeli Prime Ministers had clashed with previous presidents, including Clinton, Bush, and Carter, but the facts were irrelevant to the larger agenda of personalizing the conflict.

By portraying Netanyahu as a right-wing racist, Obama's allies had revived the old smear of Zionism as racism, while passing off their hatred of Israel under the guise of partisan and personality conflicts. The more Netanyahu tried to talk about issues, focusing on the Iranian threat, the more Obama's allies personalized everything by treating everything he did as a personal insult. The Jerusalem Strategy was the central thrust of Obama's campaign for the hearts and minds of Jewish Democrats. When Netanyahu arrived in the United States to launch a last-ditch argument against a nuclear deal with Iran, the White House spun it, above all else, as a personal insult by Netanyahu to Obama. Obama did not want an actual discussion about the Iran deal. His administration's double talk, secret agreements, illegal cash shipments, and dubious alliances with the Islamic terror state were explosive. But just as Netanyahu fought against the Iran deal by drawing on his experience as a commando and treating it as a military problem, Obama fought Netanyahu by drawing on his community organizer days. Prime Minister Netanyahu became the victim of the final Alinsky rule: "Pick the target, freeze it, personalize it, and polarize it."

While Netanyahu warned about Iran, Obama's allies claimed that Netanyahu was a political extremist. The White House countered Netanyahu's activism through covert means, by using the NSA to eavesdrop on Netanyahu and on pro-Israel advocates and members of Congress, in order to counter pro-Israel arguments, as a *Wall Street Journal* article revealed.[10] But its media campaign consisted of nastier and pettier provocations. One of Obama's media allies published an anonymous comment by a senior Obama official, calling Netanyahu, "a chickens__t." Jabs like these kept the debate at a personal level. And forced Jewish Democrats to choose between Netanyahu and Obama, rather than between Israel and Obama's policies.

Obama had gambled that his likability and politics of personal destruction would prevail. Early on, an administration official dismissed Netanyahu as "essentially a Republican." The remark warned Jewish Democrats that supporting Israel would mean backing the political opposition. In Ben Rhodes's memoir, the administration's toxic fixer, who led its political war against Israel, quoted Obama as saying, "Dealing with Bibi is like dealing with the Republicans."[11] Support for Israel had become an act of political treason, not to America, but to the Left. Even as Obama polarized support for Israel, his allies worked to fracture the pro-Israel lobby, undermining and humiliating AIPAC, [12] while bringing in an assortment of anti-Israel groups funded by political allies such as George Soros, to function as astroturf representatives of the Jewish community.[13]

AIPAC was sidelined, undermined, and humiliated, while J Street and even more vehemently anti-Israel groups, such as T'ruah, were welcomed to administration events. The White House's message, delivered directly and through its proxies, was that there was more than one way to be pro-Israel. Traditional pro-Israel organizations like AIPAC were accused of serving the interests of the Likud and "right-wing extremists." And that made them racists and right-wing extremists by extension. It also made support for Israel into a racist and right-wing position. This strategy was not, as administration mouthpieces insisted, a reaction to Netanyahu's intransigency. As far back as 2008, Obama had argued that, "There is a strain within the pro-Israel community that says unless you adopt a unwavering pro-Likud approach to Israel that you're anti-Israel."[14]

The insistence that the traditional pro-Israel position, which contended that Israel had a right to defend itself against terrorists, was actually a "right-wing" pro-Likud position, showed how supporting Israel was being transformed from a bipartisan into a partisan issue by Obama and his political allies. As the Jerusalem Strategy fractured our relationship with Israel, the Cairo Strategy was underway.

THE CAIRO STRATEGY

Athens and Jerusalem had been the paradigm of Western civilization. Obama replaced that paradigm with the paradox of Cairo, Tehran, and Jerusalem. These three cities were the fracture points between Obama and Netanyahu, between the Left and the Jews, and in the Obama era, America and Israel. Cairo, Tehran, and Jerusalem embodied Obama's foreign policy vision for the region, demanding that Israel give up territory to terrorists, including the holy city of Jerusalem, while forging a new relationship with the region through the Sunni and Shiite Islamists whose gateways were Cairo and Tehran. Iran's Tehran was the dominant Shiite Islamist power, and the Muslim Brotherhood in Cairo was the sleeping tiger of Sunni Islam with parties and terror groups lurking in countries across the region waiting to take power. American support for traditional Arab governments had restrained the ambitions of Iran and the Brotherhood. This balance of power had also restrained the Soviet Union, limited Iran's reach, and maintained stability in the region. It was a balance that leftist foreign policy, seeking revolution, had loathed.

Obama's determination to disrupt the status quo and empower Islamists was no surprise. The foreign policy speech which he gave in the fall of 2002, which helped secure support from Chicago radicals for his career in national politics, was not only noted for its opposition to the Iraq War. "Let's fight to make sure our so-called allies in the Middle East, the Saudis and the Egyptians, stop oppressing their own people, and suppressing dissent, and tolerating corruption and inequality, and mismanaging their economies so that their youth grow up without education, without prospects, without hope, the ready recruits of terrorist cells," Obama had demanded.

Seven years before he went to Cairo as the president of the United States, his vision had already been set.

The Egyptians and the Saudis were hardly saints, but in a region with far worse actors, they were an odd choice. But the Egyptians were the major obstacle to the Muslim Brotherhood, which had been born there, and the Saudis were restraining the ambitions of Iran. Even in 2002, Obama's vision was of unleashing the Muslim Brotherhood and Iran to redefine the region through Islamist takeovers. A decade after that speech, Egypt and the Saudis had become his biggest non-Jewish opponents in the region, and eventually the greatest targets of Obama's media allies, and part of Trump's coalition. The fundamental transformation of the region began not in Iran or Jerusalem, but in Cairo.

Obama's speech, "A New Beginning," laid out a vision for a new relationship, not between America and Egypt, but between America and Islam. His speech mentioned Egypt, as a nation, only twice, but Islam and Muslims, dozens of times. The Cairo speech rejected Arab nationalism and replaced it with Islamism. It did not recognize Egypt as a political entity, but as part of a global Islam community. That was not the vision of the United States or the Egyptian government, but of the Brotherhood. A New Beginning not only invited the Muslim Brotherhood to attend, and urged political changes that would bring the theocratic organization to power, but defined the world the way that they saw it.

The Cairo speech was the wellspring of the Arab Spring, signaling the withdrawal of American support for the old Arab governments, announcing support for the Islamists; and to Israel, it meant Obama was shifting support from the Egyptian government that had impeded Hamas and maintained stability, over to the Muslim Brotherhood, the parent organization of Hamas, whose governance would unleash not only the Islamic terrorist group, but also assist in the rise of ISIS in the Sinai. In Syria, the Arab Spring would bring Islamic terrorists to Israel's borders. Libya and other conflicts would unleash the flow of arms, including SA-7 anti-aircraft missiles and RPGs, into the hands of Hamas.[15] And yet the Arab Spring would also bring into being an alliance between the countries whose existence had no room in Obama's vision for the region, the Israelis, the Saudis, the UAE, and the Egyptians. The truly enduring damage inflicted by Obama's plan for Islamist regime change was ultimately to America.

Obama's betrayal of old allies led to a resurgence of Russian power in the region. The chaos and civil wars unleashed by his backing for Islamist regime change continues to tear apart the region. And the only real regional winner, Iran, expanded its influence to threaten Western oil supplies. And in America, the old bipartisan positions on traditional allies, including Israel, had been broken. The Democrats had become aligned with an Islamist coalition of Qatar, Iran, and Turkey, while growing isolated from the countries that represented the majority of the region—including Israel. By making Israel into a partisan issue, the Democrats had lost their influence over the Jewish State.

FROM THE ASHES OF BETRAYAL

The two wings of Obama's foreign policy, the pivot away from Israel and toward Islamists, came together catastrophically from Egypt to Iran to Turkey. In the political convulsions that shook the region, Israel was often collateral damage. The empowerment of Hamas, of Islamist terrorists in the Sinai and Syria, and the growth of Iran's nuclear and war-making capabilities were not directly aimed at Israel. The White House had a vision of transforming the region from one defined by allied Arab regimes struggling to restrain the ambitions of Islamists to one defined by empowered Islamist nations.

But Obama's hostility to Israel also fit into the larger belief that the only thing truly wrong with the Middle East was European colonialism. Once all the vestiges of colonialism had been withdrawn, all the allies abandoned, and the region returned to a pristine seventh-century order, then there would be peace. Israel, like Mubarak's Egypt, with its Christians, the North African governments and the oil kingdoms were unforgivably tainted by colonialism. They were all a foreign element in the region. And they had to go. In Obama's third term, that is still the Biden administration's policy which once again appeases Islamists while undermining our allies against the conquering terror of Islamism.

The new beginning would consolidate countries under populist Islamist regimes, legitimizing ethnic cleansing under the guise of democracy. Iran's Shiite allies would be allowed to dominate Iraq, while the Sunnis would push the Shiites out of Syria. The only consistent logic was that majorities would rule. Just not in Israel.

The Jews, like the Christians and Yazidis, had no place in a region divided between Sunni and Shiite Islamists. Unlike the Christians and Yazidis, Israel had a powerful military, extensive allies in America, and the support of a Jewish community that still tended to vote for the Democrats. And so, the administration adopted a tactic that was at once confrontational and passive aggressive. It manufactured disputes, turning its own confrontations into protestations of victimhood. Somehow the most powerful man on earth was portrayed as being the victim of a country the size of New Jersey. But, while the manufactured controversies blazed, Prime Minister Netanyahu and other Israeli leaders struggled to convey the magnitude of the disaster that was sweeping across the Middle East.

Obama's support for Islamist power set off murderous civil wars in Syria and Iraq that led to the rise of ISIS. His backing for regime change in Egypt led to the massacre of Christians, the empowerment of Hamas, and the rise of ISIS in the Sinai. His support for Iran led to famine in Yemen, the murder of gays in Iraq, and rockets raining down on Israel. But it also transformed the region in unexpected ways. Instead of the rise of a stable regional Islamist majority that would surround and eventually crush Israel, along with other non-Muslim minorities, out of existence, new coalitions rose out of the ashes.

The growing power of Sunni and Shiite Islamists led Saudi Arabia and the United Arab Emirates into a barely covert alliance with Israel. The Egyptian military survived the Muslim Brotherhood takeover and reemerged with more in common with Israel than its generals had ever thought they had before. For the first time in history, Israel was part of a regional coalition. The loose coalition sought to restore stability in the region by opposing the Muslim Brotherhood, its Turkish and Qatari backers, and Iran. And all it took for Israel to join the club was being kicked to the curb by Obama. The paradox of his foreign policy was that, in the name of anti-colonialism, Obama had unrolled a broad regime change strategy that had all the elements of colonialism. Israel, which the White House's foreign policy mindset had viewed as colonialist, found itself on the anti-colonialist side of the struggle.

Meanwhile the Muslim Brotherhood, which the White House saw as the anti-colonialist hope of the region, had come to be seen as the colonialist puppet of the colonialist in the White House. Within a matter of years, Hamas had gone from being the native sons to foreign puppets. And the Zionist Entity, still often reviled, had, perhaps only briefly, come to grudgingly seem not so bad after all. Wholly unintentionally, Obama's betrayal of Israel had won it new regional allies among former enemies. Much as his championing of the Brotherhood and Iran, unintentionally convinced the Saudis to allow women to drive. The law of unintended consequences is, if nothing else, reliably surprising.

Obama wanted to change the region and our foreign policy. And he succeeded. But not as expected. The White House succeeded in making Israel into a partisan issue. But instead of weakening Israel, a new Republican administration embraced it and implemented, for the first time, a pro-Israel policy. The embassy move, the recognition of the Golan Heights, and the banishing of the Palestinian Authority were the fruits of Obama's fracturing of a bipartisan consensus on Israel and the weakening of AIPAC. Obama and his proxies had repeatedly claimed that the AIPAC position was really the Likud position. The Trump administration showed what a foreign policy that adopted Likud positions would really look like.

The question is what comes next? Both in our foreign policy and in the region, much depends on the play of events. The anti-Islamist coalition may hold together, or it may not. Democrats may decide to try and rebuild a bipartisan consensus, or they may continue a leftward move that will banish pro-Israel positions entirely. As events move forward, it is vital that we understand what happened and why it happened. The Obama years serve as a demonstration of what happens when wishful thinking and distorted reasoning are allowed to dictate foreign policy. Countless lives have been lost in the region. And as the radioactive sword of Iran's nuclear program hangs overhead, those deaths may only be the beginning.

America's relationship with Israel has been at the heart of our foreign policy because it is a moral signal. It communicates our values abroad, not only to us or to the Israelis, but to the region and the world. Its impact goes far beyond a nation the size of New Jersey. Instead, it sends a message to friends and foes of our intentions, our reliability, and our vision, building and destroying alliances, and changing the world.

Daniel Greenfield, a Shillman Journalism Fellow at the David Horowitz Freedom Center, and he is an investigative journalist and writer focusing on the radical Left and Islamic terrorism.

6

HOW OBAMA FUNDED THE
MURDER OF ISRAELIS

by Daniel Greenfield

IN JERUSALEM, 2017 began with a terrorist ramming a truck into Israeli cadets who were getting off the bus. Four of the Israelis, three of them women, were killed, and over a dozen more were injured. Fadi al-Qanbar, the terrorist, was shot and killed by Israeli soldiers, but his widow was set to receive a lifetime monthly pension of 2,900 Israeli shekels from the Palestinian Authority for his crime.[1] The average salary in the West Bank is 1,720 NIS. Even though the terrorist had allegedly been inspired by ISIS,[2] the Palestinian Authority media had described him as a "Shahid" or religious martyr for Islam.[3] Despite this latest act, which demonstrated the linkage between our foreign aid to the

Palestinian Authority, Islamic terrorism, even terrorism related to ISIS, and the murder of Israelis, the money kept coming. A few weeks after the mass murder of Israelis in Jerusalem, the Obama administration rushed to transfer $221 million in funds to the Palestinian Authority that Republicans had been blocking.[4]

Hours before President Trump was inaugurated, Secretary of State John Kerry rushed the money to the terrorists. What kind of a difference would that $221 million make? The Palestinian Authority's Martyrs Fund budget for 2017 allocated $153 million in salaries to terrorists who had been or were imprisoned by Israel and another $190 million to the families of the terrorists.[5] The $221 million amounted to a sizable percentage of the "Pay to Slay" budget that was used to incentivize murders like these. And it paid off. The number of Israelis killed in terrorist attacks increased in 2017.[6] The number of lone wolf attack plots rose from 400 to 1,100. And the Martyrs Fund was a key mechanism for incentivizing these attacks, assuring surviving terrorists of a generous lifetime income and, in the event of their deaths, giving them the comfort of knowing that no matter what happens, their families will be very well taken care of.

The murders of Jews funded in 2017 included the Sabbath attack on the Salomons who were celebrating the birth of a new member of the family when an Islamic terrorist burst in with a knife and a Koran, stabbed to death seventy-year-old Yosef Salomon, wounded his wife, Tova Salomon, and murdered Chaya and Elad, Yosef's son and daughter. "I saw two houses; from one of them I heard voices and from the other I heard laughter. So I decided to get into the one that had laughter," Omar el-Abed, the terrorist, later explained.[7] The Israeli Defense Ministry estimated in 2018 that the murderer, who had smiled throughout the trial, had been paid 12,000 NIS, and would earn as much as 12 million NIS or $3.5 million throughout his life.[8]

While some argued that United States foreign aid was not meant by the Obama administration for the Martyrs Fund and its "Pay to Slay" program, money is fungible. American foreign aid allowed the Palestinian

Authority the financial freedom to invest money into funding the murder of Jews. The connection between foreign aid and violence had already been demonstrated when the rise in murders closely followed the increase in foreign aid from 2001 to 2007.[9] But the Obama era ushered in a massive increase in assistance to the terrorists running the Palestinian Authority. From an average of $170 million during the Bush years, bilateral assistance hit $400 million in 2008 and by 2009 approached $1 billion. The new annual average became $400 million, but the real price was paid by terror victims.[10] The Trump administration aggressively cut foreign aid to the Palestinian Authority, but the damage had already been done. The Israelis who had been killed by "Pay to Slay" terrorists would not be brought back to life, and the years of booming funding had built up the infrastructure of individual "lone wolf" terror. But the Obama administration's foreign aid to the Palestinian Authority was only part of the terror funding picture. The other half of the terror picture was the PA's occasional rival and ally, Hamas.

In 2016, the Obama administration had illegally transferred $1.7 billion to Iran.[11] The deputy chief of the Islamic Revolutionary Guard Corps (IRGC) claimed credit for the ransom.[12] The IRGC is a hub of Islamic terrorism in the region and was designated as a Foreign Terrorist Organization by President Trump.[13] "We can always hand it over to someone who can hand it over to the IRGC," State Department spokesman Mark Toner admitted.[14] Meanwhile the Obama administration had even tried to give Iran access to the United States financial system, converting billions into dollars and then euros.[15] After the $1.7 billion payment, Iran increased its military budget by that same amount.[16] It's been estimated that 65 percent of the military budget goes to the IRGC.[17]

And the IRGC funds, trains, and aids a variety of Islamic terrorist groups, including Hamas. That includes the missiles that Hamas has been firing at Israel and that have fallen on Jerusalem and Tel Aviv.[18] The billions in sanctions relief allowed Iran to increase its investment in conflicts in the region.[19] In 2017, Hamas announced that it had resumed receiving aid from Iran.[20] In 2019, Iran boosted aid to Hamas from $70 million a year to $30 million a month.[21] Beyond Hamas, Iran also backs Islamic Jihad (PIJ), which was at the center of the latest round of rocket attacks on Israel in the fall of 2019. These rockets were, like Hamas's rockets, developed with the assistance of the Islamic Republic of Iran. The extent of Iran's involvement in Islamic terrorism in Israel can be measured by an admission by Ali Akbar Velayati, foreign affairs adviser to the Supreme Leader of Iran that, "most of the weapons used by the Palestinians came from Iran, or that Iran help[ed] the Palestinians manufacture the weapons themselves."[22]

The Obama administration dramatically boosted aid to the Palestinian Authority. It went on pouring funds into the Palestinian Authority even though the terror network was funding the murder of Jews. It provided $1.7 billion in payments and billions more in sanctions relief to Iran. And Iran was able to use sanctions relief to increase funding to the IRGC, and increase payments to terror groups like Hamas. These numbers are not just abstractions; they translate into Israelis and Americans wounded and killed. The Obama administration was aware of the consequences of the billions it had poured into the Palestinian Authority and Iran. It knew that the money would be used to kill Jews. We will never know exactly how many Americans and Jews were killed because of those billions.

Even when the payments were made in cash, as was the case with the $400 million in foreign currency flown over to Iran, no single bill likely made its way directly into the hands of a terrorist who murdered a Jewish person. But money is fungible. When billions are poured into the infrastructure of terror, that money is blood money. The crimes committed by the terror networks feed off that infrastructure, at any level of scale from large terror groups like Hamas or Hezbollah to the individual "lone wolf" Islamic terrorist who expects to receive a generous salary from the Palestinian Authority and are on the political conscience of their funders, no matter how indirect they may claim that their contributions are.

The billions of dollars that the Obama administration injected into the infrastructure of terror was used to murder Jews. These people are not abstractions or statistics. They are as real as Chaya Salomon who opened the door at a knock and was stabbed to death by a terrorist. Chaya, a second-grade teacher, ran for help even as she was dying of her wounds.

"Dear student, when I give the report cards at the end of the semester, I am always reminded of another report card, almost like at school," she had written in a final message to her students. "It is given by our Father in Heaven, Who is everywhere. But instead of the regular subjects and exam grades, He gives grades in the following subjects: friendliness, patience, understanding, love, kindness, responsibility, gratitude, humility. And that other report card is important, even more than any other grade."[23] Chaya did not have to die. The Obama administration made a decision to keep funding the Palestinian Authority that had been funding the murder of grandfathers and grandmothers, rabbis and second-grade teachers, children and their parents. That decision may have helped lead to Chana's death.

The report card of the Obama administration reflects not mere statistics. It is marked with blood.

7

BENGHAZI BETRAYAL AND
THE BROTHERHOOD LINK

by Clare M. Lopez

IN AUGUST 2010, the Obama administration produced a document known as Presidential Study Directive 11 (PSD-11). Although PSD-11 remains classified to this day, it is understood to lay out a blueprint for US government engagement with and promotion of the Muslim Brotherhood jihad organization both domestically and abroad. Building on themes first laid out publicly in his June 2009 speech in Cairo, Egypt, with PSD-11, Obama decreed an about-face in US foreign policy strategy that "emphasized support for regime change"[1] across the Middle East and North Africa (MENA) region, according to September 2016 Congressional testimony by Pete Hoekstra, former Chairman of the

House Permanent Select Committee on Intelligence (HPSCI).[2]

Within months of taking office, President Barack Obama made it a priority to travel to Egypt, where he appeared on June 4, 2009, at Cairo University at an event co-hosted by al-Azhar University (the premier seat of orthodox Sunni Islamic learning since the tenth century). His speech, entitled "A New Beginning," was a direct expression of support for the forces of the Islamic Movement, led globally by the Muslim Brotherhood (*Ikhwan* in Arabic).[3] Although the Brotherhood was banned by the Egyptian government, Obama explicitly invited top Brotherhood operatives to attend his speech and sit in the front row, thus ensuring that then-Egyptian President Hosni Mubarak would not attend. The writing was on the wall, not just for long-time US ally Mubarak, but for leaders across North Africa.

It is not likely that Obama was unaware of the violent origins and jihadist identity of the Muslim Brotherhood, founded in Cairo in 1928 by Hassan al-Banna and other students from Cairo University. Its pledge[4] then remains the same today: "Allah is our objective. The Prophet is our leader. Qur'an is our law. Jihad is our way. Dying in the way of Allah is our highest hope." Indeed, at a 2011 presidential campaign rally following Mubarak's ouster, the White House's openly supported Brotherhood candidate, Muhammad Morsi, led a roaring crowd in chanting exactly that motto.[5]

Much closer to home, though, was the Holy Land Foundation (HLF) HAMAS terror funding trial, which concluded in 2008 in Richardson, Texas. Even as President Obama took office in early 2009, the judge in the HLF trial ordered hundreds of the Muslim Brotherhood's own documents, seized in a 2004 FBI raid in Annandale, Virginia, and used by the Department of Justice prosecution team in the case, to be posted online because he believed it so critical that the American people see exactly who and what the Muslim Brotherhood is. Key among them is the 1991 document called "*An Explanatory Memorandum on the General Strategic Goal for the Group in North America,*" written by Mohamed Akram, also known as Mohamed Adlouni, a top Brotherhood official in the US at the time, which describes in detail the Brotherhood's subversive mission in the US. Perhaps its most important section reads:

> The process of settlement is a "Civilization-Jihadist Process" with all the word means. The Ikhwan must understand that their work in America is a kind of grand Jihad in eliminating and destroying the Western civilization from within and "sabotaging" its miserable house by their hands and the hands of the believers so that it is eliminated and God's religion is made victorious over all other religions.

As I wrote in my April 2013 essay on the *"History of the Muslim Brotherhood Penetration of the U.S. Government,"*[6] by the time the Obama administration helped revolutionary jihadist forces to sweep away authoritative, but non-jihadist rulers across North Africa during the so-called Arab Spring of 2011, the Muslim Brotherhood had long established a deep and pervasive penetration of the US government and society. Without question, it was the official, active involvement of the US government to help arm, fund, support, and train both Al-Qa'eda and Brotherhood forces across the MENA region that enabled Islamic movement jihadis to advance as far and as quickly as they did. Rulers Zine El Abidine Ben Ali of Tunisia, Hosni Mubarak of Egypt, and Muammar Qaddafi of Libya were all ousted in 2011 in a series of violent uprisings that had very little to do with liberal Western-style democracy and everything to do with the Obama administration green light for the forces of the global Islamic movement.[7] Bashar al-Assad of Syria has survived to date only thanks to massive support from Iran, its Lebanese Shi'ite terror proxy Hizballah, and Russia.

The case of Libya is perhaps most illustrative of the Obama administration's betrayal of America's own foundational principles, as well as of a US ally in what was then called the Global War on Terror (GWOT), and of individual Americans, sent in harm's way and then left to fight and die alone with no effort at rescue the night of September 11–12, 2012, in Benghazi, Libya. The Citizens' Commission on Benghazi

(CCB) was formed on July 30, 2013, with a mission to "to determine the truth and accuracy of what happened in Benghazi, Libya on September 11th, 2012."[8] CCB founding members included the group's leader, Roger Aronoff; General Charles Jones (Ret.); Admiral James "Ace" Lyons (Ret., d. 12 December 2018); General Thomas McInerney (Ret.); General Paul Vallely (Ret.); former Congressman and retired Army Lt. Colonel Allen West; members of the Special Operations community; and me, Clare M. Lopez. The CCB issued two reports on events in Benghazi: the first, an interim report in April 2014, and then a final report, "Betrayal in Benghazi: A Dereliction of Duty," on June 29, 2016.[9]

Although the CCB set out specifically to learn what really happened in the months leading up to the September 11, 2012, attack on the US Mission in Benghazi as well as during and in the aftermath of the attack, what we learned in the course of our investigation proved "a sort of Rosetta Stone" that in fact revealed how the methodical, phased penetration and subordination of the US government by the Muslim Brotherhood enabled, and even made inevitable, the disastrous events of the MENA Islamic Uprising of 2011, including the murder in Benghazi of four Americans.[10]

Recalling the brazenly declared objective of the Muslim Brotherhood to eliminate and destroy Western Civilization—and above all, the Constitutional Republic of the USA—we see that the *Ikhwan* strategy explicitly has avoided terrorism and violence and instead focused on subversion from within. That strategy has been in progress since shortly after World War II and involved first and foremost the achievement of information dominance. As the Center for Security Policy (CSP) wrote in its 2010 book, *Shariah: The Threat to America. An Exercise in Competitive Analysis, Report of Team B II,*[11] the Brotherhood's brilliant and successful plan was to "co-opt the leadership of this country by fooling it into believing a counterfactual understanding of Islam and the nature of the Muslim Brotherhood, thereby manipulating or coercing these leaders to enforce the MB narrative on their subordinates."[12] By controlling the flow of information that members of the US national security community were allowed to know, the Brotherhood, amazingly, has managed not only to keep its targets ignorant of the true nature of Islam, jihad and shariah, but by way of the Muslim Brotherhood inspired-and-directed Great Purge of 2011–2012, removed all accurate references to the inspirational connection between Islam and Islamic terrorism from official USG usage, government-wide.

It is important to understanding how America switched sides in the GWOT and the betrayal in Benghazi to lay out this sequence of earlier events by which perhaps well-meaning but ultimately derelict of duty senior US officials abrogated their oath to support and defend the Constitution against all enemies foreign and domestic when they failed in their first duty to actually know that enemy. The post-9/11 scrub of the official USG lexicon of words like "jihad," "Islam," and "Muslim," began when US officials entrusted with the counterterrorism mission allowed themselves to fall under the influence of identifiable members of the Muslim Brotherhood and began substituting a garbled jumble of inaccurate words to replace the language that the Islamic enemy himself actually uses to describe his 1,400-year-old offensive to conquer the world. No later than 2012 (and in fact, much earlier), the entire executive branch of the USG, including the Departments of Defense, Homeland Security, Justice, and State, in addition to the entire intelligence community, had mounted a concerted effort to purge all instructors and training curricula that associated Islamic doctrine, law, and scriptures with Islamic terrorism.[13]

Thus, the Obama administration's pro-Muslim Brotherhood policy, as formally promulgated in PSD-11, may be seen as the culmination of the *Ikhwan*'s decades-long campaign effectively to hobble the ability of the US government to identify and counter the Islamic jihad enemy. By this point, there was no possibility left that the USG would be able to even understand the threat coming against it, and directing a national security strategy to defend against it was now completely off the table. Game, set, match to the Islamic movement.

Thus, as the PSD-11-supported Islamic Uprising got underway in early 2011, it was US government officials, led by President Obama, then-Secretary of State Hillary Clinton (with her Brotherhood-compromised deputy chief of staff Huma Abedin), and newly named Envoy to the Libyan rebels, Christopher Stevens, who leaped to provide diplomatic backing, funding, NATO warplane cover, and weapons to the Libyan Muslim Brotherhood and its subordinate Al-Qa'eda militias fighting to oust the US's GWOT ally, Muammar Qaddafi. For reasons best known still to these officials, the State Department refused to close its Special Mission Compound in Benghazi throughout 2012 or to provide it the additional security measures that were repeatedly requested, even as Libya descended into widespread armed chaos following Qaddafi's October 2011 ouster.

As the CCB's June 2016 report documents,[14] the USG also ignored repeated warnings in both intelligence and open source channels that a serious attack against the Benghazi Mission was imminent. Given the compromised situation inside senior ranks of the Obama administration, however—at the Defense Department, State Department, and intelligence community—where officers were not only deliberately deprived of accurate information about the shariah-mandated jihad objectives of Al-Qa'eda and the Muslim Brotherhood, but under pressure to present an entirely false image of "normalcy" in Libya following the USG-sponsored Islamic revolution, it becomes understandable how the disaster of September 11–12, 2012, was allowed to happen.

Egregious as was the Obama administration's failure to take steps to ensure mission security in the lead-up to the 9/11 anniversary date in 2012, what was utterly inexcusable once the attack against our Mission in Benghazi began was the refusal of the Obama White House, Clinton State Department, or Leon Panetta Defense Department to even attempt to commit forces to come to the rescue of the besieged Americans in Benghazi. The CCB ascertained that US forces at Aviano Air Base and Naval Air Station Sigonella in Italy, at the Rota Naval Base in Spain, and the Commander's In-Extremis Force in Croatia, in addition to Foreign Emergency Support Teams (FEST), were available and in range that night to have made a difference, perhaps even to have saved the lives of former Special Operations members Tyron Woods and Glenn Doherty, who died protecting the CIA Annex.[15] But they were never given a "Go" order.

The litany of failures by the Obama administration continued after the Benghazi attack. For a solid two weeks following its refusal to even attempt sending assistance to the beleaguered Americans in Benghazi, the White House, State Department, and intelligence community collaborated to stage a massive cover-up of what really happened there that night.[16] Joined by US Muslim Brotherhood front groups and government members of the Brotherhood-dominated Organization of Islamic Cooperation (OIC), the Obama team persisted in denying the role of Muslim Brotherhood–directed Al-Qa'eda militias in staging the lethal attack on our Benghazi Mission. Aside from the fact that the fall of 2012 was deep into Obama's presidential re-election campaign—which would not have benefited from truthful admission about USG collusion with the forces of Islamic jihad or the very alive-and-well status of Al-Qa'eda—all the earlier groundwork by elements of the US Muslim Brotherhood in denying critical information to our national security leadership also must be factored into any analysis about Benghazi.

Unfortunately, the nightmare of Obama-era collaboration with the Muslim Brotherhood to the massive detriment of US national security did not end when the last Americans finally were pulled out of the ruins of the US Mission in Benghazi, Libya. The influence of the *Ikhwan* persists throughout the USG, in part because the Great Purge has never been reversed, even under the Trump administration—and certainly not in the Biden administration—and in part because the seditious influence of the Islamic movement has never even been acknowledged, much less confronted in a comprehensive legal way and removed. Rather, the narrative so gradually but inexorably planted within the entirety of American society and government about the benign nature of Islam, jihad, shariah, and the Muslim Brotherhood has taken hold and been mainstreamed. While the US government was obviously a top targeting priority for the Brotherhood's "civilizational jihad," its messaging through Islamic Centers, madrassas, mosques, and myriad front groups has thoroughly penetrated academia, our courts and legal system, faith communities, local law enforcement, media, society, think tanks, and the workplace in general.

Indeed, as the Biden administration staffed out its positions for advisors and appointees in 2021, it became obvious that many of the same figures who had populated the pro-Muslim Brotherhood Obama administration were now back in office. Dominated by a worldview that sees America as a force for ill in the world, especially the Islamic world, these officials seek to remove US power and influence from the MENA region while once again doing all in their power to enable the influence of the Islamic movement domestically. The Biden administration's disastrous retreat from Afghan battlefields in August 2021, not only unilaterally ceded power to the Taliban and its jihadist allies, but equipped them with some $85 billion in top-of-the-line US equipment and weaponry left behind. Over the months since then, the US has been flooded with tens of thousands of mostly unvetted Afghan evacuees, dispersed across the country. Subsequent Biden policy discussions have involved the provision of "humanitarian aid" to the Taliban and even possible recognition of the Taliban as the *de facto* government of Afghanistan.

Outreach to jihadist regimes, such as those ruling Iran and the Palestinian Authority (PA), while shunning Abraham Accord working partners in Saudi Arabia, Bahrain, the United Arab Emirates, and elsewhere reflects the continuing malign influence of such advisors as Secretary of State Antony Blinken, National Security Advisor Jake Sullivan, CIA Director William Burns, and Director of National Intelligence Avril Haines, who were instrumental in the Obama embrace of the Muslim Brotherhood during the Islamic Uprising of 2011 as well as of the murderous Shi'ite leadership in Iran. One of the top priorities of the Biden administration through its early months was a desperate effort to convince Tehran to allow the US back into the by-now thoroughly OBE Iran nuclear deal of 2015 (JCPOA or Joint Comprehensive Plan of Action). Disregard for the PA's genocidal intentions toward Israel likewise has proven no obstacle to the Biden team's pressuring Israel to capitulate to the PA's incessant demands. [17]

The appointment of one of the most pro-jihadist, anti-Israel officials imaginable—Beirut-born Deputy Assistant Secretary of State Hady Amr—to oversee Israeli and Palestinian Authority affairs at the Department of State is a case in point. Following a career littered with sympathetic utterances for HAMAS (the Gazan branch of the Muslim Brotherhood), a gig at the Brookings Institute center in Doha, Qatar (home-away-from-home for exiled members of the Egyptian Muslim Brotherhood, including Yousef al-Qaradawi, the senior jurist of the MB), and appointment as Obama's Deputy Head of USAID's Middle East Bureau, Amr returned to the State Department in 2021 as Deputy Assistant Secretary of State for Near Eastern Affairs. Amr lost no time in reaching out to the PA's Minister Hussein al-Sheikh of the Palestinian Authority, who is a member of the PLO (Palestinian Liberation Organization) Central Council and of the Central Committee of the Fatah Party. Amr also quickly called for an immediate resumption of US financial aid to UNRWA (UN Relief and Works Agency), a frequent front for HAMAS terrorism operations.[18]

Another of the Biden administration's Muslim Brotherhood-connected appointees is Maher Bitar, who was named Biden's senior director for intelligence at the National Security Council. The position is one of the most important and powerful in the entire intelligence community (IC). Bitar has been handed authority to manage the flow of all intelligence passing between the IC and the White House as well as to determine priorities for IC-wide intelligence collection. The problem is that Bitar has been closely associated with Muslim Brotherhood (MB) front groups since his student days at Georgetown University, where he was a leader of the MB-sponsored Students for Justice in Palestine (SJP). The SJP is the campus branch of American Muslims for Palestine (AMP). According to Jonathan Schanzer, senior vice president of research at the Foundation for Defense of Democracies, "AMP is arguably the most important sponsor and organizer for Students for Justice in Palestine (SJP)."[19] AMP is a founding member of the Muslim Brotherhood's US political umbrella group, the US Council of Muslim Organizations (USCMO).[20] Bitar later worked in Jerusalem for UNWRA before serving on Barack Obama's National Security Council.

On July 20, 2020, then-US presidential candidate Joe Biden spoke via internet to the Million Muslim Votes Summit,[21] during which he cited from a hadith[22] in a way that (surely unwittingly) endorsed jihad against the US. The online event was sponsored by Emgage Action, which is a Muslim Brotherhood–linked Political Action Committee (PAC) that endorsed Biden in April 2020. Emgage Action's parent organization, Emgage USA (formerly called Emerge USA, an acronym for Empowering, Motivating, & Educating Resourceful Grassroots Entities), is a front group for the Council on American Islamic Relations (CAIR), which is the US branch of designated Foreign Terrorist Organization, HAMAS (itself the Palestinian branch of the Muslim Brotherhood). CAIR was named by the Department of Justice an unindicted co-conspirator in the 2008 Holy Land Foundation HAMAS terror funding trial.[23]

How Biden came to speak such a jihad threat against the US most likely can best be understood as words set onto his teleprompter by Brotherhood-linked advisors, perhaps including Farooq Mitha, a "Muslim engagement adviser" to the Biden campaign. Farooq Mitha, who served in the Obama administration from 2010–2011 as special assistant to the director of the US Department of Defense Office of Small Business Programs, is a long-time Brotherhood operative who worked with Emerge USA before it changed its name to Emgage USA in 2014.[24] Mitha currently is listed as an Emgage USA Board Member for Virginia[25] while also serving simultaneously in the Biden administration as the Director of the Department of Defense (DoD) Office of Small Business Programs (OSBP).[26]

These few examples are illustrative of the pro-jihadist, pro-Muslim Brotherhood worldview of the Biden administration. Still in its first year as of this writing, that administration seems to have picked up about where the Obama administration left off in terms of its links to Muslim Brotherhood–affiliated appointees, officials, and staffers. Foreign policy decisions now flowing from the Biden White House, in particular those shaping the US course of action in the MENA region and beyond, attest to the influence wielded by such officials.

Absent a concerted effort now to educate and engage the American citizenry at all levels of society—federal, state, and local—about the corrosive impact of Islamic Movement/Muslim Brotherhood information operations upon our ability to remain a Constitutional Republic free of Islamic Law (shariah), America will continue to succumb slowly to the methodical sabotage from within, "by our hands," that the Explanatory Memorandum warned of so many decades ago.[27] The Global Islamic Movement confronts us with a clear and present danger that must be faced—and soon—if this country is to remain the "last best hope of mankind on earth."[28]

Clare Lopez is a founding member of the Citizens' Commission on Benghazi and principal author of both of the Commission's reports.

8

OBAMA'S RUSSIA COLLUSION

by J. R. Nyquist

BARACK HUSSEIN OBAMA, the forty-fourth president of the United States, was conceived because his parents were students of the Russian language, who met in a Russian class. Obama's father was an African socialist. His mother was a cultural Marxist.[1] Why were they studying Russian? We don't exactly know. What we do know is that Obama's parents did not like capitalism. Perhaps they were learning Russian because their ideals aligned with those of the "socialist motherland." Sadly, Obama's parents died many years ago. We cannot ask them why they were studying Russian in the fall of 1961.

It is with this preamble I relate the following facts and testimony, to better clarify these early intimations of Obama's family allegiance. The actions and policies of President Obama, in relation to Russia, are exactly what one might expect from a president who was born of pro-Soviet parents and mentored by a likely KGB agent (*i.e.*, Frank Marshall Davis). During his presidency, Obama was eager to assist Russia technologically and economically. Obama's Russia "reset" policy, begun in 2009, was explained by Hillary Clinton with the following words: "Our goal is to help strengthen Russia."[2] First came the Uranium One deal.[3] Then came $1 billion for a Russian tech park at Skolkovo, outside Moscow.[4] All this help for Russia was facilitated by the Obama administration. This was done despite Russia's ongoing policy of transferring dangerous materials and technologies to rogue regimes. This was done despite Moscow's dismal human rights record—despite the killing of journalists like Anna Politkovskaya and the assassination of overseas dissidents like Alexander Litvinenko. This was done despite Russia's growing anti-American media campaign, which began in early 2012 and reached a fever pitch in April 2014.

In 2012 and 2013, the Russians held impromptu secret discussions with Barack Obama, Hillary Clinton, and John Kerry. These were meetings without an official record of what was said, without witnesses or even translators present. The meetings offered no transparency to the American side—no means by which other Americans could see what Obama and his secretaries of state were up to. The first of these meetings took place in South Korea when Presidents Obama and Medvedev were caught on a hot microphone exchanging confidences. Clasping Medvedev's hand, Obama said he would be "more flexible" on missile defense after the November election. Medvedev promised to "tell Vladimir." The two leaders had no idea the world was listening.

What we heard was evidence of a deeper, closer, more far-reaching set of understandings. This friendliness between Obama and Medvedev was particularly strange as US Ambassador Michael McFaul was *already* under intensive attack from the Russian media. In fact, the Russian state-controlled media was calling McFaul a child molester working to overthrow the Russian state. As McFaul later explained in his memoirs, "Denying that you are a pedophile, refuting accusations that you are plotting a regime change, explaining to the world that you are not criticizing Putin on his election night—it all became so tedious, defensive, and exhausting."[5] And yet, in the late summer of 2012, Obama scolded Mitt Romney for suggesting that Russia was our greatest threat. "The Cold War has been over for twenty years," said Obama in a lecturing tone. He accused Romney of "wanting to import the foreign policies of the 1980s."[6]

The second secret meeting in the series took place on June 29, 2012. According to Ambassador McFaul, an American delegation led by Secretary of State Hillary Clinton arrived in St. Petersburg "to agree on a common path forward" in advance of the Syria talks scheduled for the next day in Geneva, Switzerland. According to McFaul, "[Russian Foreign Minister] Lavrov took Clinton and the rest of our delegation to the roof of the building [of an upscale restaurant on the Neva River], which offered up a spectacular, panoramic view of the city." But then something odd happened. Russian Foreign Minister Lavrov took Clinton away from the American delegation "to a small room for a private chat." McFaul described the occasion further:

> Because Lavrov speaks flawless English, no translators were needed. For the next two hours or so, they spoke alone about Syria. None of us in Clinton's delegation were happy with Lavrov's move. We wanted to hear the conversation. We wanted to offer guidance and support to the secretary as needed. I knew Lavrov to be excellent at his job, playing whatever cards he held to maximum effect. In one-on-one sessions, he utilized an effective combination of persuasion and stubbornness that could wear the other side down. We fretted that Clinton was at a disadvantage.[7]

The relationship between Clinton and Lavrov, which had previously been cozy, took a strange turn. The party sat down for dinner after the meeting. Clinton and Lavrov "appeared satisfied with the progress they had made," but the Russian suddenly and inexplicably referred to Clinton's press spokesperson Victoria Nuland as the "Minister of Disinformation." It came as a slap-in-the-face to hear such an undiplomatic remark from such an otherwise smooth diplomat. According to McFaul, the Russian was not angry. He was happy with everything that had happened. McFaul wrote, "Lavrov rarely expressed such exuberance. There must be more to the story." The American ambassador made an even more curious observation: "for the rest of her time in St. Petersburg, Clinton was churning. I had the impression that she did not like what she had heard from Lavrov in their one-on-one."[8]

Nobody knows what that two-hour conversation between Clinton and Lavrov was about, except that the Russian was "exuberant" and Secretary of State Clinton was "churning." This noteworthy meeting, without witnesses or record, marked an outward shift in the relationship between Obama's White House and the Kremlin. Why was there a shift? Ukraine had not been invaded yet. The Russian reset was still considered a "success" despite the Russian media's smear campaign against McFaul. But there it was—a pivot upon which everything was about to turn. When John Kerry became secretary of state in 2013, he visited Moscow and went through the same procedure. He had a private meeting with Lavrov for an hour—no witnesses, no translators.[9]

There appeared, at roughly the same time, another element in Russia's behavior. McFaul noticed a peculiar shift in Kremlin propaganda: "Departing from Cold War tropes, Putin's regime added a new dimension to the ideological struggle—conservative, moral, nationalist Russia versus the liberal, immoral, internationalist West."[10] Already the Kremlin had developed a plan of action which would uncannily unfold along lines now familiar. Russia had been the land of Lenin and Stalin, of socialism and communism. Then came the collapse of communism. But that "collapse" was a fraud. Nothing of substance in the country had changed. Elections were still rigged, power was still centralized, businesses were controlled by agents of the regime. The ruling structures of Russia were still communist in terms of interior organization, secrecy, and allies abroad. The same communists in Africa, Asia, and Latin America were supported by Moscow as under the Soviet Union. The same *nomenklatura* sat in the same government offices as before; and they were busy reassembling the Soviet empire. In fact, communism was on the brink of a surprise comeback. The Communist Party, the Soviet Union's "friends" in America, had gotten into the White House. Thanks to Obama's policies, the US military continued to deteriorate vis-à-vis Russia and communist China (two countries now allied with each other).

What was needed at this critical juncture was an alibi for Obama and his successor. It would have been catastrophic for the communists if the American public had noticed the new ideological configuration—and the new power configuration—taking shape across the globe and in Washington. It now became necessary to initiate a policy of false opposition between the Obama White House and the Kremlin. The hot mic episode in South Korea had revealed an all-too-cozy friendship between Obama and the Russian leaders. Better to create the appearance of distance, to establish a new line of disinformation. Some clever analyst was bound to see that Russia and China—the two "former" giants of the communist world—were supporting communist regimes and movements in the Western Hemisphere.

If enough observers put those facts together with Obama's background and the true significance of his policies, there might be an inconvenient public awakening. To prevent this from happening, a strategy had long been kept in reserve—that is, of portraying Putin as a "conservative" defender of Western civilization, a Christian, and a homophobe. At the same time, Obama took up an opposing set of principles. This strategic/polemical turn would assume great importance in 2016 when Trump won the presidential election after being called "a Russian puppet" by Obama's designated successor, Hillary Clinton.

In 2015 and 2016, Obama's intelligence apparatus played a prominent role in luring Trump campaign officials to meetings with supposed Russians. These were preparatory moves, done within the context of a larger Obama/Kremlin strategy. Obama's collusion with Russia had become too hot for open continuance. It was now time for diversionary operations of the accusatory kind. We do not know as yet how widespread the effort was to manufacture evidence to prove Republicans were "colluding" with Russia, but the effort was serious, involving CIA Director John Brennan and FBI Director James Comey.

The Russians also cooperated in the effort—with the "dirty dossier" and meetings with Trump's people at the Trump Tower. The stage was being carefully set, against all previous expectations, for Obama to say that Russia was a threat to American democracy. Who would have imagined such words coming out of Obama's mouth? Yet Obama was shrewd in his distinctions. He was careful to add that Russia was not a military threat to US security. He said, merely, that Russian meddling was a threat to US democracy—by way of Donald Trump.

Keeping to his role as newly minted patriot, Obama perfected a kind of doublespeak about Russia. After Russia's annexation of Crimea in 2014, reporters reminded Obama what Romney had said about Moscow being a threat. Obama told reporters, "Russia is a regional power that is threatening some of its immediate neighbors—not out of strength but out of weakness." Despite the fact that Russia was a nuclear superpower that could level America's cities in minutes, Obama deceptively stated, "They don't pose the number one national security threat to the United States. I continue to be much more concerned when it comes to our security with the prospect of a nuclear weapons going off in Manhattan."[11]

Once again, Obama's behavior was that of someone attempting to diffuse Western vigilance. Obama was also keen to overlook Moscow's meddling in the Western Hemisphere—in Nicaragua and Venezuela. Late in his second term, Obama's sanctions against Russia were more an invitation to aggression than a method of deterrence. In fact, Obama's actual response to Russia's military aggression in Ukraine has been described by experts as "minimalist."[12] Of course, the leftist mainstream media trumpeted news of Obama's sanctions as if they were backbreaking measures. But they were not. In fact, Russia was hardly sanctioned at all. Instead, sanctions were levied against seven Russian officials and seventeen companies.[13]

Licenses were revoked for a few high-tech items, yet there is no evidence these sanctions have hurt the Russian economy in the least, for Russia's economy is a state-centered economy with many shell companies operating abroad. These are interchangeable and flexible. Therefore, the sanctions regime was not serious and, in fact, served as the pretext for repealing more effective sanctions imposed during the Cold War. The Magnitsky Act, for example, removed longstanding measures that stood in Moscow's way.[14] It also helped the Kremlin contain Russia's oligarchs by holding the threat of confiscation over their heads if they dared hide large sums of money overseas—away from the grasp of the Russian government.

It is worth noting that a large body of former US government officials signed a bipartisan document recommending the imposition of "real costs" on Russia. The recommended measures would have included serious assistance to Ukraine.[15] When Obama refused to accept these recommendations, further Russian aggression occurred in Luhansk and Donetsk. Obama continued to effectively shield Russia from the consequences of its actions even as Russian tank columns entered Ukraine's eastern territories. This was Obama's attitude in spite of America's obligation to defend Ukraine in accordance with the Budapest Memorandum on Security Assurances.

Obama's unwillingness to seriously oppose Russia carried over into the Middle East, especially with regard to the Syrian Civil War. Despite promising to bomb Syria in the event of the regime's chemical weapon use, Obama did everything in his power to avoid following through. He attempted to pass the responsibility for making a decision to the Republicans in Congress; then he secretly met with President Putin, pleading for a way out. Putin offered to persuade the Syrians to eliminate their own chemical weapons (which they did not actually do, as the world discovered in April 2017). The impression given by ambassador McFaul's account was that Obama was extremely uncomfortable with the idea of bombing Russia's ally. Some of Obama's top advisers didn't understand why.[16]

On the arms control front, by 2016 it was abundantly clear that Russia had been violating the INF Treaty; but here again Obama would do nothing to correct the situation. As defense and strategy expert Michaela Dodge noted, "A continuation of the status quo [regarding the INF Treaty] will allow Russia, which has made nuclear threats to Europe, to gain an advantage across an entire class of weapons." Dodge further stated, "The U.S. nuclear arsenal is aging, and no yield-producing tests have been conducted in over twenty years. The U.S. must modernize in order to maintain a credible deterrent."[17]

Obama was not keen on modernizing America's nuclear arsenal. At first he refused to allow modernization to proceed, initially promoting the pipedream of eliminating nuclear weapons in every country. Republicans in Congress eventually forced the issue, yet Obama's opposition kept America's nuclear arms funding to a minimum. According to an expert consulted on this matter, the US will not begin replacing its obsolete warheads until 2025 at the earliest. Obama and his ideological associates in the government made sure of this—effectively buying time for Russia to secure significant strategic advantages.

The test of Obama's true allegiance may be found in his Russia policy, outlined in the preceding paragraphs. Given that Russia remains controlled by Soviet-style apparatchiks who continue to support Marxist causes around the world, it is only obvious why an American socialist would behave as Obama has behaved. The entire case boils down to the following question: Was Obama helpful to Moscow, or did he block their way? On every key point, our survey shows that Obama was consistently helpful to Moscow.

Since 1917 Moscow has been the "General Staff" of the world revolution. This is what the communists of all countries were taught to acknowledge. As a young Marxist, Obama would have known this. It was the core of the communist catechism in the 1980s. As one Soviet text explained, "The Great October Revolution in Russia marked the beginning of the implementation of the Marxist-Leninist theory of communism. Mankind's first socialist society . . . was built in the Soviet Union."[18]

Many of the communist cadres in the West know that the collapse of communism did not happen as advertised. For many years, the communists in America and abroad have privately talked of the election of a future "stealth" communist president. I first learned of this in 1981 at a lecture given by Darek Shearer at the University of California, Irvine. Again, I listened to a more detailed description of this plan from a communist lecturer in March 1983, at the Science Lecture Hall on the same campus. The communist speaker said they were "infiltrating the left wing of the Democratic Party with the object of taking over the party to elect a 'stealth communist president.'" Given what has been presented in this book so far, who would this "stealth communist" president have been?

But is there any direct evidence or testimony that Obama is the secret creature of the Russian communists? The answer is yes. The witness is an American physicist named Tom Fife who I interviewed in 2010. As it happened, Fife lived and worked in Russia during the 1990s. Previously he had met "an Englishman who was doing relief work" in Moscow. Fife was persuaded by this Englishman to join a unique business enterprise in coordination with the Russian Academy of Sciences. The work involved the development of handheld devices for business use. Fife's testimony follows (transcribed from audio with my questions rephrased in italics for clarity):[19]

In the process of doing that work I got to know some of the people who were involved in the Russian Academy of Sciences. These guys were physics types, too, so we had an affinity. They were programmers, too, and they were very keen on a connection with some Western companies . . . and that is what we ended up doing.

The British guy had a consultancy, doing accounting. He built up an umbrella company that . . . we would be under. We had been in

Moscow, working with these people. It turns out that the Russians had already constructed this little company of their own that was within the Russian Academy of Sciences; and so we just had to hook into that. The head of that little company was a physicist and his wife. . . .

And [after a period of work] we were headed back home. It was pretty common tradition that you have a "goodbye party." And that's what this was. We were all gathered together. Some of the Russians and Americans were there. The British guy was there. We had this party in the physicist and his wife's flat.

It's a Russian tradition to do these toasts; and the way they usually do it, they work [their way] around the table and everyone will have their turn, and they'll pour a little vodka out, then they'll give the toast, and [everyone] tosses it back. Then the next in line will propose a toast and they'll go along. We were doing that and eating our meal at the same time, and just having a general discussion. Just a light-hearted thing.

My American friend who was with me didn't want to propose a toast. He, for whatever reason, didn't want that. He just wanted to go ahead and say what he thought about things; observations he made about being in Russia. For some reason he was caught by the different racial types that he saw in Russia. I think he thought they would be more homogeneous. . . . But there is a little bit a variety in the Russian people; and one of the things he was noting was the high cheek bones in some of them. So he was remarking on the influence of the Mongols, and stuff like that. I think it was that point that the wife took a little offense at the whole Mongol thing. You know, they were subjugated [by the Mongols] for four hundred years. . . . It's not something they remember fondly. The thing we're talking about, really, is her whole response to that remark; that she wanted to correct him on what true Russia is, racially. And she described what she called "a round Russian face." And she talked about what villages you could go to, to actually see the perfect Russian. And one of the funny things was, she sounded like she was describing herself. She didn't get out-of-control loud. But you could tell she was miffed, and she started to say things like, 'You Americans should talk about racism.' She was particularly talking about the black problems we have, the riots; and she said, "You are going to be quite surprised because you are going to have a black president very soon." Of course, when she said something like that it was very much a surprise, because how would she know?

The other Russians in the room were subaltern to her and they just sat there riding it out.

I asked Fife to explain this:

What they told me was, that she was an apparatchik of some sort within the Communist Party [Soviet Union], and that she was doing what they call "climbing two ladders." I got the impression she was one of these people who would be in a group, and she would be the party contact for them.

Were the other Russians in the room afraid of her?

In general, my observation was they didn't trust communists in general. And they didn't trust anyone who had been up the ladder at all. So they just sat there with their heads down waiting it out. From that point on. . . .

Did the husband of this woman try and stop her?

He did step up and say, "how about dropping this and we'll do something else." But she brushed him off and said, "No, no." She wasn't done yet. She had something else to say. He just . . . moved to the side. He also seemed to be just waiting it out, just to let her finish what she was going to say and forget about it.

The next shoe that she dropped was not only that he was black, but that he was a communist. "A Soviet," she said. Yes. She called him a Soviet. Then she made a comment that we had a chance to vote for a woman for vice president . . . but we didn't take it; and she was saying that was one of the reasons that she knew we were still backwards. . . . I said, "Well, you don't vote for vice president, you vote for president." And she just walked over that, and she started talking about this guy that was going to be president. At first it was just this fact that we were going to have this black president, and about the fact that . . . he was groomed to be president; and she said, "He's been groomed to be irresistible. And he will be president." She said he had a white mother and he had a black African father. She thought that this was great because then he wouldn't have any slave baggage to go along with it.

Did she give a name?

Yes. She named him as being "Barack," that he had that name. I said that, from what I remembered, it was an Arabic word. . . . And I said that I think it meant something like blessing or something. And she said, "Yes! He is a blessing!" I remember she said rather dramatically (this is the point where she got a little dramatic) he'll be a blessing for our world efforts; a blessing for world communism, I think is what she said.

Were you surprised that this future black president would supposedly have an Arab name?

She was convinced it was an African name, but I let her go on.

Did she provide a last name?

She was a bit muddled on that. I think she knew it but couldn't remember it quite correctly. She said maybe she was getting a country and his last name confused. That is what she said. But she . . . thought it was "Uganda." I am thinking she got that confused with "Obama." Maybe in her mind, when she heard "Obama," she thought "Uganda." And that's what stuck in her head. But she did say, definitely, "Barack." She was intent on saying this was a real person she knew about. She didn't just go with the name, and mom and dad. She said . . . he was from Hawaii. She said that he had been schooled "in the Ivy League," as she referred to it. And she said he was in New York, and went to school in California. And she said he was currently in Chicago. That's where he was. She said he would soon be entering politics, that everything was under control; you know, like he is going to check all his boxes.

Did she give you the impression Barack had been to the Soviet Union?

You know, she did not say that. There was a series of details she was giving [showing] that she knew [about] this fellow. The other thing, the way she put it, America was the biggest stumbling block to communism and its biggest hope; and that America had to be brought over for everything to work worldwide; and so, she said that's why this had to take place; because it wasn't just a woman mouthing off. She had this chilling self-assurance about everything she said, that had almost more power than the words she used. She was just so certain, like [it was] as foregone conclusion.

How did your British partner and the other American take what she said?

I think I was the one most taken aback by it. . . . I felt chilled. . . . The British guy, particularly, is the one I had little bit of a conversation with . . . and he remarked that, you know, all your life you're growing up and hear everyone talking about communists and taking over the world . . . and he said, 'I'll be damned if I didn't sit there and hear a communist say that they were going to take over the world.' That was his biggest remark about it, that she fitted the caricature. . . . But my American friend didn't have much to say about it.

Would these witnesses be willing to come forward?

It's been almost twenty years, and I was able to have some contact with the British guy; and he said he absolutely didn't want to have anything to do with this. He didn't want to talk about it. He didn't want to be involved.

Didn't he feel any responsibility?

I was trying to get him to talk about it, but he didn't.

So you told him you had been on the radio talking about this?

Yes. . . . He definitely didn't want to be involved.

How about the other American?

I'm not sure. The business venture fell apart. Somehow they brought in this other guy, and he ended up in control.

How long before you realized this Barack person was a real guy?

At the time I had an active security clearance. Whenever I went to Russia I had to be debriefed by the D.I.A. [Defense Intelligence Agency]. I was to make note of anyone who wanted to be friendly with me, and I did that. So I kept a little diary of what went on. I did make notes of this conversation because it did strike me strongly. And I was debriefed with the guy when I came back and ended up giving him the little notes I had made. You know, this was a very vivid thing. It was in my head. Matter-of-fact, it was actually so vivid that when I got home one thing I did do, was, I told my son, who was about fourteen at the time. I mentioned [it] to him, and I said, "In case I'm not around in the future, and you hear about a guy who is going to be president, and he is half white and half black," I said, "You gotta fight this guy. I just told him enough. One interesting thing, of course, my son remembers that conversation we had. That's one point of reality that's vivid for him. That's one thing he remembers very well. Of course, with me in the meantime, it was just a story for years and years. I didn't see this guy for a while. So it was in the back of my mind. . . . I'd think about it. I'd remember it. Something would remind me of it. And an interesting thing that did cause it to pop up in my head a couple times since then, when she was describing him back at the dinner, and she said he was half white and half black, she stopped and said, 'That's right. He's a chocolate baby.' And I thought that was such a queer thing to say. It was an odd turn of phrase for me, and I've heard it a couple of times since, [so] I'd immediately remember that woman saying it. So it stuck in my head. What really did it was when I saw him at the Democratic National Convention, at that famous speech of his. Even then it didn't [fully] register with me. It was only afterward I heard [all this praise of him]. When they talked about him having a white mother and father from Kenya, oh oh, it was like something was snapping. It just hit me in the head. That's what it felt like. You know, it was a story. All of a sudden it didn't seem like a story any more. I was in the middle of something real. . . . So I started googling things about him, and everything meshed. Everything she said connects with the reality of this guy.

You must have had quite a shock then.

Yeah. At first I was still kind of simmering on the back burner about this thing. I have to admit, I had an anxious feeling about it. And I felt like, how can I say to anybody what's going on. I would tell people about it. They'd half believe me, and half think I was making it up. It was enough after the fact that it wasn't like I was predicting that much, at that point in time. When I could see he really was moving toward the nomination . . . in the spring of 08 . . . I wrote emails to everyone I could think of. I wrote paper letters.

Did you get any responses?

No.

What did you write in the letters and emails?

In the first letters I said, "There's something important I have to tell you and it's about Barack Obama . . . and no one seemed to care. I got no response at all. What got something going, finally, was a friend of mine, had this rather large conservative email list and I wrote up a little story, and I have it out there on [the] Internet, and I did get a little bit of a response. Then Wiley Drake asked me to come on his show. But I couldn't get on until election day, mid-election day. Then, from that came an interview with a lady from WorldNetDaily. And after that there were a lot of emails from people, who were starting to reinforce [what I had to say]."

Such was the testimony of Tom Fife. Does it sound too outlandish to be true? Not if we consider Obama's policies toward Russia. As stated by Hillary Clinton, Obama wanted to strengthen Russia. And that is exactly what he did. Is it ludicrous to believe Obama was colluding with the Russians? To answer that question, we must first explain the baseless accusations against President Donald Trump. Why did Obama and his confederates smear Donald Trump as a traitor? In the first instance, it wasn't honest. In the second instance, it was never true. Why have they done this, and why do they persist in it—*regardless of evidence?*

The answer must be, in the case of Obama, *to cover up for his own collusion.* And now we are seeing Obama's successor, Biden, whose collusion extends to his family making money from Russian and Chinese sources. Biden takes Obama's subservience to Russia and China to the next level, for Biden is more dependent on Russia and China and therefore will more straightforwardly do what he is told.[20]

9

OBAMA'S ENABLING OF JIHAD
AND STEALTH JIHAD

by Robert Spencer

WHEN JOE BIDEN was conducting his faux campaign for the presidency, he promised a Muslim Brotherhood–linked organization that he would appoint Muslims to every level of his administration. The establishment media took no notice; nor did establishment Republicans. The acceptance of Muslim Brotherhood influence in the US government began years ago, during the Obama administration and its treatment of the so-called Arab Spring. When the Arab Spring revolutions began in Tunisia and Egypt in January 2011, the Western media reacted with unbridled enthusiasm. Ignoring signs that the Muslim Brotherhood and other pro-Sharia Islamic supremacist groups were to a large extent behind the uprisings, the media assured Americans that the "Arab Spring" uprisings heralded a new flowering of democracy and pluralism in the Middle East.

The fruit of the "Arab Spring" quickly became clear; by September 2013, less than three years after this movement began amid such hope, North Africa and the Middle East are in flames; the Muslim Brotherhood took over Egypt and then so alienated its citizens that it was driven from power after a year, ushering in a new era, not of democracy and pluralism, but of uncertainty, violence, and strife; a US consulate was attacked and a US ambassador was murdered in Libya (where President Barack Obama gave military aid to the anti-Gaddafi rebels); and Syria was engulfed in a bloody civil war that attracted Islamic jihad terrorists from all over the globe—and military aid from the United States of America for the same side for which those jihadists were fighting.

It quickly became apparent that what had happened wasn't an "Arab Spring" at all, but a new winter of jihad violence and Sharia oppression. And on April 15, 2013, at the Boston Marathon, that jihad violence once again came to America.

All of this was thanks to Barack Hussein Obama, president of the United States.

The ideology behind the Boston Marathon bombing was the same as the one that fueled the Arab Spring uprisings that were hailed by the media and the Obama administration as a new flowering of pro-Western sentiment and political and societal freedom in North Africa and the Middle East. It was also the same ideology held by the Muslim Army psychiatrist who murdered thirteen Americans at Fort Hood in November 2009—as well as that held by the 9/11 hijackers. Yet, in the face of this renewed jihad, there came from the Obama administration and the mainstream media, denial, obfuscation, and worst of all, sympathy with those who had sworn to destroy the United States as a free nation and establish an Islamic state in its place.

While terror activity was increasing, the Obama administration systematically removed any mention of Islam and jihad from counterterror training manuals for the FBI, the Department of Homeland Security, and other law enforcement and intelligence agencies—which removal played a large part in the intelligence failures that made continuing jihad activity in the US possible. In 2010, Islamic advocacy groups in the US began claiming that counterterror training was "Islamophobic," and demanding that the Obama administration scrub training materials of all mention of Islam and jihad in connection with terrorism, and stop bringing in "Islamophobic" trainers (including me). The Obama team quickly complied.

A foremost example of the human cost of all this denial and obfuscation is the Fort Hood killer, Nidal Malik Hasan. At a pretrial hearing in his military trial on July 9, 2013, one of the most notorious recent assassins inside the United States explained his creed, his allegiances, and his intentions clearly. Hasan, a major in the US Army, who admitted to having murdered thirteen people and wounded thirty at Fort Hood on November 5, 2009, complained that he was being made to wear an Army uniform. "I can't take any pride in wearing this uniform," he explained. "It represents an enemy of Islam. I'm being forced to wear this uniform."[1] During his trial, it was revealed that not long after the attack, he told a panel of mental health professionals: "I'm paraplegic and could be in jail for the rest of my life. However, if I died by lethal injection, I would still be a martyr."[2] In his context, a martyr was someone who killed on behalf of Islam and was killed in the process, in accord with the Qur'an's promise of Paradise to those who "fight in the cause of Allah" and "kill and are killed" (9:111).

During the pretrial phase, Hasan quizzed potential jurors about their opinions of the Taliban, Sharia (Islamic law), and the Islamic faith. Then during his trial, it was revealed that not long after the shootings, he had told the mental health panel: "I don't think what I did was wrong because it was for the greater cause of helping my Muslim brothers."[3] The US, he said, was targeting those Muslim brothers in an "illegal war."[4] That war, of course, was the one in Afghanistan, where Hasan was about to be deployed. Considering the war against the Taliban to be a war against Islam, he—in his own words—realized that he "was on the wrong side," and "switched sides."[5] Dr. Tonya Kozminksi, who had worked with Hasan at a hospital in Fort Hood, testified that several weeks before Hasan's jihad attack, Hasan warned that if the Army ever decided to send him to Afghanistan, "They will pay."[6]

Then on November 5, 2009, Hasan attended prayers at a mosque in Killeen, Texas.[7] Returning home, he gave a neighbor a copy of the Qur'an and told her, "I'm going to do good work for God."[8] Later on the same day, he entered a center at Fort Hood in Texas where soldiers receive medical examinations before deploying overseas. Then, shouting "Allahu akbar" (Allah is greatest, that is, Islam is superior to other religions), he drew a pistol and began firing.[9] During his trial, prosecutors showed that several days before his attack, and even just a few hours before he started shooting, he searched the internet for *jihad* and specifically for articles about Islamic jihadists and Muslim clerics calling for jihad attacks on Americans.[10] Yet, despite these abundant indications that Hasan was engaged in act of Islamic jihad akin, albeit on a smaller scale as compared to the September 11, 2001, attacks on the World Trade Center and the Pentagon, Obama's Defense Department has classified Hasan's shootings not as a terrorist act but as "workplace violence."[11] Hasan himself contradicted this at his trial, when he pointedly registered his agreement with the prosecution's contention that, unlike some others who had suddenly opened fire in public places, he hadn't just suddenly snapped or been overcome with an overwhelming paroxysm of rage: "I would like to agree with the prosecution that it wasn't done under the heat of sudden passion. There was adequate provocation, that these were deploying soldiers that were going to engage in an illegal war."[12]

Nonetheless, the Obama administration continued to ignore repeated requests from the victims' families to reclassify the murders and make the victims eligible for the Purple Heart and other benefits that are normally accorded to combatants killed or injured in the line of duty.[13] The Obama administration also downplayed the importance of Hasan's communications with jihad mastermind Anwar al-Awlaki, which took place before his attack, and, if proper steps had been taken, could have headed off that attack altogether. Those communications with al-Awlaki had been intercepted by the FBI long before Hasan's jihad attack at Fort Hood and showed that the bureau could have prevented the massacre—but Obama's FBI did nothing. Yet, in August 2013, when asked about the emails from Hasan to al-Awlaki, FBI Director Robert Mueller said that "given the context of the discussions and the situation that the agents and the analysts were looking at, they took appropriate steps."[14] This followed a long train of denial and obfuscation from government officials. Not long after the massacre, Homeland Security Secretary Janet Napolitano declared: "This was an individual who does not represent the Muslim faith."[15] The US Army Chief of Staff, George Casey, declared: "Our diversity, not only in our Army, but in our country, is a strength. And as horrific as this tragedy was, if our diversity becomes a casualty, I think that's worse."[16] And the US government's report on the massacre doesn't mention Islam even once.

All this politically correct denial cost was thirteen dead and thirty wounded.

Then in February 2012, the Obama administration purged more than 1,000 documents and presentations from counterterror training material for the FBI and other agencies. This material was discarded at the demand of Muslim groups, which had deemed it inaccurate (by their own account) or offensive to Muslims.[17] This triumph was several years in the making. The movement toward it began in earnest in August 2010, when I gave a talk on Islam and jihad to the FBI's Joint Terrorism Task Force—one of many such talks I gave to government agencies and military groups in those years. While some had counseled me to keep these talks quiet so as to avoid drawing the ire of CAIR, the possibility of that pressure seemed to me to make it all the more important to announce my appearances publicly, so as to show that the US government was not going to take dictation from a group linked to Hamas and the Muslim Brotherhood. This time, however, those who had urged silence were proven correct, for the government was indeed disposed to take dictation from CAIR. CAIR sent a series of letters to FBI Director Robert Mueller and others, demanding that I be dropped as a counterterror trainer; the organization even started a "coalition" echoing this demand, which Jesse Jackson and other leftist luminaries joined.[18]

Andrew C. McCarthy pointed out in *National Review* that CAIR was seeking total control over counterterror training material: "According to this thinking, Islamist groups like CAIR have a monopoly on what Americans—including American law-enforcement and intelligence agents—are permitted to hear about Islam from academic, media, and government sources. No dissenting views are permitted, no matter how steeped the dissenters may be in Islamic doctrine and no matter how much these dissents accord with what your lyin' eyes are seeing."[19]

Roger L. Simon added in PJ Media:

Frankly, I was pleased to hear the FBI was welcoming the likes of Spencer, especially since our Department of Justice . . . has gone out of its way to *ignore* radical Islam as a motivation for terrorism even when it couldn't be more obviously so. From Ft. Hood to Times Square, it hasn't been just the thousand pound gorilla in the room, it has been every gorilla in every room from here to Beijing and back."[20]

And indeed, Mueller made no public comment on CAIR's demand, and so it initially appeared that the effort had failed—although I was never again invited to provide counterterror training for any government agency, after having done so fairly regularly for the previous five years. This effort was, of course, not personal: CAIR targeted me because I told the truth, just as they would target everyone else who dared do so. Although Mueller was publicly silent, the Islamic supremacists and their leftist allies didn't give up. In the summer and fall of 2011, the online tech journal *Wired* published several "exposés" by far-left journalist Spencer Ackerman, who took the FBI to task for training material that spoke forthrightly and truthfully about the nature and magnitude of the jihad threat.

In a typical sally from these exposes, Ackerman reported that:

> The FBI is teaching its counterterrorism agents that "main stream" [sic] American Muslims are likely to be terrorist sympathizers; that the Prophet Mohammed was a "cult leader"; and that the Islamic practice of giving charity is no more than a "funding mechanism for combat." At the Bureau's training ground in Quantico, Virginia, agents are shown a chart contending that the more "devout" a Muslim, the more likely he is to be "violent." Those destructive tendencies cannot be reversed, an FBI instructional presentation adds: "Any war against non-believers is justified" under Muslim law; a "moderating process cannot happen if the Koran continues to be regarded as the unalterable word of Allah."[21]

Like virtually all leftist and Islamic supremacist critiques of anti-jihad and anti-terror material, Ackerman's piece took for granted that such assertions are false, without bothering to explain how or why. Apparently, Ackerman believed that their falsity was so self-evident as to require no demonstration; unfortunately for him, however, there was considerable evidence that what this FBI training material asserts is true. Ackerman condemned the training material for intimating that mainstream American Muslims were "likely to be terrorist sympathizers." Certainly, all the mainstream Muslim organizations condemn al-Qaeda and 9/11; however, as we have seen, some of the foremost of those organizations, such as ISNA, MAS, ICNA, the MSA, CAIR, and others, have links of various kinds to Hamas and the Muslim Brotherhood. A mainstream Muslim spokesman in the US, the Ground Zero Mosque Imam Faisal Abdul Rauf, refused to condemn Hamas until it became too politically damaging for him not to do so; another, CAIR's Nihad Awad, openly declared his support for Hamas in 1994.[22] Another mainstream Muslim spokesman in this country, Reza Aslan, has praised another jihad terrorist group, Hizballah, and called on the US to negotiate with Hamas.[23] Other mainstream Muslim spokesmen in the US, such as Obama's ambassador to the Organization of Islamic Cooperation, Rashad Hussain, and media gadfly Hussein Ibish, have praised and defended the confessed leader of another jihad terror group, Palestinian Islamic Jihad: Sami al-Arian.[24] Do these men and organizations represent a tiny minority of extremists that actually does not express the opinions of the broad mainstream of Muslims in this country? Maybe, but if so, they simply do not have any counterparts of comparable size or influence who have *not* expressed sympathy for some Islamic terror group.

Ackerman also claimed that the training materials called Muhammad a "cult leader." Certainly one definition of a cult is that members are not free to opt out if they choose to do so—and it was Muhammad who enunciated Islam's notorious death penalty for apostasy by saying, "Whoever changes his Islamic religion, then kill him."[25] Also, there are several celebrated incidents in which Muhammad lashed out violently against his opponents, ordering the murder of several people for the crime of making fun of him—including the poet Abu 'Afak, who was over one hundred years old, and the poetess 'Asma bint Marwan. Abu 'Afak was killed in his sleep in response to Muhammad's question, "Who will avenge me on this scoundrel?" Similarly, Muhammad on another occasion cried out, "Will no one rid me of this daughter of Marwan?" One of his followers, 'Umayr ibn 'Adi, went to her house that night, where he found her sleeping next to her children. The youngest, a nursing babe, was in her arms. But that didn't stop 'Umayr from murdering her and the baby as well. Muhammad commended him: "You have done a great service to Allah and His Messenger, 'Umayr!"[26]

Ackerman scored the training material for asserting that the "Islamic practice of giving charity" was no more than a "'funding mechanism for combat.'"[27] If this was really self-evidently false, one wonders why so many Islamic charities in the United States and around the world have been shut down for funding terrorism, including what was once the largest Islamic charity in the United States, the Holy Land Foundation for Relief and Development (HLF), as well as the Global Relief Foundation (GRF), the Benevolence International Foundation (BIF), and many others. Also while assuming that the claim was self-evidently false, Ackerman noted that the material claimed that "the more 'devout' a Muslim, the more likely he is to be 'violent,'" and that the "moderating process cannot happen if the Koran continues to be regarded as the unalterable word of Allah."[28] Yet, while certainly not all devout Muslims are terrorists, virtually all Islamic terrorists are devout Muslims, citing the Qur'an and the words and deeds of Muhammad to justify their actions. It should not be controversial to state these readily demonstrable facts. And finally, Ackerman criticized the materials for claiming that "any war against non-believers" can be "justified' under Muslim law."[29] In reality, not any war against non-Muslims can really be justified under Islamic law, but certainly Sharia delineates particular circumstances under which warfare against unbelievers can indeed be justified. As such it was hard to see how the statement was all that far off the mark. Nonetheless, in the face of Ackerman's reports, the Obama FBI went into full retreat; in September 2011, it announced that it was dropping one of the programs that Ackerman had zeroed in on.[30]

The Islamic supremacists didn't rest on their laurels. On October 19, 2011, Salam al-Marayati of the Muslim Public Affairs Council (MPAC) took this campaign to the mainstream media, writing in the *Los Angeles Times* that "a disturbing string of training material used by the FBI and a U.S. attorney's office came to light beginning in late July that reveals a deep anti-Muslim sentiment within the U.S. government." Al-Marayati warned that "if this matter is not immediately addressed, it will undermine the relationship between law enforcement and the Muslim American community—another example of the ineptitude and/ or apathy undermining bridges built with care over decades." He also noted that the FBI was beginning to move on these demands, although as far as al-Marayati was concerned, much more was needed: "It is not enough to just call it a 'very valid concern,' as FBI Director Robert

Mueller told a congressional committee this month."[31]

It was a coordinated full-court press. The same day that al-Marayati's op-ed was published, Farhana Khera of Muslim Advocates, who had complained for years about supposed Muslim profiling and entrapment, wrote a letter to John Brennan, who was then the assistant to the president on National Security for Homeland Security and Counter Terrorism. The letter was signed, not just by Khera, but by the leaders of virtually all the significant Islamic groups in the United States: fifty-seven Muslim, Arab, and South Asian organizations, including many with ties to Hamas and the Muslim Brotherhood, including the CAIR, ISNA, MAS, the Islamic Circle of North America (ICNA), Islamic Relief USA, and al-Marayati's MPAC.[32]

The letter denounced what it characterized as US government agencies' "use of biased, false and highly offensive training materials about Muslims and Islam" and emphasized that they regarded this as an issue of the utmost importance: "The seriousness of this issue cannot be overstated, and we request that the White House immediately create an interagency task force to address this problem, with a fair and transparent mechanism for input from the Muslim, Arab, and South Asian communities, including civil rights lawyers, religious leaders, and law enforcement experts."[33] This was needed because "while recent news reports have highlighted the FBI's use of biased experts and training materials, we have learned that this problem extends far beyond the FBI and has infected other government agencies, including the US Attorney's Anti-Terrorism Advisory Councils, the US Department of Homeland Security, and the US Army. Furthermore, by the FBI's own admission, the use of bigoted and distorted materials in its trainings has not been an isolated occurrence. Since last year, reports have surfaced that the FBI, and other federal agencies, are using or supporting the use of biased trainers and materials in presentations to law enforcement officials."[34] Khera complained that my books could be found in "the FBI's library at the FBI training academy in Quantico, Virginia"; that a reading list accompanying a PowerPoint presentation by the FBI's

Law Enforcement Communications Unit recommended my book *The Truth About Muhammad;* and that in July 2010, I "presented a two-hour seminar on 'the belief system of Islamic jihadists' to the Joint Terrorism Task Force (JTTF) in Tidewater, Virginia," and "presented a similar lecture to the US Attorney's Anti-Terrorism Advisory Council, which is co-hosted by the FBI's Norfolk Field Office."[35]

These were terrible things because I was, in her view, bigoted and hateful. But many of the examples Khera adduced of these "bigoted and distorted materials" involved statements that were not actually bigoted and distorted at all, but simply accurate, and what was distorted was Khera's representation of them. For instance, Khera stated:

A 2006 FBI intelligence report stating that individuals who convert to Islam are on the path to becoming "Homegrown Islamic Extremists," if they exhibit any of the following behavior:

- Wearing traditional Muslim attire

- Growing facial hair

- Frequent attendance at a mosque or a prayer group

- Travel to a Muslim country

- Increased activity in a pro-Muslim social group or political cause[36]

This FBI intelligence report didn't actually say that converts to Islam were "on the path" to becoming "extremists" if they wore traditional Muslim attire, grew facial hair, and frequently attended a mosque; it included these among a list of fourteen indicators to "identify an individual going through the radicalization process." Others included "travel without obvious source of funds, suspicious purchases of bomb making paraphernalia or weapons, large transfers of funds, from or to overseas, and formation of operational cells."[37] Khera selectively quoted and misrepresented the list to give the impression that the FBI was saying that devout observance of Islam led inevitably and in every case to "extremism." Her letter also stated that "in 2007, William Gawthrop, a [sic] FBI intelligence analyst who has stated that the Prophet 'Muhammad's mindset is a source for terrorism' taught a class at the National Defense Intelligence College, the professional education institution run by the Defense Intelligence Agency."[38] Khera left it to the reader to assume that this statement was self-evidently false. However, numerous terrorists have invoked Muhammad as their inspiration and model. In December 2003, an Iraqi jihadist invoked Muhammad to explain why he was fighting against America's presence in Iraq: "The religious principle is that we cannot accept to live with infidels. The Prophet Muhammad, peace be on him, said, 'Hit the infidels wherever you find them.'"[39]

Fawwaz bin Muhammad Al-Nashami, leader of the jihadists who attacked Americans in Khobar, Saudi Arabia, in 2004, killing twenty-two people, also invoked Muhammad: "We are Mujahideen, and we want the Americans. We have not come to aim a weapon at the Muslims, but to purge the Arabian Peninsula, according to the will of our Prophet Muhammad, of the infidels and the polytheists who are killing our brothers in Afghanistan and Iraq."[40] Al-Qaeda Sheikh Aamer Bin Abdallah Al-Aamer wrote in the Al-Qaeda's online journal *Sawt al-Jihad:* "Perform the Jihad against your enemies with your hands, sacrifice your souls and your property in fighting your enemy, as an imitation of your Prophet [Muhammad] in the month of Ramadan, enrage your enemies."[41]

Nonetheless, ignoring the factual accuracy of the material about which they were complaining, the Muslim groups signing the letter demanded that the task force "purge *all* federal government training materials of biased materials"; "implement a mandatory re-training program for FBI agents, U.S. Army officers, and all federal, state and local law enforcement who have been subjected to biased training"; and more to ensure that all that law enforcement officials would learn about

Islam and jihad would be what the signatories wanted them to learn.[42]

Brennan seemed amenable to that. He received Khera's complaints as marching orders. In a November 3, 2011, letter to Khera, that—significantly—was written on White House stationery, Brennan made no attempt to defend counterterror materials and procedures, but instead accepted Khera's criticisms without a murmur of protest and assured her of his readiness to comply. "Please allow me to share with you the specific steps we are taking," Brennan wrote to Khera, "to ensure that federal officials and state, local and tribal partners receive accurate, evidence-based information in these crucial areas."[43]

"I am aware," Brennan went on, "of recent unfortunate incidents that have highlighted substandard and offensive training that some United States Government elements have either sponsored or delivered. Any and all such training runs completely counter to our values, our commitment to strong partnerships with communities across the country, our specific approach to countering violent extremist recruitment and radicalization, and our broader counterterrorism (CT) efforts. Our National Strategy for Empowering Local Partners to Prevent Violent Extremism in the United States highlights competent training as an area of primary focus and states that 'misinformation about the threat and dynamics of radicalization to violence can harm our security by sending local stakeholders in the wrong direction and unnecessarily creating tensions with potential community partners.' It also emphasizes that our security is 'inextricably linked to our values,' including 'the promotion of an inclusive society.'"[44] Brennan then assured Khera that all her demands would be met: "Your letter requests that 'the White House immediately create an interagency task force to address this problem,' and we agree that this is necessary." He then detailed the specific actions being undertaken to ensure this, including "collecting all training materials that contain cultural or religious content, including information related to Islam or Muslims."[45] This material wouldn't just be "collected"; it would be purged of anything that Farhana Khera and others like her found offensive—that is, any honest discussion of how Islamic jihadists used Islamic teachings to justify violence. Brennan assured Khera that his view of the problem was identical to hers, and that remedies were being implemented quickly: "We share your concern over these recent unfortunate incidents, and are moving forward to ensure problems are addressed with a keen sense of urgency. They do not reflect the vision that the President has put forward, nor do they represent the kind of approach that builds the partnerships that are necessary to counter violent extremism, and to protect our young people and our homeland. America's greatest strength is its values, and we are committed to pursuing policies and approaches that draw strength from our values and our people irrespective of their race, religion or ethnic background."[46]

The letter concludes with Brennan again assuring Khera that her "concerns" would be soon assuaged: "While much work remains, I am confident that concrete actions are being taken to address the valid concerns you raised. Thank you again for your letter and for your leadership in addressing an issue that is critical to ensuring the security of the United States."[47]

The alacrity with which Brennan complied was unfortunate on many levels. Not only were numerous books and presentations that presented a perfectly accurate view of Islam and jihad purged, but in doing so, Brennan was complying with demands from quarters that could hardly be considered authentically moderate. In the face of an advancing jihad threat, the Obama administration rendered US law enforcement and intelligence agencies willfully blind to the nature, magnitude, and ideological roots of that threat. And so the jihadis were able to advance essentially unopposed and unimpeded.

10

OBAMA'S ENABLING OF ISIS

by Robert Spencer

LATE IN 2021, another catastrophic consequence of the Biden administration's weakness became evident as the Islamic State began to reas-
sert itself in Iraq and Syria.[1] In its heyday, the jihad terror group that
calls itself the Islamic State, that most of the rest of the world calls ISIS,
and that Barack Obama and officials of his administration called ISIL,
constituted a greater threat to the US than al-Qaeda, Hamas, Hizballah,
Boko Haram, and all other jihad groups *combined*. And its success was
undeniably far greater than that of any of them. The Islamic State was
the first jihad terror group to rule over a significant expanse of territory for any extended period. It was won the loyalty of other jihadis

far outside its domains—in Libya, Nigeria, and even as far away as the Philippines. It called for attacks in the West, and Muslims in the US, Canada, Britain, and France heeded its call.

In January 2014, just six months before ISIS declared itself a new caliphate, President Barack Obama dismissed the group with a now-famous analogy. After the group took over the Iraqi city of Fallujah, Obama declared that he did not take them seriously: "The analogy we use around here sometimes, and I think is accurate, is if a jayvee team puts on Lakers uniforms that doesn't make them Kobe Bryant." He added: "I think there is a distinction between the capacity and reach of a bin Laden and a network that is actively planning major terrorist plots against the homeland versus jihadists who are engaged in various local power struggles and disputes, often sectarian."[2] Just a few months later, this JV team that was "engaged in various local power struggles" controlled a nation-sized expanse of Iraq and Syria, had organized a police force, amassed an army of over 100,000 fighters, and become the world's richest (and best-armed) jihad terror group. Nonetheless, even after it established its hold on an expanse of territory larger than Great Britain, Obama administration officials and allies continued to downplay the threat it constituted. "Whether you call them ISIS or ISIL, I refuse to call them the Islamic State, because they are neither Islamic or a state," said Obama's first Secretary of State, Hillary Clinton.[3] She agreed with Obama and his second Secretary of State, John Kerry, as well as Vice President Joe Biden, that the Islamic State had nothing to do with Islam—thereby hamstringing efforts to understand its ideology properly and counter it effectively.

By August 2014, Baghdadi's Islamic State had succeeded and grown to such an extent that Defense Secretary Chuck Hagel said that it was "as sophisticated and well-funded as any group we have seen. They are beyond just a terrorist group. They marry ideology, a sophistication of . . . military prowess. They are tremendously well-funded. This is beyond anything we've seen." What's more, he said that the Islamic State was "an imminent threat to every interest we have, whether it's in Iraq or anywhere else."[4]

"Anywhere else" included the United States. As Hagel was sounding his warning, Islamic State supporters posted photos of Islamic State symbols being held in front of the White House and other American sites, with the message: "We are in your state, we are in your cities, we are in your streets."[5] Islamic State spokesman Abu Mohammed al-Adnani taunted Obama for thinking that the Islamic State could be defeated with airstrikes: "And O Obama, O mule of the jews. You are vile. You are vile. You are vile. And you will be disappointed, Obama. Is this all you were capable of doing in this campaign of yours?"[6]

In the face of all this, the Obama administration's main concern was not to counter the Islamic State's advance, but to deny that it had anything to do with Islam. On August 20, 2014, speaking a day after the Islamic State beheaded American journalist James Foley, Obama declared that "ISIL [his preferred acronym for the Islamic State] speaks for no religion. Their victims are overwhelmingly Muslim, and no faith teaches people to massacre innocents. No just god would stand for what they did yesterday and what they do every single day. ISIL has no ideology of any value to human beings. Their ideology is bankrupt. They may claim out of expediency that they are at war with the United States or the West, but the fact is they terrorize their neighbors and offer them nothing but an endless slavery to their empty vision and the collapse of any definition of civilized behavior."[7] This became administration policy: "ISIL does not operate in the name of any religion," said Obama State Department spokesperson Marie Harf not long after that. "The president has been very clear about that, and the more we can underscore that, the better."[8]

Yet, as far as the Islamic State itself was concerned, there was no question that it was Islamic, and it maintained Muslims who claimed that the group was un-Islamic are placing themselves outside the fold of true Islam. That was one principle reason why they killed other Muslims, which was one of Obama's chief points of evidence to support his claim that the group was not Muslim. In June 2014, a video circulated of a masked Islamic State commander telling a cheering crowd: "By Allah, we embarked on our Jihad only to support the religion of Allah. . . . Allah willing, we will establish a state ruled by the Quran and the Sunna. . . . All of you honorable Muslims are the soldiers of the Muslim State." He promised that the Islamic State would establish "the Sharia of Allah, the Quran, and the Sunna" as the crowed repeatedly responded with cries of "Allahu akbar."[9]

But for the Obama administration, the Islamic State was a vicious perversion of the Qur'an, the Sunnah, and the Sharia of Allah—and Obama administration officials insisted that whatever the group was called, it must not be called "Islamic" or identified in any way with the religion of Islam. It seemed much more concerned about that than about actually defeating the Islamic State. On September 10, 2014, Obama dug in, reiterating his earlier claims: "ISIL is not 'Islamic.' No religion condones the killing of innocents, and the vast majority of ISIL's victims have been Muslim."[10] When the Islamic State in November 2014 beheaded American aid worker, Peter Kassig, whom it had previously converted forcibly to Islam and given the name Abdul-Rahman, Obama said it yet again, while treating Kassig's conversion as if it had been his free decision: "ISIL's actions represent no faith, least of all the Muslim faith which Abdul-Rahman adopted as his own."[11]

The Obama administration claimed that the root cause of the popularity of the Islamic State among young Muslims from around the world was simply poverty—a problem that could be solved by the forced generosity of American taxpayers. Harf said in February 2015:

We're killing a lot of them, and we're going to keep killing more of them. So are the Egyptians, so are the Jordanians—they're in this fight with us. But we cannot win this war by killing them. We cannot kill our way out of this war. We need in the medium to longer term to go after the root causes that leads people to join these groups, whether it's a lack of opportunity for jobs—

At that point MSNBC's Chris Matthews interrupted Harf and said: "We're not going to be able to stop that in our lifetime or 50 lifetimes.

There's always going to be poor people. There's always going to be poor Muslims, and as long as there are poor Muslims, the trumpet's blowing and they'll join. We can't stop that, can we?"

Harf responded: "We can work with countries around the world to help improve their governance. We can help them build their economies so they can have job opportunities for these people."[12]

Harf was roundly ridiculed for this, but she did not originate it; many other Obama administration officials said essentially the same thing. In October 2014, Harf's boss, Obama's Secretary of State John Kerry, gave the same analysis of the rise of the Islamic State. "The extremism that we see," he said, "the radical exploitation of religion which is translated into violence, has no basis in any of the real religions. There's nothing Islamic about what ISIL/Daesh stands for, or is doing to people."

Instead, it was all about the poor envying the rich: "We're living at a point in time where there are just more young people demanding what they see the rest of the world having than at any time in modern history." They didn't have it at home because of factors, such as global warming: "And that brings us to something like climate change, which is profoundly having an impact in various parts of the world, where droughts are occurring not at a 100-year level but at a 500-year level in places that they haven't occurred, floods of massive proportions, diminishment of water for crops and agriculture at a time where we need to be talking about sustainable food." He also blamed Israel: "As I went around and met with people in the course of our discussions about the ISIL coalition, the truth is we—there wasn't a leader I met with in the region who didn't raise with me spontaneously the need to try to get peace between Israel and the Palestinians, "because it was a cause of recruitment and of street anger and agitation that they felt—and I see a lot of heads nodding—they had to respond to. And people need to understand the connection of that. It has something to do with humiliation and denial and absence of dignity."[13]

And in October 2013, the idea that poverty became terrorism was cemented even more firmly as a cornerstone of US policy at a meeting of the Global Counterterrorism Forum (GCTF), when Kerry and Turkish Foreign Minister (and soon to be Prime Minister) Ahmet Davutoglu launched what they called the "Global Fund for Community Engagement and Resilience," which was intended to counter "violent extremism" essentially by giving potential jihad terrorists money and jobs.[14] Kerry spoke about the importance of "providing more economic opportunities for marginalized youth at risk of recruitment" into jihad groups.[15] The GCTF devoted $200 million to this project, a core element of Barack Obama's "countering violent extremism" (CVE) program.[16] Kerry said this money would be used for "challenging the narrative of violence that is used to justify the slaughtering of innocent people."[17] How? By giving young would-jihadis jobs: "Getting this right isn't just about taking terrorists off the street. It's about providing more economic opportunities for marginalized youth at risk of recruitment. In country after country, you look at the demographics—Egypt, the West Bank—60 percent of the young people either under the age of 30 or under the age of 25, 50 percent under the age of 21, 40 percent under the age of 18, all of them wanting jobs, opportunity, education, and a future."[18]

This initiative was foredoomed, for in reality, study after study has shown that jihadists are not poor and bereft of economic opportunities, but are generally wealthier and better educated than their peers. A 2009 Rand Corporation report found that "terrorists are not particularly impoverished, uneducated, or afflicted by mental disease. Demographically, their most important characteristic is normalcy (within their environment). Terrorist leaders actually tend to come from relatively privileged backgrounds."[19] Rand's Darcy Noricks noted that "terrorists turn out to be more rather than less educated than the general population."[20] However, throughout the Obama administration, the focus remained on claiming that ISIS was not Islamic rather than on defeating it. White House press secretary Josh Earnest said in September 2016:

When it comes to ISIL, we are in a fight—a narrative fight with them. A narrative battle. . . . What is important in the context of political debate is to remember ISIL is trying to assert a narrative, that they represent the religion of Islam in a war against the west and in a war against the United States. That is mythology. That is falsehood. That is not true. That is bankrupt ideology they are trying to wrap in the cloak of Islam.[21]

The Islamic State itself professed contempt and amusement over all the confusion and denial in the Obama administration as to whom they were and what they were about. In a September 21, 2014, address calling for strikes in the US and Europe, Islamic State spokesman Abu Muhammad Adnani ridiculed Kerry ("that uncircumcised old geezer") and Obama ("the mule of the jews") for declaring that the Islamic State was not Islamic, as if they were Islamic authorities.[22] Meanwhile, Obama was acting as if he actually were an Islamic authority, and began arming jihad groups in Syria. He claimed, of course, that they were "moderate" and had been "vetted." In September 2014, he said: "We have a Free Syrian Army and a moderate opposition that we have steadily been working with that we have vetted."[23] That was over a year after these supposedly vetted and moderate Free Syrian Army (FSA) fighters entered the Christian village of Oum Sharshouh in July 2013 and began burning down houses and terrorizing the population, forcing 250 Christian families to flee the area.[24] Just two days after that, Free Syrian Army rebels, according to *Worthy News*:

> targeted the residents of al-Duwayr/Douar, a Christian village close to the city of Homs and near Syria's border with Lebanon. . . . Around 350 armed militants forcefully entered the homes of Christian families who were all rounded-up in the main square of the village and then summarily executed.[25]

And in September 2013, a day after Kerry praised the Free Syrian Army as "a real moderate opposition," the FSA took to the internet to post videos of its attack on the ancient Syrian Christian city of Maaloula, one of the few places where Aramaic, the language of Jesus, was still spoken.[26] Even after all that, Obama was calling them "moderates." Yet, on September 8, 2014, Bassel Idriss, the commander of a Free Syrian Army brigade, announced that this group of "vetted moderates" was actually working with the group that Obama was telling the American people it was fighting:

> We are collaborating with the Islamic State and the Nusra Front by attacking the Syrian Army's gatherings in . . . Qalamoun. Our battle is with the Assad regime, and it is on Syrian lands only.[27]

Another FSA commander, Abu Khaled, confirmed this, saying:

> Let's face it: The Nusra Front is the biggest power present right now in Qalamoun and we as FSA would collaborate on any mission they launch as long as it coincides with our values.[28]

Astoundingly, a week and a half later, the House of Representatives voted to arm these alleged "moderates." *The Hill* reported that the House had given Obama "authority to train and arm moderate Syrian rebels waging war against Islamic extremists."[29] The aid, *The Hill* said, would go to "vetted members of the Free Syrian Army."[30] Sure.

Obama expressed the hope that Muslim countries would take it upon themselves to defeat the Islamic State so as to defend the image of Islam. He stated on September 5, 2014:

> Our goal is to act with urgency but also make sure that we're doing it right, that we have the right targets, that there's support on the ground . . . that we have a strong political coalition. . . . It is absolutely critical that we have Arab states, and specifically Sunni-majority states, that are rejecting the kind of extremist nihilism that we're seeing out of ISIL, that say, 'That is not what Islam is about,' and are prepared to join us actively in the fight.[31]

Whether they would or not, the United States was not going to do much to aid those who were oppressed by the Islamic State. On September 17, 2014, according to *The Hill,* Obama "pledged that he would not send in ground troops to fight ISIS, saying it's more effective to support military allies 'so they can secure their own countries [sic] future.'"[32] Yet even this declaration that the United States would support its allies in fighting against the Islamic State was hollow. It came to light in July 2015 that Obama had blocked attempts to supply the Kurds with weapons to fight the Islamic State.[33] That same month, it came to light that a 500-million-dollar program to recruit and train Syrians to fight against the Islamic State was an embarrassing bust. Although the program's goal had been to train and equip at least 5,000 fighters to face the Islamic State, only fifty men actually graduated from the program. As soon as they had completed it, they left, never to be seen again. Hundreds of others who had been recruited for the program also left when they found out that they were expected to fight against the Islamic State rather than Syria's Assad regime.[34]

Even worse, in November 2015, former CIA agent Clare Lopez revealed "the Obama administration effectively switched sides in what used to be called the Global War on Terror when it decided to overthrow the sovereign government of our Libyan ally, Muammar Qaddafi, who'd been helping in the fight against al-Qaeda, by actually teaming up with and facilitating gun-running to Libyan al-Qaeda and Muslim Brotherhood elements there in 2011. This US gun-running policy in 2011 during the Libyan revolution was directed by Secretary of State Hillary Clinton and [the envoy to Libya] Christopher Stevens, who was her official envoy to the Libyan AQ rebels."[35] This directly aided the Islamic State. Lopez explained:

> In 2012, the gun-running into Libya turned around and began to flow outward, from Benghazi to the AQ-and-MB-dominated rebels in Syria. This time, it was the CIA Base of Operations that was in charge of collecting up and shipping out SAMs [surface-to-air missiles] from

Libya on Libyan ships to Turkey for overland delivery to a variety of jihadist militias, some of whose members later coalesced into groups like Jabhat al-Nusra [an al-Qaeda affiliate] and ISIS.

Lopez concluded:

The downstream consequences of Obama White House decisions in the Syrian conflict are still playing out, but certainly the US—and particularly CIA—support of identifiable jihadist groups associated with the Muslim Brotherhood, Jabhat al-Nusra, Ahrar al-Sham, the Islamic State and other [jihadists] has only exacerbated what was already a devastating situation.

Meanwhile, when the Islamic State expanded into Libya itself, the Pentagon in February 2016 developed plans to launch airstrikes against it there. The airstrikes, according to the *Daily Beast*, "would target ISIS resources while a small band of Special Operations Forces would train Libyans to eventually be members of a national army, the officials said."[36] Yet despite his stated intention to aid national forces in their efforts to defeat the Islamic State, Obama rejected these plans. His administration would do nothing against the Islamic State in Libya. "There is little to no appetite for that in this administration," said one appalled defense official.[37] It was getting harder all the time to escape the conclusion that Obama actually wanted the Islamic State to continue to exist in Iraq, Syria, Libya, and elsewhere.

The Islamic State did not return Obama's solicitude. In January 2015, an Islamic State spokesman said in a video: "Know, oh Obama, that will reach America. Know also that we will cut off your head in the White House, and transform America into a Muslim Province."[38] That same month, Islamic State hackers showed off their abilities by hijacking the Twitter account of the United States Central Command (CENTCOM), the Pentagon's Middle East division. The Islamic State posted what it said was "confidential data from your mobile devices" on CENTCOM's Twitter feed, and it certainly looked as if the claims were true, as the postings contained the home addresses, phone numbers, and email addresses of numerous American military officials. The hackers also wrote:

> ISIS is already here, we are in your PCs, in each military base. With Allah's permission we are in CENTCOM now. . . . AMERICAN SOLDIERS, WE ARE COMING WATCH YOUR BACK.[39]

In May 2015, reacting to reports that Islamic State leader Abu Sayyaf had been killed, an Islamic State jihadi wrote: "If your goal is killing Abu Sayyaf, then our goal is killing Obama and the worshipers of the cross. We have attacks coming against you."[40]

In February 2015, the Islamic State promised to flood Europe in the near future with as many as 500,000 refugees.[41] The Islamic State was not simply talking about engulfing the continent in a humanitarian crisis that would strain its resources to the breaking point. The jihadis were also planning to cross into Europe among those refugees, and later boasted that they had done so. An Islamic State operative claimed in November 2015 that among the flood of refugees that had begun to stream into Europe at that time, no fewer than 4,000 Islamic State jihadis had entered Europe. "They are going like refugees," he said, but they were going with the plan of sowing blood and mayhem on European streets. As he told this to journalists, he smiled and said, "Just wait." He explained: "It's our dream that there should be a caliphate not only in Syria but in all the world, and we will have it soon, inshallah."[42] These claims about the refugee stream were not unfounded. All of the Islamic jihadis who murdered 130 people in Paris in a series of jihad attacks in November 2015 were refugees who had recently been welcomed into Europe.[43] Germany's domestic intelligence agency admitted in July 2017 that hundreds of jihadis had entered the country among the refugees, and that 24,000 jihadis were active in Germany.[44]

Despite all this, Obama seemed determined to allow the Islamic

State to get an untold number of its operatives into the United States. Reuters reported on September 10, 2015, that Obama had "directed his administration to prepare to take in at least 10,000 Syrian refugees over the next year."[45] CNS News reported in May 2016 that "the Obama administration has admitted 499 Syrian refugees so far this month, with no Christians among them. Of the 499 admitted in May, 495 are Sunni Muslims and the remaining four are described simply as 'Moslem' in State Department Refugee Processing Center data."[46]

In June 2016, a Muslim named Omar Mateen murdered forty-nine people in a gay nightclub in Orlando, Florida. He told a 911 operator that he was carrying out his attack for the Islamic State. Journalist Daniel Greenfield noted: "If Obama had not dismissed ISIS early on, it would never have gained the level of support that it did. And the Orlando massacre might never have happened."[47] Middle East expert Ari Lieberman agreed, characterizing Obama's strategy as a plan to "divert America's attention from the main culprit—Islamic terrorism—to forwarding dual strawman/red herring arguments designed to confuse and mislead. By doing so, he hoped to draw America's attention away from his own flawed foreign and domestic policies which enabled the ISIS-inspired Muslim terrorist to commit mass slaughter."[48]

Yet, to the end of his presidency, Obama continued to downplay the Islamic State threat. In November 2015, Obama granted that the Islamic State posed a serious threat, but claimed that it had largely been defeated:

> This is an important moment for our nations and for the world. This barbaric terrorist group, ISIL or Daesh, and its murderous ideology pose a serious threat to all of us. It cannot be tolerated. It must be destroyed and we must do it together. . . . I don't think they are gaining strength. What is true is that from the start our goal has been first, to contain and we have contained them. They have not gained ground in Iraq and in Syria they will come in, they leave, but you don't see the systematic march by ISIL across the terrain.[49]

By April 2016, Obama was claiming that "ISIS is not an existential threat to the United States." What was? The myth of global warming: "Climate change is a potential existential threat to the entire world if we don't do something about it."[50] According to Middle East analyst Caroline Glick, Obama believed that "the threat that racist Americans will respond to the threat of ISIS with racism directed against Muslims" was "greater than the threat that ISIS poses to the US, its allies and the global order."[51] Greenfield summed it up ably in November 2015, saying: "Obama isn't trying to bottle up ISIS except as a means of bottling up America. He doesn't see the Caliph of the Islamic State as the real threat, but the average American who watches the latest beheading on the news and wonders why his government doesn't do something about it. To the left it isn't the Caliph of ISIS who starts the wars we ought to worry about, but Joe in Tennessee, Bill in California or Pete in Minnesota."[52]

And so when Barack Obama left office on January 20, 2017, he had done nothing about the Islamic State, which at that time controlled a huge expanse of territory and had attracted—because of its strict fidelity to Islamic teachings, the very fact that Obama had repeatedly denied—thirty thousand foreign fighters from a hundred countries to travel to Iraq and Syria to join the caliphate. It gained the allegiance of other jihad groups in Libya, Nigeria, the Philippines, and elsewhere. Muslims took its apparent success as a sign of Allah's favor: the caliphate had indeed returned.

A Christian resident of Qaraqosh, an Iraqi town that had been devastated by the Islamic State, was bitter, saying in November 2016: "Obama has never helped the Christians. In fact, he despises them. In the last 26 months, he has shown he despises all of them. But we have hope in the new president, Trump."[53] There was good reason for that hope. When Donald Trump replaced Barack Obama as president of the United States, Iraqi forces and others began rolling up Islamic State strongholds, such that within a year of the beginning of the Trump presidency, the Islamic State had lost 98 percent of its territory. The jihad threat posed by the Islamic State did not lessen, however, as those foreign fighters who survived returned to their home countries, often welcomed back by Western leaders who were convinced that kind treatment would compel them to turn away from jihad. Obama was gone, but his spirit and his core assumptions lived on in Joe Biden's chaotic, disastrous presidency.

11

THE IRAN DEAL

by Robert Spencer

IN NOVEMBER 2021, the Biden administration offered the Islamic Republic of Iran sanctions relief in exchange for its return to an interim nuclear deal. The offer reflected Biden's handlers' uncritical acceptance of the idea, at least publicly, that the Iran nuclear deal was a positive arrangement that would secure peace in the region. This idea, like so many others, came from Barack Obama. Over six years after winning the Nobel Peace Prize, Obama accomplished something that he clearly believed would be the foundation of lasting peace: he had brought Iran to the negotiating table and won its acceptance of an agreement that would prevent it, once and for all, from developing nuclear weapons.

The United States, Russia, China, the United Kingdom, and the European Union concluded the agreement with the Islamic Republic in Vienna on July 14, 2015. Flush with victory as he announced the conclusion of the deal, Obama proclaimed that Iran's "every pathway to a nuclear weapon" had been blocked.[1] "We have stopped the spread of nuclear weapons in this region."[2]

In his hour of victory, Obama couldn't resist taking a swipe at the naysayers—both those who had said that the US couldn't negotiate with the Islamic Republic and those who had said it shouldn't. "This deal," he declared, "demonstrates that American diplomacy can bring about real and meaningful change, change that makes our country and the world safer and more secure." The United States, he said, had "negotiated from a position of strength and principle." The president warned Congress that rejecting the deal could have severe consequences: "Put simply, no deal means the chance of more war in the Middle East."[3] To calm the fears of doubters, he insisted that the deal was "not built on trust. It is built on verification."[4]

But the spirit of peace was not exactly reigning in Tehran. The Joint Comprehensive Plan of Action (JCPOA) with Iran had just been concluded when the Islamic Republic's Supreme Leader, Ayatollah Ali Khamenei, reaffirmed his nation's hostility toward the US: "Even after this deal our policy towards the arrogant U.S. will not change. We don't have any negotiations or deal with the U.S. on different issues in the world or the region."[5] A week after the agreement was concluded, Khamenei said in a speech, "According to Qur'anic principles, fighting against arrogance and global imperialism is never-ending and today, America is the very epitome of arrogance."[6] And just four days after the JCPOA agreement was signed, Khamenei praised the Iranian people for screaming "Death to America" and "Death to Israel" at nationwide rallies on Al-Quds Day, an annual observance in Iran, during which the nation reaffirms its commitment to the Palestinian jihad against Israel. Al-Quds Day in 2015 fell on July 10, four days before the agreement was finalized. Referring to the observances in a speech on July 18,

Khamenei stated that "the slogans of the people of Iran . . . indicated what directions they're heading for."

In what directions were the Iranians heading? "You heard 'Death to Israel,' 'Death to the US.' You could hear it. The whole nation was shaken by these slogans. It wasn't only confined to Tehran. The whole of the nation, you could hear, that was covered by this great movement. So we ask Almighty God to accept these prayers by the people of Iran."[7]

In the same speech, Khamenei declared that the nuclear deal would not change Iran's hostile stance toward the US, or its support for enemies of US allies in the region: "The Islamic Republic of Iran will not give up support of its friends in the region—the oppressed people of Palestine, of Yemen, the Syrian and Iraqi governments, the oppressed people of Bahrain and sincere resistance fighters in Lebanon and Palestine."[8] Khamenei claimed, "Plainly we don't want war. But if war breaks out, it will be the aggressive, cruel American that loses."[9]

As he said all this, the appreciative crowd enthusiastically chanted "Death to America" and "Death to Israel."[10] In another address that same day, less than a week after the nuclear deal was concluded, Khamenei blamed "big powers"—that is, America and America's allies—for the disunity of Muslims worldwide: "If the Islamic Ummah were united and relied on their own commonalities, they would certainly be a unique power in the international political scene but big powers have imposed such divisions on the Islamic Ummah to pursue their own interests and safeguard the Zionist regime."[11] Khamenei was jubilant regarding the nuclear agreement: "This is the outcome of the Iranian nation's resistance and bravery and the creativity of dear Iranian scientists." He said that the US and its allies had been "forced to accept and stand the spinning of thousands of centrifuges and continuation of research and development in Iran, and it has no meaning but the Iranian nation's might."[12] Khamenei was contemptuous about the possibility of working with the US to bring peace and stability to the Middle East: "Our policies and those of the US in the region are 180 degree different, so how could it be possible to enter dialogue and negotiations with them?"[13]

A month later, Khamenei was still just as confrontational, crowing, "They thought this deal—and it is not clear if it will be passed in Iran or in America—will open up Iran to their influence. We blocked this path and will definitely block it in the future."[14]

On Friday, July 20, 2015, just two days after Khamenei's bellicose remarks, Iran's state-run media essentially declared victory outright, releasing photos of Ayatollah Mohammad Ali Movahedi Kermani—whom Khamenei had chosen to lead Friday prayers in Tehran—at a podium emblazoned in Persian, "We will trample upon America," and in English, "We Defeat the United States."[15] With the declarations of victory came new threats. On July 25, Khamenei tweeted an image of Barack Obama in silhouette, holding a pistol to his own temple. The image was accompanied by a graphic that quoted Khamenei's July 18 speech: "We welcome no war, nor do we initiate any war, but if any war happens, the one who will emerge the loser will be the aggressive and criminal U.S."[16]

That same day, Iranian Foreign Minister Mohammad Javad Zarif responded with contempt to Kerry's suggestion that if the Iranians did not abide by the agreement, the US could resort to military action: "Unfortunately the US Secretary of State once again talked about the rotten rope of 'the ability of the US for using military force.'" Zarif decried the "uselessness of such empty threats against the nation of Iran and the resistance of the nation of Iran." Such threats, he said, belonged "to the last century," and what's more, even the Americans "have repeatedly admitted that these threats have no effect on the will of the people of Iran and that it will change the situation to their disadvantage."[17]

Two days later, still less than two weeks after the agreement was signed, Zarif crowed that "Benjamin Netanyahu is ready to kill himself if it helps to stop this nuclear agreement because this agreement puts the Zionist regime in an irrecoverable danger. The abominable Zionist Regime has never been so isolated among its allies."[18] Ominously, Zarif also asserted that Iran's "violating the arms and missiles embargo" of the United Nations "does not violate the nuclear agreement."[19]

And within three months, Iran would announce that it had test-fired a precision-guided ballistic missile with a range that would allow it to reach Israel—all the while insisting that the tests were not prohibited under the terms of the nuclear deal.[20] In the months between the signing of the agreement and the ballistic missile tests, the Iranians continued to crow about their victory over the Great Satan at the negotiating table. After a spate of ballistic missile tests on March 8, 2016, Iranian Brigadier General Amir Ali Hajizadeh referred on Iranian television to "our main enemies, the Americans."[21] The next day, Iran test-fired two ballistic missiles on which "Israel must be wiped out" was written in Hebrew.[22]

"The U.S. president, fruitlessly, tries to claim the results of the nuclear negotiations, but the truth is . . . the U.S. had no alternative but giving up its excessive demands." So said Iranian foreign ministry spokeswoman Marzieh Afkham, heaping contempt on President Obama's attempts to spin the deal as victory.[23]

In September of 2015, Marzieh Afkham boasted that the US had been "forced into negotiating" with Iran because of the "failure of the U.S. policy of sanctions and threats."[24] Iranian President Hassan Rouhani dubbed the deal "evident victory," after the name in Islamic tradition of Muhammad's raids on the caravans of the pagan Arabs of Mecca. The deal, said Rouhani, was "the greatest diplomatic victory in Islamic history."[25] Not just Iranian history, but Islamic history.

Despite all the bellicosity coming out of Iran as the nuclear agreement was finalized, John Kerry insisted in a lengthy, August 2015 interview that the side that needed to show a good faith commitment to peace was not Iran, but the United States. He argued urgently that the deal should be approved by Congress because if it wasn't, it would prove to Khamenei that he had been right about the Americans all along, that we were untrustworthy. According to Kerry, the ayatollah was extremely reluctant to make a deal with the Americans and had had to be cajoled by the purportedly moderate Rouhani: "The ayatollah approached this entire exercise extremely charily. He gave a kind of dismissive OK to Rouhani and company to go do this, in the sense that he didn't want to be blamed if this didn't work. It was all Rouhani's risk. He was playing the IRGC [Islamic Revolutionary Guards Corps], and this and that. And so it was clear to me from my many conversations with Zarif and from the entire dynamic how fragile that journey was with him. The ayatollah constantly believed that we are untrustworthy, that you can't negotiate with us, that we will screw them."[26]

For Kerry, the ayatollah's suspicion of America was a major reason the US had to follow through and approve and hold to the deal—otherwise, Khamenei would lose faith in the US entirely: "This will be the ultimate screwing. We cut a deal, we stand up, it's announced, five other countries believe in it—six other countries, because Iran signs off, and we're the seventh—but you know, China, Russia, France, Germany, Britain, all sign off. Now the United States Congress will prove the ayatollah's suspicion, and there's no way he's ever coming back. He will not come back to negotiate. Out of dignity, out of a suspicion that you can't trust America. America is not going to negotiate in good faith. It didn't negotiate in good faith now, would be his point."[27]

Kerry didn't seem to have any concern about whether the ayatollah's men had negotiated with *us* in good faith—it was only American trustworthiness that was in question. Iranian good faith, in fact, was taken for granted to such an extent that the assumption of it was built into the agreement itself. On July 30, 2015, Iran's Deputy Foreign Minister, Abbas Araghchi, pointed out, "American and Canadian inspectors cannot be sent to Iran. It is mentioned in the deal that inspectors should be from countries that have diplomatic relations with Islamic Republic of Iran." International Atomic Energy Agency (IAEA) inspectors, he added, would not be given access to "sensitive and military documents."[28]

In an interview with Al Jazeera the following day, Ali Akbar Velayati, a senior adviser to Khamenei, further broadened these restrictions to apply to other signatories to the deal as well: "Regardless of how the P5+1 countries interpret the nuclear agreement, their entry into our military sites is absolutely forbidden."[29] Yet just days later, John Kerry secured the Gulf States' approval of the deal by assuring them that

Iranian nuclear sites would be subject to close inspection. After meeting with Kerry, Qatar's Foreign Minister Khalid al-Attiyah declared that the secretary of state "let us know that there is going to be live oversight over Iran not to gain or to get any nuclear weapons. This is reassuring to the region."[30] How could there be any effective "live oversight" of Iran's nuclear sites if "entry into [Iran's] military sites is absolutely forbidden" to any country whose inspectors would bring a critical eye to the process? On August 19, 2015, the Associated Press dropped a bombshell. Confirming rumors that had circulated since the agreement was signed, it reported that a secret side deal between the International Atomic Energy Agency (IAEA) and Iran allowed the Iranians to conduct *their own* inspections of *their own* sites:

> Iran, in an unusual arrangement, will be allowed to use its own experts to inspect a site it allegedly used to develop nuclear arms under a secret agreement with the U.N. agency that normally carries out such work, according to a document seen by The Associated Press. The revelation is sure to roil American and Israeli critics of the main Iran deal signed by the U.S., Iran and five world powers in July. Those critics have complained that the deal is built on trust of the Iranians, a claim the U.S. has denied. The investigation of the Parchin nuclear site by the International Atomic Energy Agency is linked to a broader probe of allegations that Iran has worked on atomic weapons. That investigation is part of the overarching nuclear deal. The Parchin deal is a separate, side agreement worked out between the IAEA and Iran. The United States and the five other world powers that signed the Iran nuclear deal were not party to this agreement but were briefed on it by the IAEA and endorsed it as part of the larger package. Without divulging its contents, the Obama administration has described the document as nothing more than a routine technical arrangement between Iran and the U.N.'s International Atomic Energy Agency on the particulars of inspecting the site.[31]

AP observed, rather mildly, that this side agreement "diverges from normal inspection procedures between the IAEA and a member country by essentially ceding the agency's investigative authority to Iran. It allows Tehran to employ its own experts and equipment in the search for evidence for activities that it has consistently denied—trying to develop nuclear weapons." Such an accommodation was unprecedented. "Olli Heinonen, who was in charge of the Iran probe as deputy IAEA director general from 2005 to 2010, said he can think of no instance where a country being probed was allowed to do its own investigation."[32]

On the evening of the day the AP story appeared, *NBC News* confirmed that report's central claim and disputed the counterclaim that Iran's self-inspections would relate only to past activity. "Iran," NBC reported, "will inspect itself at its most sensitive known military complex to clear up suspicions of past military activity, *NBC News* has confirmed." Then it invoked "two senior U.S. officials" denying the Arms Control Association's claim that the permission for self-inspections related only to "past military activity. " The same officials flatly contradicted the claim that "UN inspectors, including IAEA Director Yukiya Amano, would be on site to supervise the Iranians at every step of the way." On the contrary, NBC reported, "a senator who opposes the deal and attended classified briefings on the IAEA's role at the Parchin complex southeast of Tehran" told NBC News that it was "categorically untrue that IAEA inspectors will be inside the Parchin facility while soil samples are being taken." The senator declined to be named.[33]

The Obama White House issued a statement, assuring the world that all was well: "As we've said before, including in classified briefings for both chambers of Congress, we're confident in the [IAEA's] technical plans for investigating the possible military dimensions of Iran's former program—issues that in some cases date back more than a decade. Just as importantly, the IAEA is comfortable with arrangements which are unique to the agency's investigation of Iran's historical activities."[34] Significantly, this statement didn't deny the self-inspection claim.

Despite the lack of substance in these denials, however, AP deleted its original report and eight days later issued this correction: "In a story Aug. 19 about an arrangement over alleged past nuclear weapons work between Iran and the International Atomic Energy Agency, The Associated Press erroneously referred to Parchin as a 'nuclear site.['] In fact, it's a military site where some believe nuclear work occurred." The correction didn't touch upon the central claim of the original story—that Iran would conduct its own nuclear inspections. The "corrected version" read, "An unusual secret agreement with a UN agency will allow Iran to use its own experts to inspect a site allegedly used to develop nuclear arms, according to a document seen by The Associated Press. The revelation is sure to roil critics who argue the deal is built on trust of the Iranians. The investigation of the Parchin military site by the UN International Atomic Energy Agency is linked to a broader probe of nuclear weapons allegations."[35]

The claim that Iran would conduct self-inspections remained, unretracted and uncorrected. The correction centered upon the Parchin site, "allegedly used to develop nuclear arms." Nuclear researcher Cheryl Rofer explained, "What is the purpose of sampling at Parchin? The IAEA is looking for residues of experiments that are alleged to have been done to develop a design for a nuclear weapon. They were most likely carried out before 2003, when US intelligence estimates find that Iranian nuclear weapons work ended, although the IAEA has expressed concern that experiments may have been carried out after 2003."[36]

In other words, the inspections at Parchin were not only going to be conducted by the Iranians themselves. They were also going to be limited to looking for evidence of past nuclear weapons development. Might ongoing nuclear weapons activities be taking place at Parchin? There was nothing definitive to rule out that possibility—and it was at Parchin that Iran would be able to provide its own soil samples to the IAEA. What's more, in February 2016, satellite photos confirmed that construction had been going on at Parchin at a furious rate during the period in which the nuclear agreement was being negotiated, perhaps to conceal work on nuclear weapons.[37]

Beyond the self-inspection problem, there was a great deal more wrong with the Iran deal.

The Expiration Dates

While the Joint Comprehensive Plan of Action (JCPOA) did include real restrictions on Iran's nuclear activities, these were all slated to expire within a period of years. The agreement anticipated the "conclusion of consideration of the Iran nuclear issue by the UN Security Council 10 years after the Adoption Day"—that is, the July 14, 2015, adoption of the agreement itself.[38] It contained stipulations such as this: "There will be no additional heavy water reactors or accumulation of heavy water in Iran for 15 years."[39] What about after that? The agreement didn't say. "Iran," said the agreement, "will allow the IAEA to monitor the implementation of the voluntary measures for their respective durations, as well as to implement transparency measures, as set out in this JCPOA and its Annexes. These measures include: a long-term IAEA presence in Iran; IAEA monitoring of uranium ore concentrate produced by Iran from all uranium ore concentrate plants for 25 years; containment and surveillance of centrifuge rotors and bellows for 20 years; use of IAEA approved and certified modern technologies including on-line enrichment measurement and electronic seals; and a reliable mechanism to ensure speedy resolution of IAEA access concerns for 15 years . . . ." Another provision: "Iran will not conduct any uranium enrichment or any uranium enrichment related R&D [research and development] and will have no nuclear material at the Fordow Fuel Enrichment Plant (FFEP) for 15 years."

Such stipulations were peppered throughout the agreement, raising the inevitable question: What about after that? The Joint Comprehensive Plan of Action were silent on that key point.

The Delay in Inspections

The day after the conclusion of the Joint Comprehensive Plan of Action, Israeli Prime Minister Benjamin Netanyahu pointed out, "I think Iran has two paths to the bomb: One if they keep the deal, the other if they cheat on the deal." They can get the bomb even if they keep the deal because the JCPOA contains the provision that Iran can delay requested IAEA inspections for up to twenty-four days. "Can you imagine," Netanyahu asked, "giving a drug dealer 24 days' notice before you inspect the premises? That's a lot of time to flush a lot of meth down the toilet."[40] As preposterous as this delay sounded, Netanyahu was right. The JCPOA stated:

> If the absence of undeclared nuclear materials and activities or activities inconsistent with the JCPOA cannot be verified after the implementation of the alternative arrangements agreed by Iran and the IAEA, or if the two sides are unable to reach satisfactory arrangements to verify the absence of undeclared nuclear materials and activities or activities inconsistent with the JCPOA at the specified locations within 14 days of the IAEA's original request for access, Iran, in consultation with the members of the Joint Commission, would resolve the IAEA's concerns through necessary means agreed between Iran and the IAEA. In the absence of an agreement, the members of the Joint Commission, by consensus or by a vote of 5 or more of its 8 members, would advise on the necessary means to resolve the IAEA's concerns. The process of consultation with, and any action by, the members of the Joint Commission would not exceed 7 days, and Iran would implement the necessary means within 3 additional days.[41]

That amounted to exactly the twenty-four-day period to which Netanyahu was referring: if the IAEA feared that Iran was not complying with the agreement, first Iran would have fourteen days to "reach satisfactory arrangements" with the IAEA; then, if they couldn't come to an agreement by that point, the Joint Commission would "advise on the necessary means to resolve the IAEA's concerns," presumably including recommending inspection of Iranian nuclear sites, within another seven days, with their recommendations to be implemented within another three days. This long delay amounted to no effective right to inspect Iranian nuclear sites at all. It rendered John Kerry's confident assurance that "every facility" would be subjected to "24–7 visibility"[42] hollow.

The Removal of Sanctions

Even before the deal, it was questionable how effective the economic sanctions that the US and UN had placed upon Iran really were. In March 2015, Thomas Erdbrink, the Tehran bureau chief of the *New York Times*, a longtime resident of Iran, remarked, "As the politicians are talking for months to end the sanctions, my shopkeeper tells me he has more foreign products for sale than ever."[43] Nonetheless, the JCPOA was quite definite about removing all economic sanctions on Iran. "This JCPOA will produce the comprehensive lifting of all UN Security Council sanctions as well as multilateral and national sanctions related to Iran's nuclear programme, including steps on access in areas of trade, technology, finance and energy."[44] This included the removal of sanctions that had originally been intended to be removed only when Iran definitively gave up its nuclear program. Now the Islamic Republic was being given sanctions relief and allowed to continue its nuclear program, only with certain restrictions that would all eventually expire anyway.

American officials insisted that if Iran didn't comply with the agreement, it allowed for the "snapback"—the reapplication—of the sanctions. Barack Obama claimed, "If Iran violates the deal, all of these sanctions will snap back into place. So there is a very clear incentive for Iran to follow through and there are very real consequences for a violation." John Kerry was no less adamant: "I want to underscore: If Iran fails in a material way to live up to these commitments, then the United States, the EU, and even the UN sanctions that initially brought Iran to the table can and will snap right back into place. We have a specific provision in this agreement called 'snapback' for the return of those sanctions in the event of noncompliance."[45] The JCPOA itself, however, was ambiguous on this point, seeming to state that the sanctions, once removed, could not be put back:

The EU will refrain from re-introducing or re-imposing the sanctions that it has terminated implementing under this JCPOA, without prejudice to the dispute resolution process provided for under this JCPOA. There will be no new nuclear-related UN Security Council sanctions and no new EU nuclear-related sanctions or restrictive measures. The United States will make best efforts in good faith to sustain this JCPOA and to prevent interference with the realisation of the full benefit by Iran of the sanctions lifting specified in Annex II. The U.S. Administration, acting consistent with the respective roles of the President and the Congress, will refrain from re-introducing or re-imposing the sanctions specified in Annex II that it has ceased applying under this JCPOA, without prejudice to the dispute resolution process provided for under this JCPOA. The U.S. Administration, acting consistent with the respective roles of the President and the Congress, will refrain from imposing new nuclear-related sanctions.[46]

Any new sanctions would be a justification for Iran to pull out of the agreement—something that is also stated in the JCPOA itself: "Iran has stated that it will treat such a reintroduction or re-imposition of the sanctions specified in Annex II, or such an imposition of new nuclear-related sanctions, as grounds to cease performing its commitments under this JCPOA in whole or in part."[47]

The Lack of Any Consequences for Breaking the Agreement
The 159-page Joint Comprehensive Plan of Action went into tremendous detail about the Iranian nuclear program and how it was to be temporarily restricted in various ways. It also expatiated on exactly which sanctions are to be removed. But it was conspicuously lacking in specifying penalties for Iran's not holding to the agreement. The only specific penalty for Iranian noncompliance in the entire JCPOA was one that stood in tension with other statements in the agreement about how the sanctions would not be restored once they have been removed. The JCPOA stipulated that if a country privy to the agreement found Iran

in noncompliance, then once "the complaining participant" had made "good-faith efforts" to "exhaust the dispute resolution process," the UN Security Council would "vote on a resolution to continue the sanctions lifting."[48] That is, it could halt the lifting of sanctions, or reimpose them.

If Iran were found to be in noncompliance, the old sanctions could be re-imposed, "unless the UN Security Council decides otherwise"— a very large loophole, considering the significant number of political and economic reasons for Security Council members to avoid the re-imposition of the sanctions.[49] If Iran's friends and allies could muster the votes, it could keep the sanctions specified in old Security Council resolutions from being re-imposed. And even if the sanctions were ever re-imposed, they "would not apply with retroactive effect to contracts signed between any party and Iran or Iranian individuals and entities prior to the date of application, provided that the activities contemplated under and execution of such contracts are consistent with this JCPOA and the previous and current UN Security Council resolutions."[50] In other words, if Iran were found to be violating the terms of the deal and the old sanctions were reapplied, they wouldn't apply to deals Iran made before it was found in noncompliance. The removal of the sanctions could have been the most damaging aspect of the JCPOA. The day after the agreement was concluded, Obama acknowledged that the sanctions relief would give Iran a considerable amount of money that it could use to increase its funding of Hamas, Hizballah, and other jihad terror groups, but he insisted this was unimportant: "Do I think it's a game-changer for them? No. . . . The truth is, that Iran has always found a way to fund these efforts. And whatever benefit Iran may claim from sanctions relief pales in comparison to the danger it could pose with a nuclear weapon."[51]

But it was hard not to see this money as a game changer, especially with Iran standing to gain as much as a staggering $700 billion. Yet, in a major address defending the nuclear deal, Obama insisted that he was no Pollyanna: "We have no illusions about the Iranian government or the significance of the Revolutionary Guard and the Quds Force. Iran supports terrorist organizations like Hezbollah. It supports proxy groups that threaten our interests and the interests of our allies, including proxy groups who killed our troops in Iraq." But again he downplayed the threat: "Contrary to the alarmists who claim Iran is on the brink of taking over the Middle East, or even the world, Iran will remain a regional power with its own set of challenges."[52]

Maybe so, but the billions in sanctions relief could go a long way to helping Iran overcome those challenges. In September 2015, buoyed by the lifting of sanctions as specified in the Joint Comprehensive Plan of Action, Iran significantly increased its funding of both Hamas and Hizballah.[53] In January 2016, after the IAEA certified that Iran was in compliance with the nuclear deal and Iran released five Americans it had imprisoned (as part of a prisoner swap that involved the US dropping a $10 million claim against an Iranian engineer accused of violating the now-dead sanctions), the US released $400 million in Iranian funds that had been frozen since 1981, and added $1.3 billion in interest.[54]

In February 2016, after a spate of Palestinian stabbings of Israeli civilians, Mohammad Fathali, the Iranian ambassador to Lebanon, announced: "Continuing Iran's support for the oppressed Palestinian people, Iran announces the provision of financial aid to families of Palestinian martyrs who were killed in the 'Jerusalem intifada.'" Iran would award $7,000 to the families of Palestinians killed while trying to murder Israelis, and $30,000 to those whose homes were destroyed by the Israelis because of their jihad terror activity.[55]

Apparently aware of how bad it looked to be turning over billions of dollars to a state sponsor of terror, in March 2016, Colin Kahl, Vice President Joe Biden's National Security Advisor, claimed that $100 billion in unfrozen assets that had already been released to Iran according to the terms of the nuke deal were "being used for domestic investment, to the dismay of [Qods Force chief] Qassem Soleimani."[56] Kahl's claim was flatly false, and apparently fabricated in order to try to save some face over the increasingly obvious disaster that was the nuclear deal. In reality, the Iranians were spending all of their newfound wealth on weaponry. Flush with JCPOA cash, they had been in discussions with the Chinese about buying Chinese jet fighters, shopped for materiel in Russia, and supplied the Islamic Revolutionary Guards Corps with drones—all courtesy of Barack Hussein Obama.

12

OBAMA'S ILLEGAL MARXIST IMMIGRANT AMNESTY MOVEMENT

by Trevor Loudon

THERE IS NO DOUBT that President Barack Obama sought to secure amnesty and citizenship for America's millions of illegal immigrants. He failed, but not for lack of trying. As a consolation prize, in 2014, the president issued an executive order establishing the Deferred Action for Childhood Arrivals (DACA) program to grant temporary residence for millions of "undocumented" children and young adults.[1] None of Obama's radical immigration policies sprang from a vacuum. Obama was following a communist playbook that had been in operation for more than fifty years. The Hawaii-raised Obama surfed a wave that had been building for decades. Luckily for America, he wiped out.

Few commentators correctly understand leftists' encouragement of illegal immigration. It has little to do with compassion or the American Dream. Instead, so-called progressives pursue a deliberate program to grab permanent political control over the United States. It comes down to simple math. For years, it has been generally accepted that there are approximately 11 million illegal aliens living in the United States.[2] However, a 2018 study released by the Massachusetts Institute of Technology (MIT) gave cause to revisit that figure. The authors claimed that their research discovered a total number of 22.1 million. Even under "extremely conservative parameters," the analysts estimate a population of 16.7 million "undocumented" immigrants.[3] Following current voting patterns, if these individuals received citizenship and voting rights, the Democrats would gain millions of potential new voters overnight. It's not hard to see the huge impact this would have on future elections.

MORE VOTERS, MORE POWER

American leftists, including Obama, have long sought to use the illegal alien population to secure a "permanent progressive majority" for the Democratic Party. Communist Party USA (CPUSA) leader Emile Schepers wrote a paper on an illegal immigration amnesty for the party's 2016 national convention in Chicago, openly admitting, "For decades, the CPUSA has been involved in the struggle for the rights of immigrant workers and their families . . . A central focus has been gaining legal rights for the 11 million undocumented . . . We call for progressive legislation which legalizes as many people as possible as quickly as possible . . . We are for ease of access to U.S. citizenship."[4]

For more than twenty years the former Illinois Representative Luis Gutierrez led the fight for an illegal alien amnesty in the House. He is a former leader of the Marxist–Leninist Puerto Rican Socialist Party[5] and was an ally of the Maoist-leaning League of Revolutionary Struggle.[6] In July 2015, Gutierrez addressed the House of Representatives on the subject of the power of the Latino vote and the Left:

If millions of people naturalize, become citizens, and we add to that the million Latino citizens who this year will turn 18, plus all our allies in the African-American community, the LGBT voters and younger voters, environmental voters, women voters, Asian voters, union voters . . . [all of these] constitute a majority of Americans. Together, we are the New American Coalition that will dominate politics for decades to come.[7]

Illegal alien amnesty is the Left's road to the American one-party state. Obama was fully on board with the program, immersed in its ideas his entire adult life.

FATHER OF THE MOVEMENT
If the illegal immigration/amnesty movement can claim one father, it is undoubtedly the late California activist Bert Corona. Herman Baca, former president of the Committee on Chicano Rights, knew him well, noting that Obama and the "Gang of 8" (a bi-partisan group of senators promoting immigration "reform") reminded him of Corona. Baca regarded Corona as being "recognized by many in the Chicano community as being both the father of the Chicano and immigration movements." Baca said Corona sought to bring the problem of illegal immigration "to the forefront of U.S. public policy discussion" and that without his leadership, the movement would not exist. Baca regards Corona as prophetic, that he "predicted correctly the immigration issue grew both nationally and internationally from an Ant Hill to a Mount Everest of an issue."[8] David Bacon, a journalist and Democratic Socialists of America (DSA) comrade, claimed that, "Looking at the huge mass of Mexican immigrants populating L.A. barrios, Corona saw not just a population excluded from the political mainstream, but a future in which their votes would eventually shape the politics of the city and the state."[9]

Corona was born in 1918 in El Paso, Texas, at the height of the Mexican Revolution. His father Noé joined the Partido Liberal

Mexicano, an anarcho-syndicalist group, and served as a comandante in one of the two main insurgent armies of the Mexican Revolution, the Division del Norte. Noé Corona fled to the United States when the revolution failed.[10] In the late 1930s, Corona moved to Los Angeles to attend the University of Southern California on a basketball scholarship. Soon, he moved into labor organizing and became a protégé of the legendary ILWU leader Harry Bridges—who was later identified as a secret leader of the CPUSA.[11] Probably because of his extensive work inside the Democratic Party, Corona concealed his Communist Party membership. However, his name appeared in a congressional hearing, identifying him as a party member. He also worked with well-known CPUSA comrades including Angela Davis for decades.[12] When the Berlin Wall fell, Corona defiantly stated, "The workers of East Germany, for example, aren't about to give up easily many of the supports they had under socialism, such as low rents and free education for their children."[13]

Corona was also a founder of the Mexican American Political Association, which launched the careers of many Democratic Latino politicians. Corona also helped set up the Viva Kennedy clubs in the 1960s, which, for the first time, brought large numbers of Latinos into the Democratic Party. Corona also served as co-chair for both Lyndon Johnson's and Bobby Kennedy's presidential campaigns in California.[14] In the late 1960s, Corona broke with then-too-conservative Democrats. He allied instead with the tiny Raza Unida Party (RUP), which preached that an "occupied Chicano nation" in the southwestern United States needed to be wrested from the "Anglo" conquerors and returned to Mexico.[15]

LA HERMANDAD

After World War II, the Immigration and Naturalization Service (INS) stepped up its efforts to cancel the work visas of Mexicans living in the San Diego area. In 1951, union leaders Phil and Albert Usquiano organized La Hermandad Mexicana Nacional (The Mexican National Brotherhood) to oppose the program. In 1968, Corona brought La

Hermandad to Los Angeles and began to spread it across the country. At one point, the group boasted 30,000 members. Hermandad used leftist lawyers and mass organizing to protect illegal aliens from the INS. The group organized housing for illegal alien families and tried to unionize illegal workers where possible. But, most importantly, it tried to use their numbers to gain political leverage.

In 1964, the federal government ended the Bracero program, which gave Mexican workers temporary work permits. By the 1970s, only 20,000 Mexican workers were legally allowed into the country each year. Corona and La Hermandad organized Mexican workers, teaching them how to fight back and to legally defy or stall the INS. The organization also defended illegal alien workers in court.

In 1986, Congress passed a sweeping amnesty bill, which allowed certain illegal aliens to apply for citizenship. Corona and Hermandad reportedly helped more than 160,000 Mexicans gain US citizenship under the amnesty.[16]

A LEGACY

Corona died in 2001, but his legacy lives on through hundreds of radical leftist proteges and acolytes. Three of Corona's disciples in particular— Antonio Villaraigosa, Maria Elena Durazo, and Gilbert Cedillo—have helped transform California and the nation. According to DSA comrade and *Los Angeles Times* columnist Harold Meyerson, Villaraigosa had joined the movement by "his late teens" and "had anchored himself" to Corona.[17] Villaraigosa would work full-time organizing for Corona's Centro de Action Social Autonoma (CASA). Villaraigosa would go on to become mayor of Los Angeles. He openly opposed the enforcement of laws against illegal immigration and urged Obama to follow suit.[18] Illegal immigration enforcement virtually halted during his tenure.

Durazo became head of the California AFL-CIO, where she funded Latino voter registration drives and get-out-the-vote efforts. Her work added hundreds of thousands of new Latino voters to the California rolls—the vast majority of them Democrats. According to Richie Ross, a senior California Democratic Party operative, the state started to change in 1994 as the illegal immigrant population began to grow at an exponential rate yearly. Also that year, Durazo and her husband Miguel Contreras, the leader of the Los Angeles County Federation of Labor, began linking organizing workers with organizing voters. Ross said, "The campaigns we developed broke new ground, organized new union workers, and increased the political impact Latino voters have had on California politics—simultaneously tripling their number of registered voters, increasing the Democratic share of that vote by 50 percent, and doubling the percentage of the total votes cast in California from Latinos."[19]

While serving in the California State legislature Cedillo tried many times to pass bills that would allow illegal aliens to obtain driver's licenses. He finally succeeded in October 2013. In April 2018, Cedillo helped celebrate a "milestone" of one million licenses being granted since the law came into effect.[20]

Villaraigosa became a leading surrogate for Obama's re-election campaign in 2012. He also praised the president for instituting the unconstitutional DACA program that prevented deportation for millions of illegal immigrants.[21] Cedillo was one of the first California Latino politicians to endorse Obama in 2008.[22] Durazo was the first major California labor official to endorse Obama in 2008—and it made a difference.[23]

Fernando Guerra, director of the Center for the Study of Los Angeles at Loyola Marymount University, said that Durazo "symbolizes the new power in Los Angeles and in California—the marriage of Latinos and labor . . . and when you have those numbers, that organization and those volunteers, it makes an impact . . . There is no person in all of California who could get more people out to the street to go do something, either to march or get the vote out."[24]

Bacon described Corona as "a child of the line in the sand between the U.S. and Mexico" and that "this is not the same world Bert Corona was born into, it is certainly one he helped create."[25] Bacon claimed that now the votes of working-class Latinos were essential for gaining political power in the city.

While Corona died in 2001, there is no doubt that Obama came into the presidency intent on expanding his legacy. His administration even commissioned the Los Angeles-based "Bert Corona Leadership Institute" to find recruits. Obama's transition team sought Afro-Latino candidates for subcabinet, policy, and agency positions. The Institute's Earl Francisco Lopez, chairman and CEO, said "I have been asked to collect resumes and submit them directly."[26]   Corona's life's work has borne tremendous fruit. Once a conservative state, California is now almost totally controlled by the Left and the Democratic Party. Fifty years of deliberately encouraging and fostering illegal immigration into California has turned Ronald Reagan's Golden State into a bastion of socialism. And the California model is now being rolled out across the country. If the United States ever falls to socialism, Corona will go down as one of the communist movement's great revolutionary heroes.

ELISEO MEDINA AND THE PRESIDENT

Labor leader and "amnesty" activist Eliseo Medina is a very competent heir to the Bert Corona legacy. And he had direct access to Obama. "Before immigration debates took place in Washington, I spoke with Eliseo Medina and SEIU members," said then-Senator Obama, addressing the SEIU conference during his 2008 presidential campaign.[27]

Medina's road to power began in 1965 when, as a nineteen-year-old grape-picker, he participated in the United Farm Workers' (UFW) strike in Delano, California. Over the next thirteen years, Medina worked alongside labor leader Cesar Chavez in the UFW. Somewhere along the way Medina joined the DSA.[28] However, like many DSA comrades, Medina also worked closely with the CPUSA. Medina gave the keynote speech at the *People's Weekly World* (PWW) banquet in Berkeley, California, on November 18, 2001. The PWW quoted Medina praising the communist publication: "Wherever workers are in struggle . . . they find the PWW regularly reporting issues and viewpoints that are seldom covered by the regular media. For us, the PWW has been and always will be the people's voice."[29]

Medina is undoubtedly one of America's most influential socialists. According to Medina's Mi Familia Vota board profile, he served as a negotiator during the George W. Bush administration's immigration plans and helped get out the Latino vote during Obama's first presidential run, serving on the future president's National Latino Advisory Council. Starting in 2013, Obama and Congress pursued immigration reform with Medina acting behind the scenes. [30]

Like Corona before him, Medina's immigration activism was all about numbers and power. At the far-left "America's Future Now!" conference in Washington on June 2, 2009, Medina, then the Service Employees International Union's (SEIU) international executive vice president, addressed attendees on the vital importance of "comprehensive immigration reform"—a code phrase for amnesty. Medina didn't mention the plight of illegal aliens. He focused instead on how—if given amnesty—they would vote in huge numbers for Democrats. Speaking of Latino voting patterns in the 2008 election, he said:

"When they [Latinos] voted in November, they voted overwhelmingly for progressive candidates. Barack Obama got two out of every three voters that showed up.

So, I think there's two things that matter for the progressive community:

Number one: If we are to expand this electorate to win, the progressive community needs to solidly be on the side of immigrants. That will solidify and expand the progressive coalition for the future.

Number two: [If] we reform the immigration laws—it puts 12 million people on the path to citizenship and eventually voters. Can you imagine if we have—even the same ratio—two out of three?

"If we have 8 million new voters . . . we will create a governing coalition for the long term, not just for an election cycle."[31]

Corona would have loved Medina's concept of a "governing coalition" ruling the whole country indefinitely. That was always his goal.

FLEXIBLE SOCIALIST PRINCIPLES

Corona had worked closely with UFW leader Chavez for decades. The two, however, clashed over one vital point. Chavez actively worked to deport illegal alien farm workers lest they compete with his own members. The more politically sophisticated Corona wanted to organize illegal workers into a political force. "I did have an important difference with Cesar," Corona wrote in his autobiography. "This involved his, and the union's position on the need to apprehend and deport undocumented Mexican immigrants who were being used as scabs by the growers . . . The Hermandad believed that organizing undocumented farm workers was auxiliary to the union's efforts to organize the fields. We supported an open immigration policy, as far as Mexico was concerned."[32]

Medina moved in Corona's circles in California, and there is no doubt he knew him well. In 2010, Medina told Bacon, "That was typical of Bert . . . He didn't just put his finger up to see which way the wind was blowing. He took a principled stand and stuck to it."[33] However, socialist principles can also be very flexible. Medina's wife, Liza Hirsch, is the daughter of Fred Hirsch, a self-described "communist plumber"[34] and his even-more-radical wife Ginny. In the early 1960s, Ginny Hirsch left her husband and young children in San Jose while she drove to Guatemala with nearly a ton of smuggled ammunition destined for leftist rebels.[35]

From the age of twelve, Liza Hirsch was partially raised by Chavez. At his personal request, Liza Hirsh committed herself at an early age to earning a law degree so she could serve as an attorney for the movement. When Chavez launched his "Illegals Campaign"—an organized program to identify illegal alien workers in the fields and turn them in to the INS, Hirsch was put in charge. In 1974, just before she went to law school, Hirsch "distributed forms printed in triplicate to all union offices and directed staff members to document the presence of illegal immigrants in the fields and report them to the INS."[36] Hirsch would later marry New York DSA member Paul Du Brul.[37] After his untimely death in 1986, she married another card-carrying DSA member, Medina.[38]

WINNING THE DEMOCRATS OVER TO AMNESTY

In 1986, Medina joined the SEIU, where he helped revive a local union in San Diego, building its membership from 1,700 to more than 10,000 in five years. He rose quickly to become international executive vice president of the 2.2 million-member SEIU in 1996. The SEIU has a huge number of both legal and illegal Latino workers in its ranks. Medina used that leverage to promote amnesty in the union movement, as well as in the organized Left and the Democratic Party. In the mid-1990s, most unions were still hostile to illegal alien workers who often worked at a much lower pay rate, taking jobs away from union members. But in 1994, several far-left union leaders led by DSA member John Sweeney took over the AFL-CIO, setting the stage for a major policy change for the unions—and ultimately for the Democrats.[39]

Claiming US immigration policy was "broken and [needed] to be fixed," the AFL-CIO on February 16, 2000, called for a new amnesty for millions of undocumented workers and the repeal of the 1986 legislation that criminalized hiring them.

According to the DSA website in 2004, Medina was "widely credited with playing a key role in the AFL-CIO's decision to adopt a new policy on immigration."[40] From his union position, Medina reached across the labor movement into the social movements and the Catholic Church to create the widest possible pro-amnesty coalition.

According to Mi Familia Vota:

Working to ensure the opportunity to pass comprehensive immigration reform does not slip away, Medina led the effort to unite the unions of the Change to Win federation and AFL-CIO around a comprehensive framework for reform. Serving as a leading voice in

Washington, frequently testifying before Congress, Medina has also helped to build a strong, diverse coalition of community and national partners that have intensified the call for reform and cultivated necessary political capital to hold elected leaders accountable.

Medina has also helped strengthen ties between the Roman Catholic Church and the labor movement to work on common concerns such as immigrant worker rights and access to health care.[41]

Eventually, Medina and his movement were able to get an amnesty bill passed through the US Senate. If they could only pass a bill through the House, the United States would be set on an irreversible path to socialism. However, Tea Party–influenced Republican congressmembers refused to pass a similar bill through the House. In November 2013, Medina, along with Cristian Avila of amnesty advocacy group Mi Familia Vota started a twenty-two-day "fast for families" in front of Capitol Hill "to demand Congress approve comprehensive immigration reform." According to the CPUSA's *People's World*, the protest gained "worldwide attention." Obama, first lady Michelle Obama, and Vice President Joe Biden all dropped in to offer support.[42] Still, House Republicans would not budge. Fortunately, Republican congressmembers refused to sell out their nation. They held the line against intense pressure, and no amnesty bill passed through the House in Obama's eight years in the White House.

HILLARY TRIES TOO

On May 17, 2016, Hillary Clinton's presidential campaign announced that long-time DSA activist Dolores Huerta and Medina would join the team as senior advisers in California.[43]

In 2016, Clinton promised to introduce a "pathway to full and equal citizenship" to legalize and grant voting rights to every illegal alien in the country "within 100 days of taking office" if she were to be elected president.[44] In the hubbub of the 2016 campaign, the political significance of that historical statement did not receive the scrutiny it deserved.

Many states with high illegal alien populations, such as Arizona, Georgia, Florida, and North Carolina, are only marginally inside the Republican camp. Illegal alien amnesty would almost certainly send those states permanently "blue." Colorado and Virginia have already been lost to the Republicans. Even Republican-stronghold Texas is very vulnerable. Losing only two or three of these states could doom the GOP to minority party status and eventual oblivion. How could the Republican Party hope to counter 10–20 million new Democratic voters, possibly as soon as early 2021? Illegal alien amnesty would give the Democrats permanent control of the United States. That would mean a "one-party state" soon to be dominated by the far left. Think California nationwide, with no hope of a turnaround.

Providentially Obama let the "amnesty" opportunity slip through his fingers, but President Hillary Clinton would have almost certainly not made the same mistake. If Donald Trump had not won his shocking victory on November 6, 2016, Medina and Corona's dream of a permanent, unbeatable progressive "governing coalition" could very well have already become a reality. Under President Biden, one almost feels nostalgia for the border control regime of the Obama era. In a few short months, Biden undid almost all of the border security gains made under President Trump, and then some. Is the horrendous state of the affairs on the southern border the result of Biden administration incompetence? Or is it simply the next logical step in Obama's program to socialize America through mass illegal immigration?

Trevor Loudon is an author, filmmaker, and public speaker from Christchurch, New Zealand. For more than thirty years, he has researched radical-left, Marxist, and terrorist movements and their covert influence on mainstream politics. His latest book is White House Reds.

13

OBAMA'S DAMAGE TO
BORDER SECURITY

by Matthew Vadum

AN INSECURE BORDER and growing disrespect for the nation's immigration laws is the ugly legacy that President Barack Obama left behind. Obama invited violence and chaos on the southern border and at the nation's ports-of-entry by, among other things, doing little to build a wall to prevent migrants from illegally entering the United States from Mexico, undermining immigration law enforcement efforts, and promoting various amnesty-like schemes that shielded deportable individuals from removal. These de facto amnesties gave foreigners incentives to break US law by providing them with hope there would be more de facto amnesties. Lawlessness begets lawlessness. The Obama administration took action against state and local governments that tried to enforce immigration laws. It halted meaningful workplace enforcement efforts. It distorted statistics to make it seem as if it was vigorously enforcing the law. It stretched the meaning of "prosecutorial discretion" to write new laws without bothering to go to Congress.

Throughout his presidency, Obama used border security as a bargaining chip in his efforts to secure "comprehensive immigration reform," generally understood to be a euphemism for amnesty for illegal aliens, from Congress. Immigration enforcement itself was a waste of time, Obama told a meeting of police officers in 2014. Spending time "dealing with somebody who is not causing any other trouble other than the fact that they were trying to make a living for their families," Obama said, is "just not a good use of our resources. It's not smart. It doesn't make sense."[1]

The Obama administration also tried to blur the conceptual lines between US citizenship and illegal alien status, something open-borders advocates have been doing for years. Leftists like to refer to all migrants, including illegal aliens, simply as "immigrants" in order to muddy the waters. Those who oppose the Left's open-borders agenda can thus be smeared as anti-immigrant, even though Conservatives are generally opposed to illegal immigration, not immigration in general.

In 2013, then-Attorney General Eric Holder told the Mexican American Legal Defense and Education Fund that amnesty was a "civil right." "Creating a pathway to earned citizenship for the 11 million unauthorized immigrants in this country is essential . . . . This is a matter of civil and human rights."[2] Holder's successor in the post, Loretta Lynch, said much the same thing at her confirmation hearing in 2015.

Then-Sen. Jeff Sessions (R.-Ala.) asked Lynch "who has more right to a job in this country: citizens and legal permanent residents or illegal aliens?"

"I believe that the right and the obligation to work is one that's shared by everyone in this country regardless of how they came here," Lynch replied.[3]

Obama implied in a 2014 Labor Day speech that immigration to the United States itself was a right. "Hope is what gives young people the strength to march for women's rights, and workers' rights, and civil rights, and voting rights, and gay rights, and immigration rights."

During his time in office President Obama curtailed the enforcement of immigration law. His "catch and release" policy, which Border Patrol agents called "catch and run," overwhelmed the nation with illegal aliens. The Obama administration refused to allow illegal aliens to be pursued in areas where national parks were along the nation's borders. The Obama administration inflated deportation statistics. For example, in 2010, US Immigration and Customs Enforcement (ICE) claimed removals of illegals went up 47 percent in Obama's first year as president. It was discovered months later, the increase was a mere 5 percent.

President Obama himself admitted in a 2011 meeting with activists that his deportation figures were off. "The statistics are actually a little deceptive because what we've been doing is . . . apprehending folks at the borders and sending them back. That is counted as a deportation, even though they may have only been held for a day or 48 hours."

In 2014, the Obama administration unilaterally made it easier for persons who had given "limited" material support to terrorists to enter the country. This meant individuals who had prepared or planned a terrorist activity or given material support for such activity would be allowed into the country and to apply for green cards.[4] In addition, the Obama administration made it easier for evildoers to enter the country. In 2011, then-DHS Secretary Janet Napolitano ordered US Customs and Border Protection (CBP) agents to cut down on border inspections. Agents said they were directed to carry out checks based only on actual intelligence showing a threat, instead of suspicious behavior. Random checks were forbidden.[5]

During the Central American migrant crisis of 2014, CBP agents believed the Obama administration handcuffed them. Then-National Deputy Chief of the Border Patrol Ronald Colburn said ICE officials thought the administration "intentionally neglected to give them orders to support efforts to resolve" the problems at the southern border. "They're sitting still at their desks—reading newspapers, playing video games on their government computers—because they're not being tasked with work, and they feel like it's coming all the way down from the top. These are guys that do want to go out more, but basically they're not." Executive Vice President of the Law Enforcement Officers Advocates Council and retired Border Patrol agent Dave Stoddard said agents were "terrified" of speaking out. Some agents were reportedly threatened with ten-year prison terms.[6] In 2012, a government watchdog reported that US Citizenship and Immigration Services (CIS) officials put pressure on employees to approve applications for immigration benefits as part of a "get to yes" policy. Almost 25 percent of officers surveyed indicated a supervisor encouraged them to approve applications that should have been rejected, and 90 percent said they didn't have enough time to properly interview applicants. Employees said they feared being demoted or relocated if they failed to approve enough applications.[7]

Even figuring out the state of border security was somewhere between difficult and impossible during the Obama administration.

In February 2013, the US Government Accountability Office (GAO) reported that DHS had no official metric for determining whether the border was secure. DHS had acknowledged before that, in 2010, using the metric of the time, "operational control," the government had lost control of the nation's borders. The government had operational control over a mere 13 percent of the 8,607-mile northern, southwestern, and coastal borders, and just 44 percent operational control of the southwestern border, so the Obama administration abandoned the metric. In March 2013, the *New York Times* reported that Obama administration officials had acknowledged "they had resisted producing a single measure to assess the border because the president did not want any hurdles placed on the pathway to eventual citizenship for immigrants in the country illegally."[8] Obama refused to cut off funding from the Department of Homeland Security and the

Justice Department to so-called sanctuary jurisdictions that harbored illegal aliens as a matter of policy. He also refused to take legal action against these jurisdictions.[9] The sanctuary movement gave illegal aliens permission to rob, rape, and murder Americans by, among other things, stigmatizing immigration enforcement. Some left-wingers call sanctuary jurisdictions "civil liberties safe zones" to blur the distinction between citizens and non-citizens by implying illegal aliens somehow possess a civil right to be present in the US. Sanctuary jurisdictions defy US law by, among other things, refusing to honor detainer requests in which ICE asks local jailers to notify the agency before an inmate wanted on immigration charges is released. A detainer request also asks the jailer to hold the individual for up to forty-eight hours after when the individual would otherwise be released so ICE can take him or her into custody for processing and possible deportation.

Obama attempted to defund and abolish the so-called 287(g) program that involved state and local law enforcement agencies in immigration enforcement by getting them to help in the investigation, apprehension, or detention of illegal aliens. According to ICE, the 287(g) program "enhances the safety and security of communities by creating partnerships with state and local law enforcement agencies to identify and remove aliens who are amenable to removal from the United States." Section 287(g) of the Immigration and Nationality Act (INA) "authorizes the Director of ICE to enter into agreements with state and local law enforcement agencies, that permit designated officers to perform limited immigration law enforcement functions. Agreements under section 287(g) require the local law enforcement officers to receive appropriate training and to function under the supervision of ICE officers."

In his first year as president, the Congressional Hispanic Caucus and more than 500 other activist groups asked Obama to end the program, claiming it had been abused by law enforcement. "Although its stated purpose is to provide law enforcement a tool to pursue criminals, it is our experience that state and local law enforcement officials actually use their expanded and often unchecked powers under the program to target immigrants and persons of color. It is our opinion that no amount of reforms, no matter how well-intentioned, will change this disturbing reality," a letter to Obama from the caucus stated. "For these reasons we ask you to reconsider your evaluation of 287(g) and instead of reforming it, end it entirely."[10] Unable to end the program, the Obama administration undermined it. In June 2010, President Obama named former Houston and Phoenix police chief Harold Hurtt, a sanctuary city police chief and outspoken critic of the 287(g) program, to run the program.[11] In the fiscal 2013 budget, the Obama administration proposed cutting funding to the program by $17 million and phasing it out.[12] Under pressure from activists, Obama's DHS rescinded 287(g) agreements with various jurisdictions across the country, including Maricopa County, Arizona, and eventually, all counties in Arizona.[13]

Early in his presidency, Obama made it clear that his "preferred tool for domestic policy" was to use "'prosecutorial discretion' not to enforce statutes" with which he disagreed, according to legal scholars Robert J. Delahunty and John C. Yoo. In 2009, the administration stopped enforcing federal drug laws against individuals whose behavior complied with "existing state laws providing for the medical use of marijuana." In 2011, the administration opted not defend the Defense of Marriage Act in the courts even though federal statutes are presumptively constitutional. The administration also invoked "prosecutorial discretion" to prevent then-Attorney General Eric Holder from being prosecuted for contempt of Congress. In 2012, the Obama administration cited "prosecutorial discretion" as an excuse not to enforce removal provisions in the Immigration and Nationality Act against young illegal aliens.[14]

Obama created the Deferred Action for Childhood Arrivals (DACA) program that year with the stroke of a pen after previously admitting that creating such a program by executive fiat would be unconstitutional. "I am not king," Obama said in 2010. The next year he said that with "respect to the notion that I can just suspend deportations through executive order, that's just not the case." But Obama created DACA anyway, unilaterally, by executive action. More than a few Conservatives at the time said Obama was deliberately flooding the US with illegal aliens as a means of generating future Democratic Party voters. Conservative suspicions seemed to be confirmed in early 2018 when a leaked memo from the leftist Center for American Progress Action Fund acknowledged that passing an amnesty for DACA applicants was "a critical component of the Democratic Party's future electoral success." "The fight to protect Dreamers is not only a moral imperative, it is also a critical component of the Democratic Party's future electoral success," the memo stated. "Donald Trump and the Republican Party continue to jeopardize the futures of millions of Dreamers and their families and throw up roadblocks to meaningful legislative reform, and it is up to Democrats to stand up for them."[15]

There are now about 700,000 or more DACA-eligible individuals who came as young people to the United States. These people are a subset of around 4 million or so so-called Dreamers, many of whom did not seek relief under DACA. The term *Dreamers* is derived from the DREAM (Development, Relief, and Education for Alien Minors) Act, a legislative proposal to grant underage illegal aliens immigration amnesty that has never passed Congress. The DACA program strained federal resources. CIS put so much effort into processing DACA applications that the agency tripled wait times for US citizens seeking green cards for immediate relatives, the *New York Times* reported in 2014. "Waits for approvals for those resident visas stretched to 15 months, and more than 500,000 applications became stuck in the pipeline, playing havoc with international moves and children's schools and keeping families apart."[16]

President Obama's DACA program caused great consternation in Congress. In 2015, then-Sen. Sessions accused Obama of "systematically" dismantling the nation's immigration enforcement system. Obama's attacks on America's immigration laws are "undermining the very rule of law upon which our nation was founded and upon which its greatness depends," said Sessions, who later went on to become President Trump's first attorney general. "This unprecedented action, combined with new 'enforcement priorities' for Department of Homeland Security personnel that exempt the vast majority of illegal immigrants from the threat of removal, the Deferred Action for Childhood Arrivals directive," memos detailing plans to cripple enforcement efforts, and various executive actions have "threatened not only our constitutional system, but our national sovereignty. . . . "Indeed, the idea of national, sovereign borders is being daily eviscerated by the President's determination to write his own immigration rules in defiance of Congress and the American people," Sessions said.[17] ,

In 2014, Obama also relied on executive action to create the Deferred Action for Parents of Americans and Lawful Permanent Residents (DAPA) program to benefit illegal aliens residing in the US since 2010 who had children who were either US citizens or lawful permanent residents. Republicans have long said DACA is a brazen power grab, a usurpation of Congress's constitutionally prescribed role in making laws. At time of writing, federal courts had ordered the federal government to keep DACA operating but had enjoined DAPA. President Trump rescinded Obama's executive action that created DAPA. Trump did the same regarding DACA, but the courts refused to let him shutter the program.

The Obama administration was also openly hostile to E-Verify, which is an online system that compares information entered by an employer from an employee Employment Eligibility Verification, with records available to the US Department of Homeland Security and the Social Security Administration to confirm employment eligibility. The Obama administration threatened employers who used E-Verify with discrimination investigations. CIS and the Department of Justice entered into an information-sharing agreement in March 2010 to increase investigations of employers who used E-Verify for possible discriminatory practices.[18]

After open-borders groups criticized the Obama administration for a successful raid of an engine machine shop in Bellingham, Washington, that led to the detention of twenty-eight illegal aliens who were using fake Social Security numbers and identity documents, Obama's ICE decided in 2009 to end worksite raids. ICE agents were investigated for doing their jobs. During a conference call with employers and activists, Esther Olavarria, deputy assistant secretary of Homeland Security, said "we're not doing raids or audits under this administration."[19] From 2009 to 2012 the Obama administration reduced fines imposed on employers found employing illegal aliens. Fines fell from $52.7 million to $31.2 million, an average drop of 40 percent. Such large reductions "may diminish the effectiveness of fines as a deterrent to hiring unauthorized workers," a report by the DHS Inspector General concluded.[20] Employers that tried to comply with immigration laws were sued for discrimination by Obama's Justice Department.

For asking legal permanent residents to show their new green card when their prior card expired, Culinaire Internationale was alleged to have committed "citizenship discrimination." In a settlement, Culinaire agreed to $20,460 in civil penalties, receive training regarding the anti-discrimination provisions of the INA, create a $40,000 back pay fund to "compensate potential economic victims," change its employment eligibility reverification policies, and submit to federal monitoring for twenty months.[21]

US Service Industries (USSI) was sued for allegedly contravening the INA by supposedly discriminating against work-authorized individuals who were not citizens by making those individuals show documents issued by DHS as a condition of employment. USSI settled, agreeing to pay $132,000 in civil penalties, receive INA anti-discrimination provisions, create a $50,000 back pay fund to "compensate any workers who may have lost wages," change its employment eligibility verification policies, and be federally monitored for two years.[22]

President Obama did little to build a wall on the porous southern border. Walls and fencing now span around a third of the 1,954-mile-long border with Mexico. Construction began under President Bill Clinton in the early 1990s and carried on during George W. Bush's presidency. Obama constructed more than 130 miles, largely in his first year as president. To provide a sense of scale, between 2007 and 2015, US Customs and Border Protection went through $2.4 billion, adding 535 miles of barriers along the border.[23] But after that initial building spurt, Obama's interest in wall-building waned and actual construction was limited to repairing or reinforcing existing barriers. Although illegal aliens were still streaming across the border, in a May 10, 2011, speech in El Paso, Texas, Obama declared victory in the fight against illegal border-crossers and said the wall was "basically complete" as he mocked his critics.

"We have gone above and beyond what was requested by the very Republicans who said they supported broader reform as long as we got serious about enforcement," he said. "All the stuff they asked for, we've done. But even though we've answered these concerns, I've got to say I suspect there are still going to be some who are trying to move the goal posts on us one more time. . . . They'll want a higher fence," Obama said. "Maybe they'll need a moat. Maybe they want alligators in the moat. They'll never be satisfied. And I understand that. That's politics." The chairman of the House Homeland Security Committee at the time, Rep. Michael McCaul (R-Texas), shot back, saying "the border is not secure and it has never been more violent or dangerous. Anyone who lives down there will tell you that."[24]

President Joe Biden has been even more brazen in his efforts to erase the nation's border with Mexico, rolling out a welcome mat, beckoning illegal aliens to the United States. Biden, and his vice president, Kamala Harris, whom he named as the administration's point person on immigration, signaled that under their leadership the US government would do little to secure the porous international boundary. The message was received loud and clear throughout Latin America. In the opening months of Biden's presidency, Americans saw foreigners crashing the border in vast numbers and establishing camps nearby. They came and were continuing to come as of time of writing to claim the massive immigration amnesty Biden promised them. One individual crossing at Tucson, Arizona, told ABC that he "basically" did so because Biden had taken over as president. "Would you have tried to do this when Donald Trump was president?" the man was asked. "Definitely not," he replied.

Breitbart News published photos of "Biden for President 2020" flags flying at a migrant tent city near the border in Tijuana, Mexico. Other media outlets published video footage of border jumpers wearing pro-Biden tee shirts. The Biden administration refused to enroll would-be immigrants in the Trump administration's "Remain in Mexico" program that required non-Mexican asylum-seekers appearing at the border to wait in Mexico for their claims to be processed. The program, part of the Migrant Protection Protocols enforced by Trump, discouraged individuals from making fraudulent asylum claims.[25] The Biden administration reportedly planned to offer as much as $450,000 per person to members of families that were separated after crossing the border during the Trump administration. The proposal was roundly condemned by Republicans.[26]

After Biden's bungled military withdrawal from Afghanistan in the summer of 2021, a flood of tens of thousands of immigrants from the land of the Taliban arrived in the US with assistance from the administration. Yet, at the same time, the administration told would-be refugees from Communist Cuba–who if they became US citizens seem unlikely to embrace Democrats' radical left-wing policies—they were not welcome on American soil. "The time is never right to attempt migration by sea," Cuban-born DHS Secretary Alejandro Mayorkas told reporters in July 2021. "To those who risk their lives doing so, this risk is not worth taking."[27]

Biden also provided incentives for poor, unskilled, and unemployable individuals to make a run for the border by abandoning the so-called public charge rule. After a federal appeals court struck it down, his administration refused to defend it in court, and Biden himself separately rescinded it. The rule, which the Trump administration resurrected over intense left-wing opposition, required would-be immigrants to be able to financially support themselves. Critics argue the common-sense, pro-taxpayer rule is xenophobic and discriminates against poor aliens.[28] The public-charge principle, that is, the idea that immigrants should have to show they can survive without becoming dependent on government handouts, has been part of the American experience for centuries. Public-charge provisions have been part of American immigration law since at least 1882. One of the earliest-known, public-charge laws in colonial Massachusetts was on the books in 1645. By the end of the 1600s, many American colonies screened would-be immigrants and required bonds be posted for those thought likely to become public charges.

Biden plans to go even farther in incentivizing huge inflows of illegal aliens and effectively abolishing the border, and it's unclear if Congress, littered as it is with open-borders enthusiasts, will stop him.

Matthew Vadum is a former senior fellow and former senior vice president of Capital Research Center. He is the author of Team Jihad: How Sharia-Supremacists Collaborate with Leftists to Destroy the United States *and* Subversion Inc.: How Obama's ACORN Red Shirts are Still Terrorizing and Ripping Off American Taxpayers.

14

OBAMAGATE: OBAMA'S PERSECUTION OF GENERAL FLYNN

by Joseph Klein

FOLLOWING DONALD TRUMP'S ELECTION to succeed Barack Obama as America's forty-fifth president, Obama abused his powers during the transition period in an attempted coup against the incoming Trump administration. Fifteen days before Obama left office, he personally gave the critical direction leading to the continued government persecution of three-star retired General Michael Flynn, who had already been named as President-elect Trump's national security advisor designate. Obama did so at a fateful Oval Office meeting, just a day after career FBI investigators had indicated that they were ready to close the Flynn case. They had found no incriminating evidence against

Flynn. Obama colluded with the disgraced former FBI Director James Comey to continue going after Flynn, nevertheless. Incredibly, Obama instructed his team not to advise the president-elect that Flynn still had a Sword of Damocles hanging over his head, courtesy of Obama himself. Former Whitewater Independent Counsel Robert Ray said that the Flynn imbroglio, known as Obamagate, was at the very least a "political scandal of the highest order."[1]

By comparison, President Richard Nixon's Watergate scandal was small potatoes. What brought Nixon down was a "smoking gun" tape in which Nixon was recorded hatching a plot to use the CIA to intervene with the FBI's ongoing investigation into the Watergate break-in. Nixon wanted the CIA's leadership to ask the FBI's acting director to halt the FBI's Watergate investigation on the grounds that it was a national security matter. Nixon was exposed trying to weaponize the intelligence agency defensively to serve his own personal political purposes. The Watergate tape did not evidence any plot by Nixon to send the CIA or FBI on a mission to destroy a patriotic American hero.

Barack Obama's direct role in persecuting Flynn did not come to light from White House tapes. It came to light when the Trump Justice Department released bombshell documents as exhibits to the government's motion to dismiss the case against Flynn. Obama wanted the FBI, which was ready to close its investigation of Flynn, to keep its Flynn investigation open on totally spurious grounds. The persecution of Flynn that Obama launched continued after he left office, including the duress imposed on Flynn to plead guilty to lying to the FBI. Flynn tried to reverse this plea as new information about the corruption behind the persecution of Flynn emerged. Trump pardoned Flynn on November 25, 2020.

The plot against Flynn unfolded at a White House meeting on January 5, 2017 attended, in addition to Obama, by former Vice President Joe Biden, former Obama national security advisor Susan Rice, former Deputy Attorney General Sally Yates, former FBI Director James Comey, former CIA Director John Brennan, and former Director of

National Intelligence James Clapper. All were avowed political enemies of Trump who sought to undermine his presidency at every opportunity.

Obama has a long history with General Flynn, who once served as the Obama administration's head of the Defense Intelligence Agency. Flynn opposed Obama's appeasement policies in the Middle East and distanced himself from Obama's lies that ISIS was nothing to worry about. So, in April 2014, General Flynn was forced out of his job, presumably for "insubordination." Since General Flynn served at the president's pleasure, there was nothing improper about his removal. But Obama carried on his personal vendetta against Flynn right up to the final days of his presidency. Obama and his senior officials were also no doubt concerned about what dirty secrets the national security advisor designate might uncover regarding the Obama administration's nefarious activities. Flynn, who was no fan of Obama's disastrous nuclear deal with Iran, would have left no stone unturned to get to the bottom of the secret concessions the Obama administration made to close the deal. Flynn would also have had free rein to expose how Obama's top FBI and intelligence officials were using the infamous Clinton campaign-funded Steele dossier to sabotage Donald Trump's election and presidency.

The FBI opened its original investigation of Flynn on August 16, 2016, as part of its overall probe of possible collusion between the Trump campaign and Russia, under the codename Crossfire Razor. The investigators wanted to know whether Flynn was somehow engaged in inappropriate Russian contact. Of particular concern to some FBI agents as the investigation proceeded were intercepted conversations between Flynn and Russian ambassador to the United States Sergey Kislyak. However, then-FBI Assistant Director William Priestap was skeptical about their significance and was worried that Flynn's enemies would weaponize the intercepts to prolong the investigation.[2] The FBI was ready to shut down Crossfire Razor by early January 2017. Indeed, the day before the fateful White House meeting on January 5, 2017, when Obama intervened, an FBI agent involved with Flynn's case wrote a memo declaring, "The FBI is closing this investigation."[3]

Priestap's worries about weaponizing the Flynn investigation were prescient. An e-mail from the then-lead agent in the larger Russia case, the infamous Peter Strzok, gave instructions to keep the Flynn investigation open, adding that "the 7th floor" of FBI headquarters was "involved." Comey and then-Deputy Director Andrew McCabe worked on the seventh floor.[4] Obama himself initiated the setup of General Flynn directly from the Oval Office, exploiting the revelation of Flynn's identity as a participant in the intercepted conversations with Russia's ambassador Kislyak. Although these conversations were harmless, Obama was invested in using them to go after Flynn.

Normally, intelligence agents listening in on calls with foreign persons of interest to US intelligence conceal in their transcriptions—"mask"—the identities of US citizens incidentally swept up in the surveillance. There is some question as to whether Flynn's identity was masked in the first place.[5] However, even if Flynn's identity was masked initially, US officials in the government with proper security clearance would have been able to request that his identity be revealed—that is, that Flynn be "unmasked." Susan Rice requested the unmasking of US individuals associated with Donald Trump's campaign and transition, which could well have triggered Flynn's unmasking if his identity had, in fact, been originally masked.[6] Whether Flynn's identity was not masked in the first place or his identity was unmasked pales in comparison with what Obama did with the information once it came to his attention. Obama abused his presidential powers by directly intervening in the Flynn investigation, after the FBI was ready to close it, despite having learned of Flynn's identity on the intercepts with the Russian ambassador.

During the January 5, 2017, meeting that Obama presided over in the Oval Office, Biden is believed to have suggested dusting off the antiquated 1799 Logan Act as a pretext to go after Flynn, according to federal court filing by Flynn's defense lawyers.[7] Biden's Logan Act suggestion was reportedly echoed by Comey, who stayed behind with

Obama, along with Yates, at the conclusion of the larger meeting. According to Rice, she and Biden also participated in the follow-on discussion with Obama.[8] During its 200-year-plus history, nobody has ever been convicted of violating the Logan Act, which prohibits private citizens from engaging in unauthorized discussions with foreign governments having disputes with the United States. Yet Obama was prepared to wield the Logan Act, and whatever else his minions could dig up, to persecute Flynn.

Handwritten notes reportedly written by Strzok of all people appear to summarize what he was told about the fateful Oval Office meeting. The handwritten notes, which were included with the government's dismissal motion, indicated that Obama (referred to as "P") gave the order at the meeting to "'make sure you look at things'" and to "'have the right people on it.'"[9] The career FBI investigators who had concluded that Flynn had done nothing wrong were evidently not "the right people" as far as Obama was concerned. No doubt, Obama was hoping to prolong the baseless investigation in order to entrap Flynn, which is what eventually happened.

The pliant press was all too happy to aid in Obama's vendetta against Flynn. "According to a senior US government official, Flynn phoned Russian Ambassador Sergey Kislyak several times on Dec. 29, the day the Obama administration announced the expulsion of 35 Russian officials as well as other measures in retaliation for the hacking," wrote David Ignatius for the *Washington Post* on January 12, 2017.[10] This article was published just a week after Obama's Oval Office meeting. It doesn't take a rocket scientist to figure out that the senior US government official who illegally leaked the classified information about Flynn to the *Washington Post* was among Obama's "right people." In short, Obama personally set in motion one of the gravest abuses of the nation's law enforcement and judicial processes in American history. Out of sheer vindictiveness, Obama used the instruments of the state to destroy an innocent man. The anti-Trump press was Obama's willing partner.

The icing on the cake is a face-saving memo in the form of an e-mail that Susan Rice wrote to herself on the day of President Trump's inauguration, memorializing her version of the Oval Office meeting that had been held two weeks earlier. Rice, as noted above, was one of the attendees at this meeting. She concocted an after-the-fact whitewashing of Obama's handling of the Flynn matter in a pitiful attempt to cover up Obama's guilt. Here are excerpts from Rice's memo:[11]

> "President Obama began the conversation by stressing his continued commitment to ensuring that every aspect of this issue is handled by the intelligence and law enforcement communities '*by the book.*' . . . The president stressed that he is not asking about, initiating, or instructing anything from a law enforcement perspective. He reiterated that our law enforcement team needs to proceed as it normally would *by the book.*" (Emphasis added)
>
> "From a national security perspective, however, President Obama said he wants to be sure that, as we engage with the incoming team, we are mindful to ascertain if there is any reason that we cannot share information fully as it relates to Russia."
>
> "Director Comey affirmed that he is processing '*by the book*' as it relates to law enforcement. From a national security perspective, Comey said he does have some concerns that incoming NSA Flynn is speaking frequently with Russian ambassador Kislyak. Comey said that could be an issue as it relates to sharing sensitive information.
>
> President Obama asked if Comey was saying that the NSC should not pass sensitive information related to Russia to Flynn. Comey replied 'potentially.' He added that he has no indication that Flynn has passed classified information to Kislyak, but he noted that 'the level of communication is unusual.'" (Emphasis added)

Obama and Comey did everything but operate "by the book." Obama used the FBI, with Comey's help, to maliciously target Flynn for no reason other than that Flynn was a political enemy. When then-Attorney General Bill Barr made the decision to drop charges against Michael Flynn and try to restore justice to the military hero that Obama's persecution had taken away, Obama shamelessly claimed in response that the "rule of law is at risk."[12] Obama's multiple abuses of presidential power, including Obamagate, put the rule of law at risk constantly during his administration.

The rule of law is at risk once again during the Biden administration. It turns out that the Obama administration's persecution of General Flynn was but a prelude to the persecution of American citizens during Biden's first year in office. The Biden administration is painting many ordinary Americans with the same broad brush as alleged "racists" and "domestic extremists" for strongly advocating conservative points of view on controversial subjects that differ from the radical left's orthodoxy. Not content with lies and smears, the Biden administration has exploited its law enforcement tools to discourage vigorous dissent from conservative voices. Subverting the rule of law, President Biden's Department of Justice and FBI are targeting law-abiding American parents who have expressed their anger to school boards, teachers, and administrators for indoctrinating their children in classrooms across the country with far-left dogma such as critical race theory. Attorney General Merrick Garland responded to accusations contained in a letter sent by the National School Boards Associations, which coordinated with the Biden White House, that some of these parents were engaging in "a form of domestic terrorism" by issuing an extraordinary memorandum on October 4, 2021. He ordered the FBI to work with federal prosecutors and local law enforcement officials to investigate complaints of "harassment, intimidation, and threats of violence against school administrators, board members, teachers, and staff." Following Garland's directive, the FBI's Criminal and Counterterrorism Divisions then put in place a process to track such so-called threats. In short, the Biden administration has established a mechanism to track the activities of American parents for vehemently standing up for their children. Barack Obama's legacy includes laying the groundwork for the Biden administration's egregious abuse of federal law enforcement powers.

15

OBAMA'S ENABLING OF RACIAL STRIFE AND DOMESTIC TERROR

by Daniel Greenfield

IT WAS THE SUMMER OF '14 and the men and women in windbreakers and sunglasses, touting government IDs and a secrecy code, came to Ferguson just as the riots were breaking out. That hot August in Missouri was the beginning of a turning point that would change America. Barack Obama had leaned heavily on racist dog whistles in his reelection campaign. But Black Lives Matter had still been in its nascent stage, and the spectacle of reviving the nationwide race riots that had terrorized the nation a generation ago was a work in progress. Now that long labor of terrorizing the country with an outbreak of race riots was ready for its first major field test. The United States had not seen nationwide race riots on the scale of the Black Lives Matter riots since the 1970s. There had hardly been any significant race riots since the early 1990s. But now race riots have once again become the norm.

Biden has met with Black Lives Matter leaders and endorsed their hateful riots. Kamala Harris even raised bail money for the rioters. How did America go from a handful of incidents to a sustained series of nationwide riots? Why did a phenomenon that most people associated with black-and-white photos and shaky camera footage not only make a comeback, but dominate the nation as it never had before? And why did some of the biggest bursts of rioting tend to take place around election years?

In '14, Obama was no longer on the ticket, personally, but Congress was. And black turnout, always challenging in midterm elections, was not going to happen without some racial strife. "There is not a Black America and a White America and Latino America and Asian America—there's the United States of America," a younger Chicago community organizer had declaimed at the DNC convention a decade before his men came to enable race riots in Missouri.[1] Obama had once run as a unifying candidate who pitched his message to white liberals, but in one of his many reinventions, the community-organizer-in-chief had radicalized. "Punish our enemies," he was urging Latinos after two years in the White House.[2] It was no coincidence that Obama's broadly racist appeals coincided with national elections.

In 2010, Obama was polling badly among the same white voters who had historically backed the country's first black president because he promised them hope and change. They had seen plenty of change, but little hope. And the polls showed that voters were going to oust his party. Urging Latinos to "punish our enemies" was the cry of a racial agitator turned racial healer who was returning to his racist roots. But unlike the racial healer, this incarnation of Obama was here to stay. And, like a tribal totem, the face that Obama showed to the world was also his regime's façade. By 2012, Joe Biden, a former friend of segregationists, had hit the campaign trail to tell black voters that Republicans are going to "put you all back in chains." [3]

The naked racial rhetoric helped put Obama back in the White House but didn't reclaim Congress. It did however deeply fracture the country and set the stage for a divided America. When Obama told the Democratic National Convention and the nation that, "There is not a Black America and a White America," he was describing the reality of the country in 2004. A decade later, he had transformed America into a war-torn nation deeply divided by race. In 2008, the majority of Americans had anticipated the onset of better race relations.[4] As the protests and the riots, the tidal wave of divisive racial rhetoric from the White House, burned through the years and the cities, incinerating entire neighborhoods, turning communities against each other, and shattering families, a majority of Americans saw race relations as bad and growing worse.

Before Obama, 71 percent of Americans had thought that relations between black and white people were generally good. A year after Ferguson, more than half the country thought relations were bad.[5] Change had arrived, but hope was gone. It was America's worst race relations low until now[6] where, with the revival of the Black Lives Matter race riots, 55 percent of Americans believe race relations are bad. Of these, a quarter believe that they are very bad.[7] That fundamental division has been Obama's true enduring legacy.

Obama had brought into being the "Black America and a White America," not with mere rhetoric, poisonous as it was, but by lending government authority to the racist agenda of the radicals. That's what the arrival of the government men in Ferguson signaled. The race riots were no longer makeshift local affairs. They had the DOJ at their backs. The men and women in sunglasses and windbreakers, who refused to speak to the media claiming that they had to operate secretly, might have sprung from some crank's conspiracy theory, but they and the arm of the Justice Department they belonged to were all too real. The *St. Louis Post-Dispatch* described the Community Relations Service as a "secretive unit of the US Department of Justice" that had "held dozens of meetings with police, residents and community leaders, nearly all of them in secret."[8]

The eight CRS agents, including its director and deputy director, were the first federal boots on the ground[9] while working under orders that gave them "broad authority to act in secrecy." "Department officials in Washington," the paper noted, "won't even provide basic information on its employees or their work here." [10] The Community Relations Service was one of the many paragraphs buried in the mammoth text of the Civil Rights Act of 1964, which created it and attached it to the Commerce Department to monitor discrimination affecting "interstate commerce": the pretext for the 1964 power grab. There were tremendous problems with the organization from the start. The Civil Rights Act defined the CRS as offering "to provide assistance to communities and persons therein in resolving disputes, disagreements, or difficulties relating to discriminatory practices." This function has led the Community Relations Service to dub itself as "America's Peacemaker." Despite this pretense of mediation, the Community Relations Service was a clearinghouse for complaints about racism, and yet had no investigatory or prosecutorial powers. But that didn't stop LBJ from moving it into the Justice Department a few years later. [11]

Suddenly an organization tasked with intervening whenever "in its judgment, peaceful relations among the citizens of the community involved are threatened" at "the request of an appropriate State or local official or other interested person" was wedded to the muscle of the law enforcement arm of the United States government. And its scope and power grew with bills like Senator Ted Kennedy's Matthew Shepard Hate Crimes Prevention Act.[12] The Community Relations Service had spent generations as an obscure appendage of a federal government overrun with croft, where each cabinet member presides over departments that have dozens of components with million-dollar budgets whose names he will never even know. But the CRS was the perfect tool, an activist group operating out of the DOJ with its authority. When "America's Peacemakers" arrived in Ferguson, they weren't there to make peace or love. They had come to a war zone with a message of racial divisiveness and animosity. Or, as they told local officials, they were from the government, and they were here to help.

"How does white privilege impact race relations in our community?" the DOJ's community organizers berated local residents. "Is there a need for personal commitment to race relations?" [13] The Obama administration wasn't making peace; it was subjecting local residents to a struggle session by men and women who had the authority of the Justice Department behind them. The CRS personnel who went down to Ferguson included Rita Valenciano, a former diversity trainer and consultant who had no law degree but did have a BA in Sociology. [14] As the former head of the Latino Civil Rights Task Force, Valenciano had gone after Frances Semler, a seventy-three-year-old grandmother who had been serving on the Park Board in Kansas City over her opposition to illegal immigration. [15]

In 2008, Valenciano joined the CRS and has been there ever since. Like Valenciano, CRS personnel tended to have a background in diversity training, multicultural consulting, and political activism. They were federal community organizers and they were there to organize, to work with protesters, mobilize locals, and push officials in the right direction. But the CRS was only one arm of a multi-pronged effort to exploit the Ferguson crisis. While CRS worked with the protesters, the more conventional parts of the DOJ came after the police. But the operatives of Attorney General Eric Holder's DOJ soon found that their first job in Ferguson was a cover-up. Despite the familiar chant of, "Hands up, don't shoot," that and just about everything involving the shooting of the violent criminal was one big lie. [16] Worse still, the convenience store he had robbed had a video of him attacking a store clerk.

The Ferguson police were sitting on evidence that would exonerate the department of the false accusation that its officer had murdered an innocent man. Holder's DOJ received a copy of it and sat on the evidence that would prove that the Ferguson race riots were based on a hoax. A source told *NBC News* that the DOJ had never considered releasing the video to the public. [17] But not only did the DOJ refuse to reveal the truth, its personnel were pressuring Ferguson police to suppress the evidence.

The DOJ warned the police that releasing the video would lead to violence. Even while one arm of the DOJ was working with the protesters, another was using the threat of violent protests to force local authorities to cover up evidence of their hoax.[18] The release of the video ended the hoax,[19] but the DOJ still took its revenge on the local police.

At a press conference, Attorney General Eric Holder argued that while, "violence is never justified," Ferguson authorities had created a "highly toxic environment" that "set off the city of Ferguson like a powder keg."[20] The Attorney General of the United States was defending riots. Holder's DOJ justified its grotesque abuse of power by digging through thousands of emails until it found a racist joke about Obama from 2008 and a 2011 email, which "included jokes that are based on offensive stereotypes about Muslims."[21] Ferguson was about a lot more than one place. It was both a naked effort to drive turnout for the midterm elections, a time when Democrat voters are traditionally less likely to show up, and a testbed for a massive power grab by the DOJ over local law enforcement and communities.

The following year, on his way out, and fantasizing about a run for the White House, Holder pushed a lower standard of proof for civil rights cases. The radical AG who had aggressively fought for greater protections for criminals wanted to make it easier to seize power and terrorize cities. Holder had already pioneered the use of disparate impact when suing lenders,[22] and his assault on the Ferguson police leaned heavily on that discredited nostrum of critical race theory.

The dual use of Ferguson captured the racist game plan of the Obama administration. Race riots were a voter turnout tool and a power grab. The Obama administration manufactured the crisis, using racial strife and terror to drive turnout during election years, and also used it to enable a much-larger agenda of creating a national police state in response to the riots. The worse the violence became, the more the government was justified in intervening.

The Obama administration started the fires and then led the fire brigade, but instead of water, its hoses were filled with oil. The DOJ went after law enforcement officers in fundamentally flawed cases, not because it expected to win them in a court of law, but because its failure would unleash more violence and allow it to push for stronger laws and lower standards of proof. In Ferguson, a machine was unleashed, and that machine was only partly a government entity. Barack Obama was, first and foremost, a community organizer. It was central to how he thought and acted. America was just a larger community to organize through the familiar tactics of division. As a candidate, Obama had preached healing and unity, but as a national leader, his overriding agenda was to convince some that they were the oppressed and others, oppressors.

Obama was not just offering racial appeals, he was transforming the template of his party. Under his administration, the Democrat showing in the South entirely collapsed. After eight years, Democrats had become so poisonous to much of their working-class base, that they were left unable to win through any means except radical and minority turnout. That was the plan. Under and after him, the Democrats were hopelessly wedded to racist and divisive politics. Black Lives Matter and the resulting nationwide violence and terror were a political strategy. Even after Obama left office, the Democrat response to a national election came in the form of race riots. By early 2020, Black Lives Matter might have appeared to be a relic of another time, but the infrastructure was biding its time waiting, not for another shooting, but for another election.

In 2016, the Ford Foundation, Borealis Philanthropy, and a number of other left-wing organizations, created the Black-Led Movement Fund.[23] The goal was bringing in $100 million. Another $33 million came from the Soros network.[24] Even with Obama heading for the exit, the financial infrastructure of the Left was making big investments in a movement of race riots. The connections between the financiers and thugs were welded by an Obama pro.

Patrick Gaspard had served as Obama's national political director in the 2008 campaign before going on to become his director of the White House Office of Political Affairs. In 2017, he became the head of Soros's

Open Society Foundation.[25] Gaspard had, like Obama, started out as a community organizer. He had followed Obama into the White House and, after Obama, to the network that would determine the future of the Left. By 2020, the Soros group, under Gaspard, announced that it would pump $220 million into "racial justice."[26] Black Lives Matter had not gone quiet. The organizations behind it were building capacity. That the capacity was unleashed in an election year with so much at stake was no coincidence. Obama had built the machine. Now the machine had become the election strategy of his party.

"Where Have All the Rioters Gone?" an *Atlantic* article wondered two years ago. "Cities should be exploding—but they aren't."[27] The answer was that it wasn't time to pull the trigger. Yet. Race riots were not the "language of the unheard" nor were they the "outcry of the oppressed." Some riots have been spontaneous, but most riots are the work of political organizers seeking to profit from violence, terrorism, and the sheer spectacle of massive destruction. But no race riots in our nation's history came close to their level of organization, their massive amounts of funding, and their level of government backing as the Black Lives Matter riots.

Under Biden, overt racists, like Assistant Attorney General for Civil Rights Kristen Clarke, occupy the Justice Department and wage their racial wars under the government's seal. Clarke told Congress that she would try to find "common ground" with the police. It is a measure of just how far the third term of the Obama administration has drifted from even the pretense of law and order that its Justice Department nominee talks of finding common ground with law enforcement as if there was a huge gulf between the DOJ and the police. But under Obama there was and now under Biden, there is.

16

AN EX-PRESIDENT'S POST-PRESIDENTIAL
WAR ON AMERICA

by Joseph Klein

INTRODUCTION

Barack Obama finally left office on January 20, 2017, after foisting
on the American people one of the most destructive presidencies in
American history for eight long years. As the nation's forty-fourth president, Obama took a wrecking ball to the US Constitution. He repeatedly overstepped his executive authority and usurped legislative powers.
Obama and his senior administration officials infringed on freedoms
of speech, press, and the exercise of religious beliefs. Barack Obama's
rhetoric sowed class warfare and racial divide, while his domestic policies
strangled economic growth. The former president also wreaked havoc
abroad. Obama appeased our nation's enemies, most notably the Iranian

regime, while throwing our closest ally in the Middle East, Israel, under the bus. He was the nation's apologist-in-chief for radical Islam. By pulling all US combat troops out of Iraq prematurely and against military advice, Obama allowed ISIS to emerge as a global terrorist threat.

In short, Barack Obama was a disastrous president. His quest to radically transform America came perilously close to causing irreparable damage to the nation's security and constitutional liberties. But Obama wasn't done once he finally left the White House. Motivated by his contempt for Donald Trump, who threatened to puncture Obama's delusions of grandeur and myths of great accomplishments, Obama aimed to sabotage the legitimacy of his duly elected successor. He used prominent platforms afforded to him as a former president for that very purpose. For example, Obama demonized Trump in speeches he delivered on foreign soil in Germany and South Africa, trying to undercut Trump's standing as president of the United States in negotiations with the leaders of other countries.

Barack Obama has also been busy spurring on a generation war. He scorned "old people" for not getting out of the way and allowing space for young progressive "leaders" to take over. To that end, Obama expanded the mission of his Obama Foundation. He is using his foundation to nurture the next generation of community-organizing Obama mini-mes. They are to be Obama's foot soldiers, combatting the supposed "social injustices" for which older generations are responsible, according to Obama's "us versus them" philosophy. All the while, as he lectures the rest of us about the evils of conspicuous consumption and continues to sow class warfare, Barack Obama and his wife Michelle have been living the life of the rich and famous. This essay discusses Barack Obama's destructive post-presidency to date.

OBAMA'S JIHAD TO DELEGITIMIZE PRESIDENT TRUMP

During the waning days of his own disastrous presidency, Barack Obama promised his followers that once Donald Trump took over as president: "We're going to be in a position where we can start cooking up all kinds of great stuff."[1] The "great stuff" would turn out to be the lies and poisonous rhetoric Obama cooked up to demonize then-President Trump and insult his supporters. Barack Obama could not accept the fact that Donald Trump won the 2016 presidential election because he out-campaigned Hillary Clinton with a superior message that resonated with the forgotten men and women of America. According to Obama's deputy national security adviser, Ben Rhodes, Obama was deeply shaken. Obama lamented to his aides shortly after Donald Trump's victory, "Maybe people just want to fall back into their tribe." He dismissed Donald Trump as a "cartoon."[2]

Obama was lashing out in desperation. He faced the prospect that the self-proclaimed accomplishments he had rammed through with executive orders and highly partisan legislation were in jeopardy of being thrown into the dustbin of history. As Charles Krauthammer, the late Pulitzer Prize-winning political commentator, explained, Obama was facing the very real possibility that his "legacy is toast" and that he's going to end up as "a parenthesis in American history."[3] Thus, Barack Obama felt he had no choice but to deviate sharply from the long-established presidential tradition of not publicly bad-mouthing one's successor. Simply criticizing specific Trump administration policies on the merits was not even enough for Obama. At home and abroad, Obama used thinly veiled barbs to malign then-President Trump and his policies as bigoted, racist, isolationist, and representative of a dark period in American history. Obama sought to instill fear of imaginary "dangers," lurking around every corner so long as Trump remained in office.

Obama Scorned Trump's US Border Policy During His German Visit with Open-Borders Advocate Chancellor Merkel

Barack Obama visited Germany in May 2017 and met with his old pal German Chancellor Angela Merkel who shares Obama's disdain for Trump and his immigration policies. Obama knew that just hours later, on the first day of then-President Trump's own first state trip to Europe, the chancellor would be meeting with Trump at a NATO summit in

Brussels. Obama couldn't resist the opportunity to upstage his successor by appearing alongside Chancellor Merkel in a photo op and criticizing Trump's southern border wall policy on foreign soil.[4] "In this new world we live in, we can't isolate ourselves—we can't hide behind a wall," Obama said in his typical moralizing manner. He added that "we have to push back against those trends that would violate human rights or suppress democracy or restrict individual freedoms."

Building effective barriers at America's southern border with Mexico, as part of a multi-pronged strategy to stem the flow of illegal immigrants and drugs into the country, is sensible policy to anyone but an open-borders advocate. As a senator, Obama had supported a border barrier. But because Trump had made such border protection a centerpiece of his anti-open-border policy, Obama claimed it was an abuse of human rights. Similarly, as a senator, Joe Biden supported building a long border fence, mainly to stop "tons" of drugs from entering the United States from Mexico.[5] But on his first day in office as president of the United States, Biden took Obama's criticism of Trump's border wall to heart and pulled the plug on any further construction. The result is a crisis at the southern border with Mexico of historic proportions, including the dramatic rise of drug smuggling on Biden's watch.

On display in Berlin was an example of what *Politico* described as "Obama's approach to Trump: present the contrast by continuing to pop up, push back on the sense that Trump's winning, while barely saying a word explicitly about Trump."[6] Obama knew full well that Trump would be meeting with Chancellor Merkel for difficult negotiations only hours after Obama's own very public meeting with the chancellor. Obama exploited his friendship with Chancellor Merkel by using their shared platform to sabotage Trump's ability to negotiate from a position of strength. As much as Trump has frequently criticized his successor's disastrous domestic and foreign policies, Trump has not done so on foreign soil as Obama did. And Trump has not replicated Obama's outrageous exploitation of a post-presidency meeting hosted by a foreign leader to bad-mouth his successor who was meeting shortly thereafter on behalf of the United States with that very same foreign leader.

Obama Took His Thinly Veiled "Smear Trump" Show to South Africa

Barack Obama gave a long-winded speech in Johannesburg, South Africa, on July 17, 2018, a day intended to honor the 100th anniversary of Nelson Mandela's birth. Instead of delivering an uplifting speech devoted to Mandela's life, Obama used his remarks as an occasion to attack the bogeyman of "rabid nationalism and xenophobia," with Donald Trump obviously in his sights.[7] He did not have to mention then-President Trump by name for those listening to his speech to get the message. One article reporting on the speech, for example, was headlined: "Obama on Trump: 'We see the utter loss of shame.'"[8] The Associated Press's article on the speech was headlined, "Obama delivers veiled rebuke to Trump in Mandela address."[9] Obama warned about a world he saw as "threatening to return to an older, a more dangerous, a more brutal way of doing business." That is rather rich coming from the former president who presided over the dangerous spread of brutal jihadist terrorism.

As president, Barack Obama allowed ISIS to emerge from the ashes to become a global menace, controlling extensive territory and exporting terror worldwide. Obama neither took ISIS seriously enough when it was in its early stages nor faced squarely its underlying ideology rooted in Islam. Hence, ISIS became a mortal danger to regional and world peace and security, reversed only after Obama left office and then-President Trump allowed the US military to take the gloves off. To this day, Obama refuses to acknowledge that fundamentalist Islamic doctrine is the inspiration for the jihadist terrorists' mass murders, rapes, and persecution of non-believers. In his July 2018 South Africa speech, he portrayed "9/11 and the emergence of transnational terrorist networks" as a "backlash against globalization." He repeated his oft-recited claim that Islamist terrorism was "fueled by an ideology that perverted one of the world's great religions." To the contrary, ISIS derived its ideology from a literal reading of Islam's holy texts themselves.[10]

Barack Obama did not just load his South Africa speech with thinly veiled insults of Trump. He delivered a not-so-subtle dig aimed in part at the groundswell of voter support leading to Trump's electoral victory. Obama claimed that in the United States and Europe "populist movements" had "tapped" the "unease" felt by "many people who lived outside of the urban cores" and the "fears" that "their cultural identities were being threatened by outsiders." Obama was reprising his condescending characterization of Trump voters shortly after the 2016 election: "Maybe people just want to fall back into their tribe."[11] Only now he was doing so on foreign soil.

Dishonest Defense of Disastrous Obama–Kerry "Legacy" Nuclear Deal With Iran

Between Barack Obama's two trips to Germany and South Africa, Obama went on Facebook to decry what he called then-President Trump's "misguided" announcement of his decision to withdraw the United States from the nuclear deal with Iran, known formally as the Joint Comprehensive Plan of Action (JCPOA).[12] Obama regarded the JCPOA as one of his most prized legacies and was horrified that Trump would dare take it away. Obama need not worry, however. President Biden is doing everything he can to bring the JCPOA back to life with more concessions to Iran. In his May 8, 2018, post, Obama laid out his distorted version of the "facts" to prove, in his words, that the "JCPOA is working." He added that because of these "facts" he believed that "the decision to put the JCPOA at risk without any Iranian violation of the deal is a serious mistake." As usual, Obama has it backwards. The nuclear deal itself was the serious mistake that Donald Trump was trying to correct.

Obama claimed in his May 8, 2018 Facebook post that the JCPOA has "significantly rolled back Iran's nuclear program." That is misleading, at best. Obama foolishly committed the United States to providing the Iranian regime with immediate relief from economic sanctions and a huge cash infusion upfront. In return, Iran agreed to a temporary suspension of elements of its nuclear program that it had already mastered. One of the elements of nuclear weapons–related work the Iranian regime has not mastered involves integrating nuclear warheads on missiles. Iran's longstanding interest in developing this technology is documented in Iranian archives that Israeli intelligence managed to find and seize.[13]

"Even after the deal, Iran continued to preserve and expand its nuclear know-how for future use," Israel's former Prime Minister Benjamin Netanyahu pointed out, no doubt having the deal's sunset clauses in mind. As DEBKAfile commented, "The material presented by the prime minister demonstrated that Iran's nuclear program had been secretly stored intact for use at a time of its choice and posed an ever-present peril."[14] The Obama administration negotiators, led by then-Secretary of State John Kerry, agreed to Iran's demand that its ballistic missile program remain outside of the JCPOA's nuclear-related restrictions. Never mind that such missiles are capable of delivering nuclear weapons. The Obama administration figured that a weak provision regarding missiles appearing separately in an annex to United Nations Security Council Resolution 2231 endorsing the JCPOA (but not part of the JCPOA itself) would suffice. It called on Iran "not to undertake any activity related to ballistic missiles designed to be capable of delivering nuclear weapons."[15] The Obama administration was wrong, as usual. This resolution replaced unambiguous prohibitions on Iran's ballistic missile activity, contained in prior UN Security Council resolutions, with an unenforceable call to behave. Iran has not behaved. It has continued its nuclear-related ballistic missile program with more missile launchings.

Obama boasted in his May 2018 Facebook post of the "far-reaching inspections and verification regime" built into the JCPOA. Obama told us that "Iran's nuclear facilities are strictly monitored" and that "we can catch them if they cheat." Not true. Iran has claimed it has the absolute right to deny the International Atomic Energy Agency (IAEA) inspectors access to any of its military sites, even where suspected nuclear-related activity may be taking place. The IAEA backed off asking to inspect such sites in the face of Iranian resistance.

Section T of the JCPOA prohibits activities by Iran, which could contribute to the development of a nuclear explosive device, including designing, developing, acquiring, or using computer models to simulate nuclear explosive devices. We know from the final assessment report of past nuclear-related activities conducted by Iran, released by the IAEA on December 2, 2015, that Iran had in the past worked on the development of a nuclear explosive device, including modeling and calculations related to nuclear explosive configurations.[16] After the JCPOA went into effect, the Iranian regime may well have continued performing its nuclear explosive device development work at military sites from which IAEA inspectors are barred. The IAEA has no way of conducting verification and monitoring to ensure Iran's compliance with this portion of the JCPOA.

In short, the inspection regime that Obama boasts about is full of enough holes to drive a missile launcher truck through. The IAEA was confined to verifying that Iran's uranium stockpiling and enrichment activities remained within the limits set forth in the JCPOA. While the IAEA was fixated on these shiny objects, Iran remained free to conduct secret research and development into nuclear explosive and ballistic missile warhead integration technologies at undeclared military sites. And now even the benefits of the uranium stockpiling and enrichment constraints have proven to be easily reversible. The Iranian regime first decided to openly breach these constraints to put pressure on the remaining parties to the JCPOA and got away with it. Then, the Iranian regime decided to end its compliance with the JCPOA's constraints altogether and is undermining the IAEA's ability to continue monitoring Iran's uranium enrichment program.

John Kerry, like his former boss Barack Obama, continued as a private citizen to defend the JCPOA and downplay any concessions he made to close the deal. He claimed in September 2018 that Trump's decision to pull out of the Iran nuclear deal was "a very dangerous and ill-advised move."[17] Quite the opposite is true. Kerry's concessions were both very dangerous and ill-advised. Kerry subsequently wrote an op-ed column for the *New York Times* that criticized the killing of Maj. Gen. Qassim Soleimani.[18] This terrorist mastermind had American blood on his hands and was plotting to kill more Americans when he was eliminated. Kerry claimed that "the drone strike that eliminated" Soleimani, coming on top of then-President Trump's withdrawal of the US from the JCPOA, "nailed" the "door shut" on dealing with Iran "through constructive diplomacy."

Kerry evidently has amnesia regarding the Iranian regime's seizure of two United States Navy patrol boats and ten crew members in January 2016, which occurred shortly after the completion of the JCPOA.[19] The sailors were finally released after sixteen hours in captivity. They had been photographed on their knees with their hands over their heads. Rather than publicly protest Iran's clear violation of international law, Kerry thanked the regime for its cooperation in the care and release of the captured sailors. Groveling is Kerry's idea of how to engage in "constructive diplomacy" with the Iranian regime.

Kerry also conveniently forgot his own admission in 2016 that he thought it likely some of the billions of dollars in sanctions relief negotiated as part of the nuclear deal "will end up in the hands of the IRGC or other entities, some of which are labeled terrorists."[20] That is precisely what happened. Qasem Soleimani was all too happy to get his hands on the money made available as a result of the JCPOA. He was the head of Iran's Islamic Revolutionary Guard Corps (IRGC) Quds Force that funded the activities of various Iranian-backed Iraqi terrorist groups, including Kata'ib Hezbollah, which killed a US civilian and assaulted the US embassy in Baghdad on December 31, 2019. Kerry argued in in his op-ed article that President Trump's decision to withdraw from the JCPOA played into Soleimani's "hard-line strategy by weakening voices for diplomacy within the Tehran regime." Precisely the opposite is true. The concessions made by the Obama administration to secure Iran's agreement to the nuclear deal and the billions of dollars made available as a result to fund Soleimani's terror campaign had played perfectly into Soleimani's hands.

Private citizen Kerry went further than just using media outlets to vent his anger. He met with Iran's then-Foreign Minister Javad Zarif three or four times by his own admission.[21] Kerry was conducting unauthorized shadow diplomacy with Zarif in an effort to keep the disastrous Obama administration nuclear deal with Iran alive. Too late. Iran has dealt a death blow to it anyway. Trump responded to Kerry's outrageous attempt to interfere in his administration's foreign policy with the usual Trump-style bluntness: "John Kerry can't get over the fact that he had his chance and blew it! Stay away from negotiations, John; you are hurting your country!"[22]

Kerry engaged in an even more outrageous attempt to interfere in the Trump administration's policies regarding the Israeli-Palestinian conflict. "Mr. Kerry recently met with Hussein Agha, a close associate of Palestinian President Mahmoud Abbas," the *Independent* reported on January 25, 2018, citing a report in the *Jerusalem Post*. "During the meeting, the former US diplomat reportedly asked Mr Agha to tell the Palestinian leader to 'hold on and be strong,' and not 'yield to [Mr Trump's] demands.'" Kerry predicted that President Trump "won't last the year."[23] Kerry crossed the line of permissible behavior by a private citizen. He actively sought to undermine the foreign policy of the then-duly elected president of the United States by acting as an unauthorized quasi-negotiator with Iranian and Palestinian leaders. This is illegal under the Logan Act, which prohibits US private citizens from communicating with any foreign government or its officers, in the absence of authorization by the US government, "with intent to influence the measures or conduct of any foreign government or of any officer or agent thereof, in relation to any disputes or controversies with the United States, or to defeat the measures of the United States."[24] Unlike the Obama administration's corrupt intent in using the Logan Act as a pretext to persecute General Flynn, the Trump administration would have had solid legal grounds to go after Kerry for violating the Logan Act.

We do not know what Barack Obama himself may have been saying to foreign leaders behind closed doors to undermine the foreign policies of Donald Trump's presidency. However, from the thinly veiled barbs he aimed publicly on foreign soil against Trump, it is not much of a leap to presuppose Obama's willingness, à la Kerry, to go considerably further in his private discussions with foreign leaders. In any case, one can easily imagine how proud Obama was that his secretary of state had chosen to continue pursuing a shadow diplomacy reflecting the Obama–Kerry appeasement policies. Obama and Kerry are cut from the same cloth when it comes to placating the Iranian regime and the Palestinians.

Obama Served Up Lies and Hypocrisy to an Adoring College Audience

Barack Obama appeared at the University of Illinois to deliver a highly anticipated speech in September 2018.[25] As The Associated Press reported, "More than 17 times as many University of Illinois students registered to hear" the speech "as there are seats in the auditorium."[26] They were not disappointed. Obama delivered plenty of red meat in his denunciations of "the crazy stuff that's coming out of this White House." Obama's speech also exploited existing generational divides. He pitted the college students "coming of age" during the Trump administration against those he claimed were seeking to "maintain the status quo and keep their power and keep their privilege."

According to Obama's telling, everything was fine until he left office. Then all hell broke loose. Donald Trump and Republicans in Congress, Obama charged, were guilty of sowing divisiveness, attacking freedom of the press, using the criminal justice system as a cudgel to punish their political opponents, and cozying up to Russia. Obama should have looked in the mirror and taken responsibility for his own sordid record as president before lashing out at Trump and congressional Republicans. He was guilty of virtually every charge that he threw at then-President Trump and the Republican Party.

Barack Obama was not content to limit his criticisms of the Trump administration to specific policies with which he disagreed. Instead, he portrayed then-President Trump in stark terms as a "symptom" of a "backlash" coming from resentful people "fearful of change." He accused President Trump of "capitalizing on resentments that politicians have been fanning for years." But it was Obama who stoked class warfare while he was president, which he continued to do in his inflammatory, post-presidency speech at the University of Illinois. This fearmonger-in-chief tried to scare his impressionable student audience into believing that, with Donald Trump in office, these were "dangerous times." Obama also told the students that they were facing "a time of growing inequality, of fracturing of economic opportunity." Obama was dishing up one of his customary lies. Thanks to Trump's reversal of the high taxes and the burdensome regulations of the Obama era, college students were then coming of age during a time of unprecedented employment opportunities in a robust economy.

Obama boasted to his college audience that by the time he left office "poverty rates were falling." What he did not say was how paltry the decline was. During the eight years of the Obama administration, the "percentage of Americans living with income below the official poverty line went down to 12.7 percent of the population in 2016, a half-point drop compared with 2008," according to FactCheck.[27] During the first two years of the Trump administration, the "percentage of Americans living with income below the official poverty line went down to 11.8% of the population in 2018, the lowest level since 2001," according to FactCheck.[28]

Obama was just getting started. He threw out loaded phrases such as "racial nationalism" and "politics of fear" before asking his audience, "Sound familiar?" Then, to make sure that the audience understood his meaning, Obama added that the "politics of division, resentment and paranoia has unfortunately found a home in the Republican Party." That is vintage Barack Obama on his high horse, accusing his opponents of bad behavior for which he and his own party are guilty.

Aside from the division and resentment that had often found a home in the Obama administration, anti-Semitic sowers of hate and discord have increased their ranks in the Democrat House of Representatives caucus. Barack Obama could not care less. Indeed, he endorsed one of them—Alexandria Ocasio-Cortez.[29] And he posed proudly for a photo with another—Rashida Tlaib.[30]

After launching his broadside against Republicans, Obama listed a few of his specific grievances—each one more absurd than the last. Three examples will suffice to demonstrate how far Barack Obama was willing to go with his lies, false accusations, and hypocritical protestations. Republicans, Obama said, "embraced wild conspiracy theories like those surrounding Benghazi." Wrong. Former President Obama and his secretary of state Hillary Clinton were the ones embracing wild theories they knew to be untrue. Even after Obama and Clinton knew that the assault commencing on September 11, 2012 against the US consulate and the nearby annex in Benghazi was a pre-meditated terrorist attack, they persisted with their own concoction of events. They continued to insist that the assault was a spontaneous mob outburst that got out of control in reaction to an obscure Prophet Mohammed–mocking video.

Barack Obama also told his college audience that the Republicans were "cozying up to Russia . . . cozying up to the former head of the KGB." Wrong again. It was former President Barack Obama who had placated Russia. Obama gave in to Russian demands by scaling back missile defense plans in Europe, for example.[31] It was all part of his Russia "re-set" policies. Obama was also caught on an open mic telling former Russian President Dmitry Medvedev that he will have "more flexibility" to deal with difficult issues, such as missile defense, after the US 2012 presidential election. "This is my last election . . . After my election I have more flexibility," Obama said, considering his own re-election to be a foregone conclusion. "I will transmit this information to Vladimir," said Medvedev, referring to Vladimir Putin, the incoming Russian president and former head of the KGB.[32]

Obama feigned concern for freedom of the press. "I complained plenty about Fox News," he said to his University of Illinois audience, "but you never heard me threaten to shut them down or call them enemies of the people." Obama once again demonstrated his shameless hypocrisy. The Obama administration went beyond verbal attacks on the press. "Under Mr. Obama," wrote *New York Times* journalist James Risen, "the Justice Department and the F.B.I. have spied on reporters by monitoring their phone records, labeled one journalist an unindicted co-conspirator in a criminal case for simply doing reporting and issued subpoenas to other reporters to try to force them to reveal their sources and testify in criminal cases."[33] The journalist who was labeled an unindicted co-conspirator by the Obama Justice Department was then Fox News' chief Washington correspondent, James Rosen.[34] The purpose was to justify secretly subpoenaing and seizing his telephone and e-mail records.

After lying about Trump and the Republican Party and projecting onto them his own wrongdoing, Barack Obama concluded his University of Illinois speech by putting on his hope-and-change hat. "I believe you will help lead us in the right direction," he told his college audience, "and I will be right there with you every step of the way."

Hoover Institution's Victor Davis Hanson once described Barack Obama as the "mysterious Pied Piper figure of 2008, who mesmerized and then marched the American people over the cliff."[35] Obama still wants to be that "Pied Piper figure" for the next generation of aspiring radical progressives. He wants to lead them into battle against those he believes are part of the reactionary old guard. Obama blames the "old people, usually old men, not getting out of the way"[36] for the ills of the world today and is anxious to replace them. So, he transformed his Obama Foundation into a training ground for that purpose, as discussed in the next section. Obama wants to "be right there" with his followers "every step of the way," as he promised his University of Illinois audience. If Obama succeeds, he will be creating future leaders in his image. Like Obama, they, too, will be in position to march the American people over the cliff.

The spirit of the Obama Foundation is already present in the Biden administration. Its former president, Wally Adeyemo, was sworn in as

President Biden's Deputy Secretary of the Treasury on March 26, 2021. Adeyemo had previously served in the Obama administration. In fact, out of the top 100 positions filled in the Biden White House during Biden's first 100 days in office, seventy-four previously had worked in the Obama administration.[37]

CREATING THE NEXT GENERATION OF
OBAMA RADICAL PROGRESSIVES

"The single most important thing I could do is to help develop the next generation," Mr. Obama said at a March 2018 conference in Tokyo. Discussing his Obama Foundation, Obama said he hoped that its work "would create a hundred or a thousand or a million young Barack Obamas or Michelle Obamas."[38]

Barack Obama told attendees at the Obama Foundation Summit on November 18, 2018, that the United States has failed to make progress on many issues "because we are still confused, blind, shrouded with hate, anger, racism, mommy issues."[39] Reflecting on his own time as a young community organizer in Chicago and as a politician, he added, "You should be extraordinarily impatient about the injustices and nonsense and foolishness you see around you and you should be finding opportunities at every juncture to challenge those things." With its fellowship and scholarship programs, the Obama Foundation seeks to find, train, and connect "rising young leaders" committed to social action.[40] The Obama Foundation is enlisting recruits for Barack Obama's generational war to displace members of the "old" guard with impatient young progressives.

One such recruit is Colette Pichon Battle, a 2019 Obama Foundation Fellow. She has been described as a climate justice advocate.[41] The Obama White House had previously recognized Ms. Battle in 2016 as one of the "White House Champions of Change for Climate Equity."[42] Colette Pichon Battle is the executive director of Gulf Coast Center for Law & Policy. The stated mission of the organization she is leading, and for which she was singled out to participate in the Obama

Foundation fellowship program, is to advance "structural shifts toward ecological equity and climate justice in Gulf Coast communities of color on the frontline of climate change."[43] The Gulf Coast Center for Law & Policy is anchoring what is called Gulf South for a Green New Deal. The website of Gulf South for a Green New Deal links approvingly to the Green New Deal Resolution sponsored by Socialist-Democrat Rep. Alexandra Ocasio-Cortez.[44]

Ms. Battle said during a November 2019 interview with Radical Imagination[45] that she thought the Ocasio-Cortez resolution was "a great and bold vision to put out into the world," although it did not go far enough. "So we just took it upon ourselves to declare that we're gonna make our own policy platform," Ms. Battle said.[46] Ms. Battle became a core editor of the Gulf South for a Green New Deal Policy Platform. Among other things, the platform proclaims: "A Gulf South economy first built by enslaved labor has transitioned to a toxic economy fueled by environmental racism." The platform calls for "climate reparations" and for recognizing "all Indigenous tribes of the Gulf South as sovereign nations." It criticizes "a market based approach to climate resiliency and equity." It demands a ban on "new pipelines and drilling leases for extractive industries on Gulf South lands and territorial waters."[47]

In a speech that Ms. Battle delivered in 2019 at a conference hosted by TED Talks, she displayed her radical anti-capitalist sentiments.[48] The 2019 Obama Foundation Fellow claimed that climate change is the "most horrible symptom of an economic system that has been built for a few to extract every precious value out of this planet and its people, from our natural resources to the fruits of our human labor." Ms. Battle called for restructuring our social and economic systems towards a more "collective" future for humanity. Colette Pichon Battle has trained well to become an emerging radical progressive leader in the image of Barack Obama.

Alice Barbe, co-founder of the French organization SINGA, was a 2018–2019 Obama Foundation Scholar at Columbia University. She tweeted to Obama, "It is an honor for me and #SINGA to work with you @BarackObama and @ObamaFoundation. Migration is an opportunity, not a crisis, and your support is priceless!"[49] Since returning to France, she has worked to expand SINGA into a global organization to "encourage citizens mobilization to radically transform migration."[50] In March 2019, Ms. Barbe derided then-President Trump's immigration policies. "One of the political reactions to migration," Ms. Barbe wrote, "is that chosen by Donald Trump on numerous occasions (anti-immigration decree, declaration of a state of emergency at the Mexican border for the construction of a border wall)," which she said, "consists in categorically refusing immigration. To scare and make more noise than the others."[51] Like her mentor Barack Obama, Ms. Barbe engaged in gross distortions of what Trump was actually trying to accomplish. The Trump administration did not categorically refuse immigration. It refused opening the nation's borders to a flood of illegal immigrants or allowing all those whom Ms. Barbe collectively calls "new arrivals" to become the "full citizens" Ms. Barbe would like them to be.

In short, the Obama Foundation is serving as Barack Obama's vehicle to search for and incubate the next generation of Obama social activist mini-mes to fight social "injustices" they see around them. But, as discussed in the next section, Obama is rather blasé when it comes to addressing complaints raised by community activists about his own foundation.

THE SELF-RIGHTEOUS HYPOCRITE

One of the foundation's prized projects is the construction of the Obama Presidential Library in the Southside of Chicago. But neighborhood activists have objected, fearing that the location of the library would result in the displacement of low-income residents, gentrification, and the privatization of public park space. There have also been complaints about lack of transparency regarding the foundation's biggest donors.[52] At a community meeting to discuss some of these concerns, Obama came across as dismissive.[53] While he was president, Barack Obama lashed out at the "fat cat bankers on Wall Street," whom he held mainly responsible for the financial crisis he had to deal with during his first year as president.[54] After he left office, during the speech he delivered at the University of Illinois in September 2018, Obama told students that "the reckless behavior of financial elites" had triggered "a massive financial crisis, 10 years ago this week."[55]

A funny thing happened on Obama's post-presidency journey, however. Obama managed to become one of the highest-paid public speakers in the country. This self-righteous hypocrite has been paid handsomely for speeches hosted by financial elites of the type he has regularly scorned.[56] And Obama has returned the favor. High-finance fat cats are serving on the Obama Foundation board. One of "anti-fat cat Obama's own foundation directors," the *Washington Times* reported, is "an offshore tax haven sheltering fat catter" named Penny Pritzker.[57] Obama has picked "private equity, hedge fund, venture capital, and banking veterans to oversee his foundation, and an alumnus of Goldman Sachs Group Inc. to advise him on investments," Bloomberg's Max Abelson reported.[58]

As of the end of 2019, Barack Obama's own net worth was estimated at around $40 million. Michelle Obama's net worth was reportedly about the same.[59] As of 2021, Barack Obama's net worth grew to an estimated $70 million.[60] With all their newfound wealth, the former president and first lady have chosen the life of luxury since leaving the White House, including a cruise on a multibillionaire's $590 million luxury yacht[61] and other lavish vacations.[62] And the Obamas purchased toward the end of 2019 a 6,892-square-foot home on Martha's Vineyard for $11.75 million, consisting of seven bedrooms, eight-and-a-half baths and several stone fireplaces.[63] This house is in addition to the home they own in Washington, DC.[64] The Obamas also like to spend time in California. Michelle Obama "rented one of the most exclusive and amazing homes in all of the Hollywood Hills" for a couple of days in July of 2019, TMZ reported. "One realtor, who's very well connected in the area, tells TMZ the buzz is that Michelle might be scoping out the neighborhood and/or that particular house to set down roots."[65]

Of course, the Obamas have every right, as private citizens, to spend as they wish the money they earn lawfully from their books, memoirs, speaking engagements, Netflix productions, and so forth. But please stop lecturing the rest of us on the evils of conspicuous consumption. Without a trace of self-reflection, Barack Obama deplored during his 2018 South Africa speech that "there's only so much you can eat, there's only so big a house you can have, there's only so many nice trips you can take. I mean, it's enough."[66] Evidently, Obama has not had "enough" yet to satisfy his own expensive tastes.

CONCLUSION

Barack Obama promised as a presidential candidate to "fundamentally transform America." He came perilously close to destroying the liberties and security of America's Constitutional Republic. Oblivious to the grave harm he had done as president, Obama declared at the 2016 Democratic National Convention that "there's still much I want to do."[67] He added, "I'm ready to pass the baton and do my part as a private citizen." Obama looked to Hillary Clinton to take the baton and carry forward his legacy. He urged voters "to do for Hillary Clinton what you did for me. I ask you to carry her the same way you carried me."

The election of Donald Trump on November 8, 2016 came as a shock to Obama. The baton he intended to pass on to Hillary Clinton fell instead into the hands of his nemesis, who had promised to upend the Obama "legacy." Obama used some of his time as a private citizen to nurse his wounds at luxurious vacation destinations. He also filled his pockets with lavish fees he received for his speeches to fat-cat audiences. But Obama could not accept the defeat of his legacy at the hands of Donald Trump. Thus, he set out to delegitimize the Trump presidency by demonizing Trump, his policies, and his supporters, including doing so on foreign soil.

Barack Obama is also using his foundation to enlist recruits for his battle against those he considers to be the "old" guardians of the "status quo." He wants to replace them with young radical progressives trained to carry his social justice banner forward. Obama has not been shy about his goal to "create a hundred or a thousand or a million young Barack Obamas or Michelle Obamas."[68] Obama did enough major damage to America while president. Now this narcissist wants to create more future "leaders" in his own radical image. In the meantime, the Biden presidency gives Obama hope that he can save his disastrous legacy, with what is amounting to a "third Obama term" of destructive foreign and domestic policies.

17

WHY OBAMA SHOULD HAVE
BEEN IMPEACHED

by Joseph Klein

INTRODUCTION

This essay reviews the case that should have been brought to impeach and remove from office the forty-fourth president of the United States, Barack Obama. He committed multiple impeachable offenses by abusing his presidential powers and willfully subverting the American republic's constitutional system of checks and balances. No other president in the history of the United States has come anywhere close to the depth and breadth of misconduct in office, meriting the application of the Constitution's most serious remedy against a runaway presidency. The author Ben Shapiro went so far as to describe the Obama administration as a "quasi-criminal syndicate," led by a president who sent the signals of what he wanted accomplished by his subordinates while remaining "an expert at hiding from his own crimes."[1]

Former federal prosecutor Andrew C. McCarthy, who was the lead prosecutor in the charges against the "blind sheikh," Omar Abdel Rahman, and eleven others in connection with the 1993 World Trade Center bombing and plots to attack other New York City landmarks, warned during Barack Obama's second term in office about the unprecedented degree of "presidential lawlessness" that the United States was experiencing under then-President Obama. Mr. McCarthy laid out a compelling case for impeaching Obama in his 2014 book entitled *Faithless Execution: Building the Political Case for Obama's Impeachment*.[2] He described seven main offenses that he considered to be impeachable. These included the forty-fourth president's failure to carry out the laws passed by Congress and usurpation of legislative authority, particularly with respect to immigration; his dereliction of duty as commander in chief; perpetrating multiple frauds against the American people and their representatives in Congress and those acting under his direction; and the multiple violations of Americans' constitutional rights.

Barack Obama sought to impose his radical transformational policies on the nation he swore to serve in accordance with the Constitution by grossly unconstitutional means, including by executive fiat. The House of Representatives conducted a hearing into the Obama administration's abuses of power in 2012.[3] After he was re-elected less than two months later, however, no serious effort was launched to impeach Obama. Andrew McCarthy had hoped that the credible case he laid out in 2014 for Obama's impeachment would at least make Obama think twice during the remainder of his second term before engaging in any further presidential misconduct. It didn't work. Obama's unprecedented record of cumulative presidential lawlessness and subversion of America's constitutional system of government continued right to the end of his presidency. Barack Obama managed to leave the White House personally unscathed. However, that does not mean we should simply ignore how seriously he damaged the Constitution's design of separation of powers and limited government. It is worth examining why Obama's abuses of power, not seen before or since from any other president, merited his impeachment and removal from office.

First, by reviewing the compelling evidence of Obama's multiple usurpations of legislative power, his repeated failure to faithfully execute the nation's laws, and abuses of his executive powers in trampling on the fundamental freedoms of speech, press, and religion, we see what a real case for impeachment should look like. It is certainly not like the wafer-thin partisan cases against former President Trump that the House Democrats have mounted, including the second impeachment trial that took place after Trump was no longer in office. Ironically, this impeachment trial of former President Trump sets a precedent for conducting impeachment and trial proceedings against former President Obama so that Obama can never hold any federal office again. More importantly, if we do not learn from the past by subjecting Obama's record to a constitutional critique of the type that would have been conducted in an impeachment hearing and trial, Obama's egregious abuses may end up becoming accepted practice. History will then repeat itself, but with one dangerous twist. Next time the damage to the Founding Fathers' design of separation of powers and limited government may be irreversible.

PRESIDENTIAL IMPEACHMENT BACKGROUND

Article II, Section 1 of the US Constitution vests the "executive Power" in a single person—the duly elected president of the United States. Before entering "on the Execution of his Office," the president "shall take the following Oath or Affirmation:—'I do solemnly swear (or affirm) that I will faithfully execute the Office of President of the United States, and will to the best of my Ability, preserve, protect and defend the Constitution of the United States.'" Article II, Section 3 commands that the president "shall take Care that the Laws be faithfully executed."

The president is responsible for the acts of his subordinates in the Executive Branch. As Mr. McCarthy observed, "If you look at the

Constitution carefully, you'd find that all the executive power in the government is invested in one person. It is not endowed in this vast array of executive agencies. It is singularly the president who is responsible."[4]

Pursuant to Article II, Section 4 of the US Constitution, the president "shall be removed from Office on Impeachment for, and Conviction of, Treason, Bribery, or other high Crimes and Misdemeanors." A majority vote in the House of Representatives to impeach the president sends the articles of impeachment over to the Senate where a trial is conducted. A two-thirds vote of the Senate is required to convict the president and remove him from office.

Two of the three stated bases for impeachment and conviction are treason and bribery. *Treason* is a criminal offense that is defined in the Constitution itself in Article III, Section 3: "Treason against the United States, shall consist only in levying war against them, or in adhering to their enemies, giving them aid and comfort." *Bribery* of public officials is a criminal offense, which has been codified in a federal statute (18 USC. § 201). It requires proof that a public official, with corrupt intent, demanded that someone provide him with a "thing of value" as a condition for performing an "official act." Andrew McCarthy has argued that the Founding Fathers had a different notion of what "bribery" meant when they wrote the impeachment clause so many years before the federal bribery statute was enacted. According to Mr. McCarthy, the bribery offense for impeachment purposes applies when "a president was bribed by a foreign power to put the might of the United States in the service of the foreign power at the expense of the American people."[5]

The third stated basis for impeachment and conviction is the more amorphous offense of "*Other High Crimes and Misdemeanors.*" The Founding Fathers did not view policy differences or a parliamentary-type vote of loss of confidence in the president as rising to the level of a high crime and misdemeanor impeachable offense. Alexander Hamilton described such offenses in Federalist Papers No. 65 as "those offenses which proceed from the misconduct of public men, or, in other words, from the abuse or violation of some public trust. They are of a nature which may with peculiar propriety be denominated POLITICAL, as they relate chiefly to injuries done immediately to the society itself."

It is certainly plausible to conceive of a spectrum of presidential misconduct that ranges from relatively minor acts, which may constitute technical breaches of law but do not rise to the level of violation of the president's oath of office and his duties to faithfully execute the nation's laws in the public interest, to very serious wrongdoing that subvert the nation's constitutional system of limited government and separation of powers and violates the public trust. Where on the spectrum a president's actions lie becomes the central question in defining a credible impeachable offense. To date, however, we have scarce congressional precedent to shed light on the answer to this question.

Four presidents in US history have faced a serious threat of impeachment. This includes former President Donald Trump, who was impeached twice in proceedings initiated by the Democrat-controlled House of Representatives. The House Democrats' first highly partisan case for Trump's impeachment revolved around allegations, based on hearsay and presumptions, that he abused his presidential powers by exerting improper pressure on Ukraine to open investigations into his political opponents. The Democrats had added to the mix obstruction of Congress. Trump was impeached a second time by the Democrat-controlled House in which he was charged with "incitement of insurrection," arising from the January 6, 2021, riot at the Capitol. In both cases, Trump was acquitted by the Republican-controlled Senate.

In addition to Trump, only two past presidents were, in fact, impeached by the House of Representatives. Andrew Johnson was impeached in 1868 for breaching the Tenure of Office Act by removing Edwin Stanton, Secretary of War, from the cabinet. Bill Clinton was impeached in 1998 for perjury and obstructing justice, relating to sexual harassment charges against him. Both presidents were acquitted by the Senate.

Richard Nixon resigned before being formally impeached by the full House of Representatives on grounds recommended by the House

Judiciary Committee. The recommended charges were obstructing justice, misusing his power, and contempt of Congress—focusing primarily on the Watergate break-in scandal and coverup. One of the articles of impeachment drafted by the committee held Nixon accountable for "failing to act when he knew or had reason to know that his close subordinates endeavoured to impede and frustrate lawful inquiries by duly constituted executive, judicial and legislative entities concerning the unlawful entry into the headquarters of the Democratic National Committee, and the cover-up thereof."

While the particulars vary, all decisions on whether or not to press forward with a case for impeachment are ultimately political in nature. Not all crimes in the legal sense are necessarily impeachable. At the same time, not all impeachable offenses must technically be criminal acts. Impeachable offenses, as Alexander Hamilton said, are offenses against the public trust that are injurious to society itself. However, the House's impeachment power should not be abused to serve narrow partisan purposes. Mr. Hamilton warned in Federalist Papers No. 65 that in the heat of the moment, "there will always be the greatest danger that the decision will be regulated more by the comparative strength of parties, than by the real demonstrations of innocence or guilt."

Republicans held the majority in the House of Representatives during the last two years of Barack Obama's first term in office and throughout his second term. However, they held back from commencing formal impeachment proceedings against Obama. Instead, they held an oversight hearing and issued their majority report on the Obama administration's multiple abuses of power.[6] That turned out to be insufficient. Rather, as the remainder of this essay will demonstrate, Barack Obama should have been impeached for the serial offenses he committed in violation of the public trust. These violations resulted in significant damage to the Constitution's separation of powers and protected freedoms. When any credible threat of impeachment failed to materialize, the Obama administration became even more emboldened.

THE OBAMA RECORD OF MULTIPLE IMPEACHABLE OFFENSES
Acting personally or through his subordinates for whom he was responsible as the nation's chief executive officer, Barack Obama displayed a persistent pattern of violating his public trust as president of the United States, to the manifest injury of the rule of law and the American people. The following are among the most egregious offenses that merited Barack Obama's impeachment and removal from office.

Repeated Usurpations of Legislative Authority and
Refusals to Faithfully Execute the Nation's Laws
Andrew Johnson was impeached on account of his violation of a single statute, for which he avoided conviction and removal from office by just one vote. Barack Obama unilaterally changed or refused to enforce a whole slew of laws he did not like. He also made unconstitutional appointments. And, he entered into what the United Nations considered to be a treaty by the way it was presented to the UN by the Obama administration, although the administration had not secured the constitutionally required approval by the US Senate.

More specifically, Barack Obama himself or through his subordinates:

- Unilaterally "amended" Obamacare without legislative action, including continuing to pay insurance companies to compensate them for losses even though there was no appropriation from Congress to pay for these subsidies.

- Unilaterally "amended" the statutory Temporary Assistance for Needy Families non-waivable welfare to work requirement without legislative action by using artifice to get around the work requirement.

- Abused the presidential recess appointment power under Article II, Section 2 of the Constitution by making three unilateral appointments to the National Labor Relations Board, as well as appointing the head of the Consumer Financial Protection Bureau. Obama did so, even though the Senate was holding "pro forma" sessions every three days during which it could conduct business and did not consider itself to be in recess. In a case regarding three of the four appointments Obama had made, the Supreme Court unanimously ruled that Obama had exceeded his constitutional authority, noting that "the Senate is in session when it says it is, provided that, under its own rules, it retains the capacity to transact Senate business."[7]

- Obstructed congressional oversight by withholding on bogus executive privilege grounds many thousands of documents directly bearing on the Obama administration's disastrous "Operation Fast and Furious" program, through which many firearms were smuggled into Mexico under the direction of US government agencies and officials as part of an anti-drug cartel initiative. The guns ended up in the wrong hands, resulting in the death of a border patrol agent. Obama and his attorney general, Eric Holder, deliberately tried to conceal from Congress, which was exercising its constitutionally authorized oversight powers, evidence of executive branch misconduct. The misconduct included false representations that Justice Department officials made to Congress.

- Submitted to the United Nations Secretary General an instrument of "acceptance" on behalf of the United States with regard to the Paris Agreement on Climate Change, which the UN website defines as expressing "the consent of a state to be bound by a treaty." This instrument of "acceptance" was then deposited as a treaty with the UN and listed as such in the United Nations' Treaty Collection under the heading "Multilateral Treaties Deposited with the Secretary-General," despite the absence of Senate concurrence.[8] For domestic consumption, however, Obama administration officials had described the Paris Agreement as an "executive agreement" that did not require Senate concurrence as a treaty. In short, by sleight of hand, Barack Obama enlisted the United Nations in a scheme to transform his "executive agreement" on the domestic stage into a legally binding treaty under international law on the global stage, even though it was not approved by the US Senate pursuant to Article II, Section 2 of the US Constitution.

- Repeatedly refused to enforce selective portions of the nation's immigration laws and unilaterally "amended" the law through executive action. "To contend that the obligation imposed on the President to see the laws faithfully executed implies a power to forbid their execution is a novel construction of the Constitution, and entirely inadmissible," the Supreme Court declared more than 180 years ago.[9] That fundamental principle has not changed. Even Obama originally recognized the constitutional limitation on his executive prerogatives but ultimately ignored them.

  In March 2011, Barack Obama said that with "respect to the notion that I can just suspend deportations through executive order, that's just not the case . . . There are enough laws on the books by Congress that are very clear in terms of how we have to enforce our immigration system that for me to simply through executive order ignore those congressional mandates would not conform with my appropriate role as president."[10]

  Yet, in defiance of the constitutional limitations on his presidential powers that he himself had acknowledged on several occasions, Obama used an executive order to bypass Congress and establish the Deferred Action for Childhood Arrivals program (DACA) all by himself. Obama's program purported to create by executive fiat a protected class of illegal aliens who had been brought to the United States as children. Obama also provided, to the broad protected class of illegal aliens he had created, work authorizations and access to federal government benefits, despite the lack of congressional authority to do so. This was no mere exercise in "prosecutorial discretion," as Obama contended. He abused his presidential powers by legislating eligibility for significant protections and benefits bestowed on broad classifications of people. A president cannot simply nullify portions of a law passed by Congress with which he disagreed on policy grounds. Yet that is precisely what Obama did.

In 2014, Obama doubled down. He unilaterally instituted a parallel program for a certain class of illegal alien adults called the Deferred Action for Parents of Americans and Lawful Permanent Residents program (DAPA). Obama himself acknowledged what he had done in remarks he delivered to a Chicago audience in November 2014—"I just took action to change the law."[11] He claimed he had the legal authority to do so because he was simply "reprioritizing how we enforce our immigration laws generally." The Fifth Circuit Court of Appeals disagreed. It upheld a nationwide injunction issued by a lower federal district court judge against DAPA and an expanded version of DACA, declaring that an enforcement decision not to remove particular illegal immigrants "does not transform presence deemed unlawful by Congress into lawful presence and confer eligibility for otherwise unavailable benefits based on that change." The Obama administration then showed its contempt for the judiciary. It violated the district court's injunction order by continuing to hand out work permits to deferred action beneficiaries. Obama Justice Department lawyers also misrepresented material facts in submissions and statements made to the court, which found "a steady stream of misconduct" on their part.[12]

An equally divided eight-member US Supreme Court affirmed the Fifth Circuit's decision without an opinion, effectively upholding the lower court's injunction, halting the expansion of DACA and the implementation of DAPA. On the one hand, Obama finally admitted that "I have pushed to the limits of my executive authority" and said, "We now have to have Congress act." At the same time, however, he declared he would not change his enforcement priorities—in other words, pursuing the goals of his illegal executive orders by failing to fully execute the immigration laws as enacted by Congress. And he excoriated the Supreme Court for taking "us further from the country that we aspire to be."[13]

Barack Obama aspired to govern a country on which he could impose by executive edict his design for "fundamental transformation." As he tweeted in August 2013, "If Congress won't act, I will."[14] Obama willfully and repeatedly violated the limitations imposed on his executive authority by the Constitution, which he once declared to be inadequate because it "doesn't say what the federal government or state government must do on your behalf." There were too many constitutional constraints on government action, he believed, that prevented bringing about the kind of rapid "significant redistributional change" he was after.[15]

In sum, as president, Barack Obama treated the Constitution's fundamental separation of powers principles as inconvenient hurdles he could simply jump over whenever they got in his way. He should have been impeached and removed from office for engaging in a pattern of deliberate usurpation of legislative authority and refusal to faithfully execute the nation's laws.

The failure to do so made it much easier for President Biden to take up where Obama left off. Biden has willfully refused to enforce America's immigration laws, substituting his own policy judgments for those of the legislative branch. He has knowingly put Americans in harm's way by letting hundreds of thousands of illegal immigrants into the United States and releasing them to settle in communities across the country, regardless of whether they have been tested or vaccinated for COVID-19. Obama's legacy of impeachable usurpation of legislative authority and refusal to faithfully execute the nation's laws lives on in Joe Biden's presidency.

Treacherous Dereliction of Duty as Commander in Chief.
Article II, Section 2 of the Constitution specifies that the president is entrusted with the responsibility of serving as the nation's commander in chief. One would think that this responsibility would involve invoking his ultimate authority over military resources to protect US military and diplomatic personnel who are thrust into the middle of armed hostilities. President Obama did the opposite. He released high-level enemy combatants from captivity, allowing them to possibly return to the battlefield against American soldiers. He provided furtive cash payments to an enemy country, which it has used to fund terrorists with American blood on their hands. And he turned his back on diplomats and military personnel in danger for their lives.

- American troops were in harm's way in Afghanistan when Obama decided in 2014 to release five key Taliban figures from Guantanamo in exchange for captive US soldier Bowe Bergdahl, who had abandoned his post before he was captured. As Andrew McCarthy explained at the time, "we have a commander in chief who is replenishing the enemy in wartime when the enemy is still on the battlefield conducting offensive, jihadist operations against our guys. That's about as shocking a dereliction of duty as I can imagine."[16] In other words, Obama's reckless release of Taliban fighters was a boon to an enemy of the United States then fighting US soldiers for whom Obama was ultimately responsible as commander in chief.

- The murders of US ambassador to Libya John Christopher Stevens and three other Americans during an assault that commenced on September 11, 2012, against the US consulate and nearby annex in Benghazi were the direct result of the failure of the Obama administration to take adequate security measures that Ambassador Stevens had requested. Even after the attack had commenced, American lives might have been saved if there had been a quick US military response, according to Greg Hicks, who was the US deputy chief of mission in Libya at the time of the attack.[17] Four US Special Forces troop members in Tripoli were prepared to board a Libyan plan to travel to Benghazi to help their besieged colleagues, but they were told to stand down. That's on Barack Obama's head as commander in chief. Obama should have taken command and pulled out all stops in a rescue mission. Instead the commander in chief was AWOL. Following the attack, Obama himself, along with his then-secretary of state Hillary Clinton and UN Ambassador Susan Rice, participated in a coverup of the facts. They continued to insist that the assault was a spontaneous mob outburst that got out of control in reaction to an obscure Prophet Mohammed–mocking video, rather than the premeditated Islamic jihadist attack that they knew it was. Obama and senior members of his administration shamelessly blamed the video for the violence in order to divert attention away from their abysmal failure to secure the consulate and annex against a predictable Islamist jihadist assault on Americans on the anniversary of 9/11.

- Shortly after the implementation of the disastrous nuclear deal that Barack Obama concluded with Iran without the concurrence of the Senate, Obama surreptitiously paid Iran a $1.7 billion cash ransom for the release of several, but not all, American hostages then held by the regime. "Iran has used the funds to pay its main proxy, the Lebanon-based terrorist group Hezbollah, along with the Quds Force, Iran's main foreign intelligence and covert action arm and element of the Islamic Revolutionary Guards Corps," according to Bill Gertz, the national security columnist for the *Washington Times*, citing knowledgeable sources.[18] These militants have American blood on their hands. Nevertheless,

Commander in Chief Barack Obama supplied these enemies of the United States with more money to fund their bloodlust.

Barack Obama failed in critical ways to carry out his duties as the nation's commander in chief. Indeed, in at least two instances described above, the effect of his actions was to provide aid to America's enemies— the Taliban and Iran. For this shameful dereliction of duty alone that put Americans' lives in jeopardy, Obama deserved to be impeached and removed from office.

In his first year of office, President Biden also forsook his constitutional responsibilities as commander in chief with his reckless withdrawal of all American troops from Afghanistan in August 2021. Thirteen US service members needlessly lost their lives in a suicide bombing attack near the Kabul airport as thousands of desperate people tried to reach planes taking off from Afghanistan amidst the chaos that Biden's hasty retreat precipitated. Biden removed all the American troops before securing the safe passage out of Afghanistan of every single American civilian who wanted to leave out of fear for his or her life under Taliban rule. Biden left many of these fellow Americans behind to fend for themselves. Biden also abandoned billions of dollars' worth of sophisticated military equipment for the Taliban to use or to transfer to other enemies of the United States, most notably al Qaeda, China, Russia, and Iran. The Taliban's al Qaeda friends have their own home base again from which to plan and launch terrorist attacks against Americans everywhere. Obama's legacy of impeachable dereliction of duty as commander in chief lives on in Joe Biden's presidency.

Attacks on First Amendment Rights

Barack Obama directly, and through the acts of his subordinates with his knowledge and at least tacit approval, systematically undermined Americans' First Amendment rights of freedom of the press, freedom of speech, and freedom of religion.

- *Persecution of journalists*—The Obama administration went far beyond rhetorical attacks on the press. "Under Mr. Obama," wrote *New York Times* journalist James Risen, "the Justice Department and the F.B.I. have spied on reporters by monitoring their phone records, labeled one journalist an unindicted co-conspirator in a criminal case for simply doing reporting and issued subpoenas to other reporters to try to force them to reveal their sources and testify in criminal cases."[19]

Here's one example of the Obama administration's trampling on freedom of the press that drew the ire of journalists. In a May 14, 2013 letter to Attorney General Eric Holder and Deputy Attorney General James M. Cole,[20] the Reporters Committee and fifty news organizations stated, "The nation's news media were stunned to learn yesterday of the Department of Justice's broad subpoena of telephone records belonging to The Associated Press . . . The scope of this action calls into question the very integrity of Department of Justice policies toward the press and its ability to balance, on its own, its police powers against the First Amendment rights of the news media and the public's interest in reporting on all manner of government conduct, including matters touching on national security which lie at the heart of this case."

In a second example of Obama administration overreach against journalists doing their job, the Obama Justice Department secretly subpoenaed and seized telephone and e-mail records of the Fox News chief Washington correspondent, James Rosen, in connection with the Espionage Act prosecution of a contract analyst in the State Department with access to classified information. It further abused the law enforcement powers of the executive branch and violated its own guidelines by filing an FBI affidavit in support of the federal court application for a secret search warrant, declaring that "there is probable cause to believe that the reporter has committed or is committing a violation" of the Espionage Act—"at the very least, either as an aider, abettor and/or co-conspirator."[21]

According to the House Committee on the Judiciary Majority Staff Report dated July 31, 2013,[22] Obama's attorney general at the time, Eric Holder, misled Congress when he denied ever being involved in or having heard of "the potential prosecution of the press" for the disclosure of classified material. Holder's testimony, the report said, "was an attempt, through verbal gymnastics, to circumvent proper congressional oversight and accountability by distorting the truth about the Justice Department's investigative techniques targeting journalists." Holder reportedly signed off on the search warrant application, according to a Justice Department official cited by CNN at the time.[23] Even the *New York Times* editorial board declared that "the Obama administration has moved beyond protecting government secrets to threatening fundamental freedoms of the press to gather news."[24]

Yet Obama continued to express confidence in his attorney general, who had misled Congress under oath concerning what he knew about this sordid abuse of power and when he knew it. This was not the first time that Obama gave Holder a pass for lying to Congress. Holder did so regarding what he knew about Fast and Furious. Holder also was held in contempt by the House of Representatives for obstruction of Congress's oversight investigation of the Fast and Furious scandal. By doing nothing to rein in Holder, Obama signaled to his attorney general and other high-level Obama officials that their significant misconduct would be overlooked if it served Obama's own agenda—a flagrant abuse of presidential power.

- *Abridged freedom of speech*—Under Barack Obama's leadership, his administration, including his secretary of state Hillary Clinton, did everything they could to stifle so-called blasphemy against Islam. Obama set the tone during his first year as president when he vowed to the Muslim world in his June 2009 Cairo speech: "I consider it part of my responsibility as President of the United

States to fight against negative stereotypes of Islam whenever they appear."[25]

In remarks to the United Nations General Assembly in September 2012, Obama paid lip service to the First Amendment's protection of free speech but then declared to the whole world, "The future must not belong to those who slander the prophet of Islam."[26] Indeed, his administration had worked with the Organization of Islamic Cooperation (OIC) in 2011 to repackage the OIC's "Combating defamation of religions" resolutions that the OIC had successfully steered through the UN for years into a less ominous-sounding resolution entitled "Combating Intolerance, Negative Stereotyping and Stigmatization of, and Discrimination, Incitement to Violence and Violence Against, Persons Based on Religion or Belief." But the resolution was merely old wine in a new bottle, a backdoor way of helping the OIC get closer to achieving its objective, which remains stamping out speech deemed offensive to Muslims.

Hillary Clinton worked behind the scenes with her OIC partners to find ways to stifle speech offensive to Muslims and end run the First Amendment's protection of free speech. For example, the former secretary of state had no problem promising to apply "some old-fashioned techniques of peer pressure and shaming, so that people don't feel that they have the support to do what we abhor."[27] But the Obama administration did not stop there.

On September 14, 2012—three days after the Benghazi terrorist attack—a memorial service attended by Obama, Clinton, and family members of the fallen heroes was held at Andrews Air Force Base. When approached by the father of Navy Seal Tyrone Woods, who lost his life in the Benghazi attack, Hillary Clinton vowed to him that the Obama administration would "arrest and prosecute" the producer of the video offensive to Muslims. That target of the Obama administration's wrath turned out to be Mark Basseley Youssef, an Egyptian-born US resident formerly known as Nakoula Basseley Nakoula.[28] He was arrested on September 27, 2012, and held without bail. Probation violations served as the convenient pretext to arrest and prosecute the video producer. The day after Obama's re-election victory lap, the individual who had dared produce the obscure video denigrating Islam was sentenced by a federal district court judge to one year in prison for violating the terms of his probation. His real "crime" was blasphemy against Islam—which is a crime under Sharia law but is supposed to be protected speech in the United States under the First Amendment. That is, until Obama promised to "fight against negative stereotypes of Islam whenever they appear."

As George Washington University law professor Jonathan Turley wrote:

> The distrust shown by many free speech advocates, including myself, is that the Administration has a checkered history of claiming to support free speech while supporting the creation of an international blasphemy standard.[29]

Barack Obama arrogantly proclaimed to the world, "The future must not belong to those who slander the prophet of Islam." He abused his presidential powers by using federal law enforcement and the State Department to stamp out speech that did not accord with his mission to protect Islam from criticism.

- *Used the IRS against political opponents*—Barack Obama took the unprecedented step during his 2010 State of the Union address[30] to insult several Supreme Court justices sitting right in front of him to their faces. He was angry about the Supreme Court's decision in *Citizens United v. Federal Election Commission*[31] that struck down, on First Amendment grounds, a legislative prohibition on corporate independent expenditures in connection with candidate elections. "With all due deference to separation of powers," Obama said, without a trace of self-awareness, "last week the Supreme Court reversed a century of law that I believe will open the floodgates for special interests—including foreign corporations—to spend without limit in our elections." He urged "Democrats and Republicans to pass a bill that helps to correct some of these problems." That did not happen. But Obama had sent a signal to his subordinates at the IRS to use the tools of one of the most punitive agencies in the executive branch to slow down any adverse effects that the *Citizens United* decision might have on his 2012 re-election campaign.

Following the Supreme Court's *Citizens United* decision, there was a significant increase in the number of nonprofit organizations engaged in limited amounts of political activities that applied for tax-exempt status. Some IRS employees got Obama's message. They discriminated against conservative groups opposing the Obama agenda in their administration of applications for tax-exempt status in the run up to the 2012 presidential election. Groups with names, such as "tea party" and "patriot," were singled out. IRS employees screened their tax-exempt applications, significantly delaying the processing of those applications, and made unconstitutionally burdensome requests for information based on the names, associations, and/ or political viewpoints. In May 2013, then Acting Director of Exempt Organizations, Lois Lerner, admitted that certain organizations with tea party or patriot in their titles had been targeted. The treasury inspector general for Tax Administration came out with a critical report around the same time.

At first, Obama expressed concern and vowed to get to the bottom of the scandal. However, he didn't follow through. Although Ms. Lerner was found to have been directly involved in the targeting, having written in one 2011 e-mail "Tea Party Matter very dangerous,"[32] for example, Obama did not demand her resignation or fire her. After being on paid leave for four months, she retired with a full pension. How convenient it was for Ms. Lerner that her hard drive had crashed, following which the IRS just happened to destroy her blackberry even though a Congressional inquiry was already under way.[33]

Obama blamed Fox News for promoting the idea that the IRS had acted corruptly to help Democrats. "Not even a smidgen of corruption," Obama declared with a straight face during a 2014 interview with Bill O'Reilly, who was then with Fox News.[34]

Years later, in a 2017 consent decree,[35] the IRS formally apologized for what it had done. The federal district court minced no words in the declaratory judgment it issued accompanying the consent decree: "The Court hereby declares that discrimination on the basis of political viewpoint in administering the United States tax code violates fundamental First Amendment rights. Disparate treatment of taxpayers based solely on the taxpayers' names, any lawful positions the taxpayers espouse on any issues, or the taxpayers' associations or perceived associations with a particular political movement, position, or viewpoint is unlawful."

• *Abridged free exercise of religious belief*—The Obama administration sought to impose government regulations abridging the constitutional right of churches and synagogues to choose their clergy according to the free exercise of their religious beliefs. The administration argued to the Supreme Court that the First Amendment guarantee of religious freedom does not protect religious organizations in such cases. This flagrant disregard of one of the First Amendment's core protections was summarily dismissed by the Supreme Court in a 9–0 decision.[36] "We cannot accept the remarkable view that the Religion Clauses have nothing to say about a religious organization's freedom to select its own ministers," Chief Justice Roberts wrote in the Court's opinion.

Even after its embarrassing loss in the Supreme Court,

the Obama administration continued to run roughshod over Americans' constitutional right of free exercise of religion. As part of its implementation of Obamacare, the administration issued a regulation requiring all employer health plans to provide contraceptives, sterilization, and abortion-causing drugs. Individuals and organizations were forced to choose between following their faith and paying steep government fines. "That regulation, 'the Mandate,' applies . . . to many business owners who want to ensure their practices are consistent with their faith," Lori Windham, Senior Counsel of the Becket Fund for Religious Liberty, testified at a House Judiciary Committee hearing on the Obama administration's abuse of power. "The government has effectively said that you forfeit your free exercise rights when you open a business."[37] After being challenged, the administration played games to delay judicial review with phony offers of compromise. The Supreme Court, in a 5–4 decision, held that, as applied to closely held corporations, the regulations promulgated by the Department of Health and Human Services requiring employers to provide their female employees with no-cost access to contraception violated the Religious Freedom Restoration Act.[38]

Barack Obama and his administration repeatedly trampled over the Constitution's First Amendment guarantees of fundamental freedoms, using the enormous powers of the executive branch to encroach on freedom of speech, freedom of the press, and the free exercise of religious beliefs. For such overbearing intrusions on the liberties of the American people, Barack Obama deserved to be impeached and removed from office.

FAILURE TO IMPEACH AND REMOVE OBAMA EMBOLDENED FLAGRANT SPYING ON AMERICANS

Congress's abdication of its responsibility to impeach and remove from office the serially lawless forty-fourth president of the United States paved the way for Obama's audacious abuse of law enforcement tools to persecute General Flynn, as discussed in chapter 14. It also paved the way for the Obama administration's untrammeled abuse of the government's surveillance powers against the American people. This abuse first came to light in a Foreign Intelligence Surveillance Act (FISA) Court ruling issued in April 2017, written by the Presiding Judge Rosemary Collyer. The decision stated that unwarranted and illegal surveillance of American citizens had been going on from at least as far back as 2012 and continuing through 2016. The decision noted that, at an October 26, 2016 hearing, the FISA Court had criticized the Obama administration's "lack of candor" in failing to disclose reports of past National Security Agency (NSA) abuses and "emphasized that this is a very serious Fourth Amendment issue."[39] But the abuse did not stop there.

During the final days of the Obama administration, Obama's then-Attorney General Loretta Lynch signed off on widespread dissemination of raw intelligence information collected by NSA to multiple intelligence agencies within the government, including the intelligence branches of the FBI.[40] This move considerably heightened the potential for breach-of-privacy protections for Americans caught up in NSA's vast web of collected data and for leaks that could embarrass political opponents. Most notably, Obama's highly partisan United Nations Ambassador Samantha Power, as the American Center for Law and Justice reported, "made numerous requests seeking the 'unmasking' (or unredacted identification) of names and other information about members of the Trump campaign team whose communications had been incidentally caught up in intelligence surveillance efforts."[41]

Where might some of these Trump campaign team communications that Ms. Power wanted to learn more about have come from? During October 2016, the same month that the FISA Court took the Obama administration to task for past NSA abuses, the Obama Justice Department submitted a highly questionable application for a surveillance warrant against American citizen Carter Page, a former Trump campaign adviser.[42] This action was part of the FBI's investigation, known as "Crossfire Hurricane," into whether individuals associated with the Trump presidential campaign were coordinating with the Russian government's efforts to interfere in the 2016 US presidential election. The application relied largely on unsubstantiated claims contained in the notorious dossier compiled by former British intelligence agent Christopher Steele, funded by the Democratic National Committee and Hillary Clinton's presidential campaign.

The initial application, certified by then-FBI Director James Comey and approved by then-Deputy Attorney General Sally Yates on behalf of then-Attorney General Loretta Lynch, exaggerated the reliability of its principal source of information, Christopher Steele. The Office of Inspector General for the Justice Department determined in its report on the FBI's surveillance of Mr. Page and related matters that the receipt of Steele materials in September 2016 by the Crossfire Hurricane investigatory team "played a central and essential role in the FBI's and Department's decision to seek the FISA order."[43] The first application contained "seven significant inaccuracies and omissions," including the omission of several exculpatory facts regarding Carter Page.[44] The warrant was granted, providing senior members of the Obama administration a backdoor means of secretly surveilling members of the Trump campaign who had any contact with Carter Page.

In January 2017, the Obama Justice Department successfully applied for a renewal of the surveillance warrant, relying again on the Steele dossier. Missing from the second application was critical information the FBI had found out from Steele's direct sub-source, which raised "significant questions about the reliability of allegations included in the FISA applications."[45] The application also omitted details that some in the FBI had reason to suspect by that time regarding the specific partisan source of the dossier's funding. These and other glaring material omissions and misrepresentations were nothing less than fraud on the FISA Court. The fraud that the Obama administration had set in motion against Carter Page rolled on for a brief time after Obama left office. Two more renewal surveillance warrant applications were successfully submitted in April and June 2017, certified by James Comey (while he was still the FBI Director) and Andrew McCabe (then FBI Deputy Director) respectively.

The Justice Department's inspector general, Michael E. Horowitz, testified before the Senate Judiciary Committee that his office's report was not vindicating "anybody who touched this."[46] Barack Obama's senior-level appointees, for whom Obama was directly responsible, failed to exercise appropriate supervision of such a sensitive FISA surveillance application process all the way up the chain of command. These appointees included former FBI Director James Comey, former Attorney General Loretta Lynch, and former Deputy Attorney General Sally Yates. They evidently took their cues from how much Obama himself had gotten away with and turned a blind eye.

CONCLUSION

It did not take long after Barack Obama left office for the mythologization of his presidential legacy to begin. Presidential historians surveyed by C-Span in February 2017 rated Obama as the twelfth-best president of all time, ranking him eighth as to his "moral authority."[47] Pulitzer Prize-winning author and presidential historian Doris Kearns Goodwin claimed, "There will be a certain kind of dignity Obama brought to the office that people will remember, a kind of classiness."[48] Historians who airbrush Barack Obama's legacy with towering words of praise are doing a disservice to the institution of the presidency of the United States. By glossing over Obama's record of multiple impeachable offenses, they become his apologists rather than objective chroniclers of his presidency. Revisiting the case for why Obama should have been impeached shines critical light on Obama's betrayal of the public trust during his time in office. The purpose is not to relitigate the past but to counter the misguided attempts to soft-pedal or completely ignore his egregious presidential misconduct. Without such a day of reckoning, the misconduct that Barack Obama got away with while in office is more likely to become accepted practice for future presidents. Indeed, President Biden is already following the example of his former boss's malfeasance.

18

OBAMA'S REVISIONIST "PROMISED LAND"

by Dov Lipman

EDITOR'S NOTE: This article first appeared in the *Jewish News Syndicate* in its November 26, 2020 issue. It is reprinted here with permission from *Jewish News Syndicate* and the author Lipman.[1]

I HAVE NEVER CRITICIZED former US President Barack Obama publicly—neither during my time in the Knesset nor anywhere else—despite my having disagreed with many of his policies. I am of the strong opinion that Israelis should not engage in or interfere with American politics, and I regularly offer a blanket thank you to all American presidents, including Obama, for their economic and military support for Israel.

However, his memoir, *A Promised Land*, is filled with historical inaccuracies that I feel the need to address. His telling of Israel's story (at the beginning of Chapter 25) not only exhibits a flawed understanding of the region—which clearly impacted his policies as president—but misleads readers in a way that will forever shape their negative perspective of the Jewish state.

Obama relates, for example, how the British were "occupying Palestine" when they issued the Balfour Declaration calling for a Jewish state. But labeling Great Britain as an "occupier" clearly casts doubt on its legitimacy to determine anything about the future of the Holy Land, and that wasn't the situation.

While it is true that England had no legal rights in Palestine when the Balfour Declaration was issued in 1917, that changed just five years later. The League of Nations, the precursor to the United Nations, gave the British legal rights over Palestine in its 1922 "Mandate for Palestine," which specifically mentions "the establishment in Palestine of a national home for the Jewish people."

The League also said that "recognition has thereby been given to the historical connection of the Jewish people with Palestine and to the grounds for reconstituting their national home in that country."

The former president's noted omission of the internationally agreed-upon mandate for the British to establish a home for the Jews in Palestine misinforms the reader, who will conclude that the movement for a Jewish state in Palestine had no legitimacy or international consent.

"Over the next 20 years, Zionist leaders mobilized a surge of Jewish migration to Palestine," Obama writes, creating the image that once the British illegally began the process of forming a Jewish state in Palestine, Jews suddenly started flocking there.

The truth is that Jews, who maintained a continual presence throughout the 2,000 years that most were exiled from the land, had already been moving to Palestine in large numbers way before then; considerably more than 100,000 immigrants arrived in the late nineteenth century and beginning of the twentieth century. Then, in the 1920s, high numbers fleeing anti-Semitism in Europe could only find safe haven in Palestine due to the United States having instituted quotas in 1924 on the number of Jews who could enter America.

The number of immigrants rose even more in the 1930s when Adolf

Hitler rose to power and began his conquest of Europe while the world remained silent.

Historical context is important, and once Obama chose to write about the history, he should have provided the full context and portrayed the Jews as they were: a persecuted and desperate people searching for safety, and not, as he implies, strong conquerors flooding into Palestine.

His claim that the new immigrants "organized highly trained armed forces to defend their settlements" is also misleading. A more accurate way to describe it would have been: "Because the Arabs in the region mercilessly attacked the Jewish areas, the Jewish refugees had no choice but to take up arms to defend themselves."

Acknowledging that the Arabs were attacking Jews before there was even a State of Israel is important historical context for understanding the Israeli-Arab conflict.

A Promised Land recounts, as well, how the United Nations passed a partition plan for Palestine in November 1947, by dividing the country into a Jewish and Arab state, which the "Zionist leaders," as he calls them, accepted, but to which the "Arab Palestinians, as well as surrounding Arab nations that were just emerging from colonial rule, strenuously objected."

Obama's use of "Zionist leaders" instead of "Jewish leaders" plays right into the current international climate, in which it is politically correct to be "anti-Zionist," while unacceptable to be anti-Jewish. (In reality, Zionism is the movement for Jews to live in their biblical and historic homeland, so being against that actually is anti-Semitism, but that's for another discussion.)

The description of "Arab nations that were just emerging from colonial rule" is a clear attempt to justify the Arab refusal of the UN Partition Plan. Those poor "Arab nations" that have been suffering due to outsiders colonizing their "nations" simply could not accept another "colonial" entity, the Jews, entering the region.

But the truth is that with the exception of Egypt, which was not colonized, none of the neighboring countries that rejected the partition plan had been established states before World War I. Yes, the post-war mandates of the League of Nations gave control in the region to the British and the French for a few decades, but this was in place of the Ottoman Empire that had controlled the region for centuries. Thus, the image of countries emerging from long-standing colonial rule as a subtle attempt to justify their objection to the Partition Plan is simply false.

Obama tells the story of the establishment of the State of Israel in two sentences, which are nothing short of outright revisionist history: "As Britain withdrew, the two sides quickly fell into war. And with Jewish militias claiming victory in 1948, the state of Israel was officially born."

Wow. I don't even know where to begin. The two sides didn't "fall into war" when Britain withdrew; the two sides had been fighting for decades, with the Arabs—who rejected more than half-a-century' of efforts to establish a Jewish state in the region—attacking the Jews, and the Jews defending themselves. When the British then left the area in May 1948, the Jews made a very difficult decision to declare their independence based on the UN Partition Plan, which gave the right for a Jewish state alongside an Arab state.

There were no "Jewish militias claiming victory." There was a unified Jewish army that formed the Israel Defense Forces, which knew that the surrounding Arab countries would begin an all-out assault to destroy Israel the moment its Jewish leadership declared an independent fledgling Jewish state. And that is exactly what the Arab armies did. The new State of Israel fought off that assault for months, emerging in 1949 both weakened and fragile.

Obama's perspective on the formation of the State of Israel no doubt affected his foreign policy regarding the Jewish state. If one sees Israel as a colonial force occupying the land as a result of its armed militias, then it will be treated as an outsider that wronged others to establish itself as a state. The former president misleads others into believing this, as well.

The most disingenuous sentence of Obama's history of Israel is in his description of what happened during the thirty years following Israel's establishment: "For the next three decades, Israel would engage in a succession of conflicts with its Arab neighbors. . . ."

What? I had to read that sentence many times because I could not believe that a president of the United States could write such misleading, deceptive, and damaging words about his country's close ally.

Israel did not "engage" in any conflict with the surrounding Arab countries. The Arab armies and their terrorists attacked Israel again and again, and Israelis fought to defend themselves.

A straightforward history of Middle East wars involving Israel yields this basic truth. Facts are facts, and the former president's misrepresentation of Israel as a country that sought conflict instead of peace—one that willingly engaged in wars with the Arabs—does an injustice to peace-seeking Israel and riles up anti-Israel sentiment.

Obama's description of the 1967 Six-Day War continues this revisionism: "A greatly outnumbered Israeli military routed the combined armies of Egypt, Jordan and Syria. In the process, Israel seized control of the West Bank and East Jerusalem from Jordan, the Gaza Strip and the Sinai Peninsula from Egypt, and the Golan Heights from Syria."

Here he fails to address what led up to the war, when all those Arab armies gathered along Israel's borders and declared their intention to wipe it off the map. He doesn't describe Israel's pleading with Jordan not to enter the war, nor that Jordan altogether had no legal rights to the West Bank, which it occupied in 1948 and annexed against international law in 1950.

Most significantly, Obama fails to mention Israel's willingness, immediately after the war, to withdraw from all the areas that it won in its defensive battle in exchange for peace; and by extension, he also fails to tell of the Arab League's "Three No's" in response to that offer: no peace with Israel, no recognition of Israel, and no negotiations with Israel.

This omission serves once again to portray Israel as the aggressive occupier that seeks conflict and not peace.

The former president continues with another outright falsehood, which helps give insight into his policies regarding Israeli settlements in the West Bank.

The "rise of the PLO (the Palestinian Liberation Organization)" was a "result" of the Six-Day War he writes. That makes it seem like the Palestinian liberation movement, including its violent and murderous attacks against Israelis, was only a result of Israel's taking control over the West Bank, eastern Jerusalem and the Gaza Strip.

It strengthens the message that if only Israel would vacate these areas, there would be peace between Israel and the Palestinians. This is what spurs leaders around the world to suggest that Israeli settlements in these areas are the obstacle to peace in the region.

But there is one flaw with this story and logic. It's not true. The PLO was established in 1964—three years before Israel was in control of any of those "occupied" areas and three years before there were any settlements.

What exactly was this Palestinian organization liberating at that time? Is there any conclusion other than the liberation of the Jewish state in its entirety? What other option could there be?

This is why the "Free Palestine" movement chants, "From the river to the sea, Palestine will be free." They are against the existence of Israel anywhere between the Jordan River and the Mediterranean Sea. They see such a state as a colonial enterprise with armed militias grabbing the land of others, just as Obama leads readers to believe when describing the formation of the state.

The false description of the PLO rising after 1967 serves the narrative that the "occupation" and the settlements are the cause of the conflict, and this, no doubt, had a direct impact on Obama's "not one brick" policy, including freezing settlement construction, in an effort to bring about peace between Israel and the Palestinians.

Obama describes the failed Camp David accords of 2000, in which former Israeli Prime Minister Ehud Barak offered the Palestinians more than 90 percent of what they were asking for. "Arafat demanded more concessions, however, and talks collapsed in recrimination," he writes. But the talks didn't simply "collapse." Sixty-six days later, Arafat unleashed the Second Intifada, in which 1,137 Israeli civilians were murdered and 8,341 were maimed by Yasser Arafat-funded terrorists who blew themselves up in Israeli buses and cafes.

Don't trust my word on this. Mamduh Nofal, former military commander of the Democratic Front for the Liberation of Palestine, revealed that following Camp David, "Arafat told us, 'Now we are going to fight so we must be ready.'"

In addition, Hamas leader Mahmoud al-Zahar said in September 2010 that in the summer of 2000, as soon as Arafat understood that *all* of his demands would not be met, he instructed Hamas, Fatah, and the Al-Aqsa Martyrs Brigades to begin attacking Israel. And Mosab Hassan Yousef, son of Hamas founder Sheikh Hassan Yousef, has verified that the Second Intifada was pre-planned by Arafat.

Not only does Obama fail to accurately connect the Second Intifada to Arafat's not receiving everything the Palestinians asked for at Camp David—demands that would have prevented Israel from being able to defend itself against Palestinian terrorism—but he seems to place the blame for the intifada on Israel.

He describes the September 2000 visit of Israel's opposition leader and subsequent prime minister, Ariel Sharon, to the Temple Mount in Jerusalem as "provocative" and a "stunt" that "enraged Arabs near and far."

But Obama neglects to mention that Sharon only visited there after Israel's Interior Ministry received assurances from the security chief of the Palestinian Authority that no uproar would arise as a result of the visit.

In fact, Jibril Rajoub, head of Preventive Security in the West Bank, confirmed that Sharon could visit the sensitive area as long as he did not enter a mosque or pray publicly, rules to which Sharon adhered.

Even more incredibly, Obama describes the Temple Mount as "one of Islam's holiest sites," making no mention that it is *the* holiest site in Judaism.

An innocent reader who is unfamiliar with the region and its history reads this and concludes that it was simply wrong for a Jewish leader to walk onto a Muslim religious site. On the other hand, if he or she knew that it is the holiest site for Jews, then they would more likely wonder why there was anything wrong with Sharon's having gone there—except Obama omits that part, leading anyone to conclude that Sharon was in the wrong.

That omission, together with the exclusion of Arafat's plans for the intifada right after negotiations at Camp David failed, can only lead one to conclude that Israel was responsible for the five years of bloodshed during the Second Intifada.

Obama's history lesson continues with the tension between Israel and Gaza. Remarkably, he makes zero mention of the Israeli disengagement from Gaza in 2005, when Israel pulled out all of its troops from the strip while forcing 9,000 Jewish citizens to leave their homes.

Anyone reading the president's description of the wars between Israel and Hamas would never know that Israel no longer "occupies" Gaza, and that the Palestinians have been free to build a wondrous "Israeli-free" Palestinian state there for the last fifteen years. That omission is glaring.

Finally, Obama's misleading words describing Israel's response to Hamas rocket fire on its civilian population only serves to inflame and incite anti-Israel sentiment worldwide. That response, he writes, included "Israeli Apache helicopters leveling entire neighborhoods" in Gaza—Apache helicopters that he identifies as coming from the United States, a subtle or not-too-subtle questioning of whether the United States should be providing Israel with military aid if it is used in this manner.

More importantly, what does he mean by "leveling entire neighborhoods," other than to imply that Israel indiscriminately bombs Gazan neighborhoods, willfully murdering innocent people? And what human being on Earth wouldn't be riled up to condemn Israel for such inhumane activity?

The problem is that it's false. Israel targets terrorist leaders and the rockets that they fire into Israeli cities. Tragically, Hamas leaders use innocent Palestinians as human shields by hiding behind them in civilian neighborhoods and by launching rockets into Israel from there and from hospitals and mosques.

Israel does its best not to kill innocent people, even airdropping leaflets announcing an imminent airstrike, and calls off missions to destroy rocket launchers or kill terrorist leaders when there are too many civilians in the area. Israel most certainly does not launch retaliatory attacks that aimlessly "level" entire neighborhoods.

I have no problem with criticism of Israel. We can debate the issues in intellectually honest discussions, and in the end, we may have to agree to disagree about Israel's policies. But no one should accept a book that is filled with historical inaccuracies that invariably lead innocent and unknowing readers to reach false conclusions. Such a devastating book has real-life ramifications and consequences.

It is terribly disappointing. I surely would have expected truth, accuracy, and fairness from Barack Obama, America's 44th president. But the falsehoods and inaccuracies in this memoir only feed the theory that Obama was, in fact, anti-Israel. Now, through *A Promised Land,* he seeks to convince others to join him.

Dov Lipman served as a member of the 19th Knesset.

EPILOGUE

by Robert Spencer

THE EVIDENCE MARSHALED TOGETHER in this book is truly dis-
quieting. Considering it in the aggregate, one finds it difficult to escape
the conclusion that Barack Hussein Obama, as president of the United
States, was not only uninterested in working for the general welfare of
the United States and the benefit of American citizens, but was actively
working against the interests of the United States. Now those who share
his perspective and goals are back in power in Joe Biden's ostensible
presidency. Even worse, the all-pervasive influence of the establishment
media, which served for the eight years of his presidency and beyond
as essentially a propaganda apparatus to secure popular approval of

his program, was extremely successful in normalizing Obama's radical, far-left agenda for the American people. The unanimous support of the Democratic Party, pursuing its own narrow self-interest and the continuation of programs that profited its elected officials, also served to ensure that Obama and his allies would be able to pursue their dangerous vision with virtually no opposition at all. All of this could have been seen before it unfolded, and it was. However, any dissenting voices that did materialize, meanwhile, were and are stigmatized and demonized as "racist," opposed to Obama not because of his socialism, his internationalism, and his disdain for both national security and for America's allies, but solely because of the color of his skin. This charge was bitterly ironic in light of all that Obama did to exacerbate, rather than calm, racial tensions.

Barack Obama himself gave a hint of what was to come during his first campaign for the presidency in 2008. A wire service photo captured him crossing an airplane tarmac holding Fareed Zakaria's book *The Post-American World*; Obama was holding his place in the book with his finger, as if he didn't dare put it down and lose his place. Zakaria described his book this way: "This is not a book about the decline of America, but rather about the rise of everyone else." In it, he detailed a scenario that leftists are doing their best to bring upon America, or to which they are endeavoring to draw us back. Zakaria's ideal world is one in which the United States would "no longer dominate the global economy, orchestrate geopolitics, or overwhelm cultures." He asserts that the "rise of the rest" is the "great story of our time, and one that will reshape the world. The tallest buildings, biggest dams, largest-selling movies, and most advanced cell phones are all being built outside the United States. This economic growth is producing political confidence, national pride, and potentially international problems."

Zakaria's book predicting America's inevitable decline turned out to be a veritable blueprint for Obama's presidency. Throughout his eight years in office, as this present book abundantly illustrates, Obama seemed determined to make Zakaria's "post-American world" a self-fulfilling prophesy. Obama went to work from his first day in office to make Zakaria's wishful thinking about America's decline become a reality. As the most powerful man in the world, he would level the playing field, even if it meant cutting America off at the knees. Good and evil would be made equivalent, with evil sanctioned by the world's only remaining superpower: democracy and tyranny, dictator and elected leader would be given the same moral sanction.

Now, after four unexpected years of an America-First president who did all he could to restore the safety and prosperity of Americans after the devastation of eight years of Obama's socialist internationalism, Barack Obama's third term has begun, in the guise of the Biden/Harris administration. The defeat of Donald Trump and the restoration of the political establishment's power makes this present book not just a record of the recent past, but a warning for the Biden years and their aftermath.

After evidence of widespread election fraud of 2020 and the theft of the presidency and the Senate from under the noses of a complacent and compromised Republican establishment, the Trump administration has ended, but the pro-American policies that Trump offered and implemented as an antidote to the managed decline of the Obama years are not dead. This book stands as a warning and as a primer on just how devastating Obamaism was for the United States and will be again unless vigilant, courageous, and patriotic American citizens stand, determined to employ all lawful means to defend freedom.

Barack Obama is no longer president, although suspicions remain that it is he who is calling the shots in the Biden administration. Thus the scourge of his administration is now being revisited upon the American people. This is the book to give to those who are skeptical or uninformed about just how much damage this shadowy and ultimately mysterious individual has done and is still doing.

ENDNOTES

Foreword by General Michael Flynn

1   Alexandra Del Rosario, "Barack Obama Explains to Stephen Colbert the Satisfaction of Being President, What A Third Term Could Have Looked Like," *Deadline,* November 30, 2020.

2   "Yemeni Nationals on Terror Watch List Arrested at California-Mexico Border," *CBSLA,* April 5, 2021.

3   Robert Spencer, "Is Customs and Border Protection Covering Up the Arrest of Two Yemenis on the Terror Watch List?, *PJ Media,* April 6, 2021.

4   Adam Kredo, "Palestinians Funneled Hundreds of Millions to Terrorists, State Dept Report Reveals," *Washington Free Beacon,* March 22, 2021.

1: "Obama: The Young Communist I Knew"

1   Barrington Moore, *Social Origins of Dictatorship and Democracy: Lord and Peasant in the Making of the Modern World*, Beacon Press, reprint edition, 1993.

2: "The Marxist Origins and Goals of Obamacare"

1   Brett Samuels, "Trump: I think Sanders is a Communist," *The Hill*, Feb. 2, 1920: https://thehill.com/homenews/administration/481112-trump-i-think-sanders-is-a-communist

2   National Nurses United Press Release, "Largest U.S. Nurses' Union Champions New Medicare for All House Bill," Feb. 26, 2019:https://www.nationalnursesunited.org/press/largest-us-nurses-union-champions-new-medicare-all-house-bill

3   Randi Storch, *Red Chicago: American Communism at Its Grassroots, 1928–35*, University of Illinois Press, Dec. 12, 2008, p. 207.

4   "Appendix IX," *Publication of the Special Committee on Un-American Activities*. House of Representatives, Seventy-Eighth Congress, Second Session, on "House Resolution. 282," "Committee Print, Appendix—Part IX, Communist Front Organizations with Special Reference to The National Citizens Political Action Committee." p. 261–248, Item 30, *American Student Union*, p. 514–523, Quentin Young on p.523.

5   "Dr. Quentin Young with Sen. Barack Obama," *Physicians for a National Health Program newsletter.* July 9, 2008: http://www.pnhp.org/news/2008/july/dr_quentin_young_wi.php

6   John Dittmer, *The Good Doctors: The Medical Committee for Human Rights and the Struggle for Social Justice in Health Care*, University Press of Mississippi, Jan. 31, 2017 reprint edition, p.199.

7   "Ben Green," *Keywiki:* https://keywiki.org/Ben_Green

8   William H. Tucker, *Princeton Radicals of the 1960s, Then and Now*, McFarland & Company, Sept. 9, 2015, p.181.

9   "The Theory and Practice of Communism, (People's Republic of China), Hearings," *United States Congress, House Internal Security,* page 2690; "Ben Green," *Keywiki:* https://keywiki.org/Ben_Green; "The Theory and Practice of Communism, (People's Republic of China), Hearings," *United States Congress, House Internal Security,* page 2690.

10   "Young, Quentin, 1923–2016," Northwestern University Archival and Manuscript Collections: https://findingaids.library.northwestern.edu/agents/people/1812

11   Theodore M. Brown, Elizabeth Fee, and Michael N. Healey, "Quentin Young (1923–2016): Advocate, Activist, and 'Rebel Without a Pause,'" *Am J Public Health,* June 2016: https://www.ncbi.nlm.nih.gov/pmc/articles/PMC4880246/

12   "About PNHP," *Physicians for a National Health Program* website, Accessed Jan. 1, 2020: https://pnhp.org/about/

13   Steve Tarzynski, M.D., "Health Care: The Crucial Year Ahead," *Democratic Left,* January/February 1994, pp.2 and 23: https://democraticleft.dsausa.org/files/sites/6/2018/12/DL_1994_V022_01_final.pdf.

14   "On the Struggle for Universal Health Care: A statement from the DSA National Political Committee," *Democratic Left,* June 2009, pp.3 and 16: https://democraticleft.dsausa.org/files/sites/6/2018/12/DL_2009_V037_01.pdf

15   Michael Lighty, "The Fight for Single-Payer, Version 2007," *Democratic Left,* Winter 2007, p.14: https://democraticleft.dsausa.org/files/sites/6/2018/12/DL_2008_V035_03.pdf

16   Russell Mokhiber, "My Work is Unfinished: Quentin Young, MD, Doctor to MLK and Single-Payer Advocate," *Counterpunch*, March 10, 2016: https://www.counterpunch.org/2016/03/10/my-work-is-unfinished-quentin-young-md-doctor-to-mlk-and-single-payer-advocate/

17   Ben Smith, "Obama once visited '60s radicals," *Politico*, Feb. 22, 2008: https://www.politico.com/story/2008/02/obama-once-visited-60s-radicals-008630

18   "Chicago DSA Debs Dinner 2002 program," *KeyWiki:* https://keywiki.org/File:8002.jpg; Leon Despres and Kenan Heise. *Challenging the Daley Machine: a Chicago Alderman's Memoir,* Northwestern University Press, April 20, 2005, p. 24; *Daily Herald,* March 6, 2000, Sec. 1, p.7.

19   Amy Goodman, "Dr. Quentin Young, Longtime Obama Confidante and Physician to MLK, Criticizes Admin's Rejection of Single-Payer Healthcare," *Democracy Now!,* March 11, 2009: https://www.democracynow.org/2009/3/11/dr_quentin_young_obama_confidante_and

20   "Quentin Young, Early Supporter of Obama, Now Disappointed and Saddened," *Corporate Crime Reporter,* Jan. 28, 2008: https://www.corporatecrimereporter.com/obama012808.htm

21   Bruce Dixon, "Barack Obama: Hypocrisy on Health Care," *Thomas Paine's Corner,* Feb. 3, 2007: https://web.archive.org/web/20070704224554/http://civillibertarian.blogspot.com/2007/02/barack-obama-hypocrisy-on-health-care.html

22   Nancy Kleniewski, "Socialist Notes," *Democratic Left,* May 1989, p.7: https://democraticleft.dsausa.org/files/sites/6/2019/01/DL_1980_V008_05_final.pdf

23   Ibid.

24   John McDonough, *Harvard School of Public Health,* July 21, 2012: https://www.hsph.harvard.edu/john-mcdonough/

25   Trevor Loudon, "The Enemies Within: Healthcare Agenda," *YouTube,* May 2, 2017: https://www.youtube.com/watch?v=KiAZfk6nWks

26   David McLanahan, "Dr. Quentin Young at Physicians for a National Health Program Western Washington Chapter's Annual Public Meeting-YouTube Sharing.mov," YouTube, Mar 9, 2012: https://www.youtube.com/watch?v=zSHxSdVh4T8; Robin Huebner, "Fargo man first in ND to get medical degree in Cuba," *Grand Forks Herald,* Jan. 2, 2018: https://www.grandforksherald.com/news/4382173-fargo-man-first-nd-get-medical-degree-cuba.

27   Gerald Friedman, "I-1600 is a giant step forward for Washington, and for the United States," *Medium,* April 22, 2018: https://web.archive.org/web/20200217195049/https://medium.com/@geraldfriedman/i-1600-is-a-giant-step-forward-for-washington-and-for-the-united-states-9fed46efeae0

28   Gerald Friedman, "A Century and Counting: The Campaign for National Health Insurance," *Democratic Left,* Sept. 30, 2013: https://www.dsausa.org/democratic-left/national_health_insurance/

29   David McLanahan, "Gerald Friedman, Ph.D. on economics of health care reform, 8th Annual Public Meeting of PNHPWW," *YouTube,* May 11, 2013: https://www.youtube.com/watch?time_continue=520&v=chTFyxXhW1E&feature=emb_logo

30   Ibid.

3: "Muslim Brotherhood's Penetration of the US under Obama"

1   "Living the Purge, Not Loving It" is adapted from a larger work on Stephen Coughlin's experience with the Muslim Brotherhood in the Pentagon. This portion covers some key aspects of the Muslim Brotherhood influence in the Obama administration.

2   Testimony of FBI Director Mueller, *Federal Bureau of Investigation, HEARING Before the Committee on the Judiciary,* House of Representatives, One Hundred Twelfth Congress, Second Session, Serial No. 112–151, U.S. GPO, May 9, 2012, 30, Mueller stated; "So it is not as if we have purged a substantial amount of our training materials." **NOTE:** The hearing memorialized how brazen, heavy-handed, and un-American the purge was. From the transcript, on page 23 of the testimony, *Rep Coble* made clear he was aware of the purge and its reasons; *"The bipartisan Senate report on the Fort Hood massacre, the, quote, worst terrorist attack on U.S. soil, close quote, since 9/11, found that political correctness inhibited Hasan's superiors from taking actions that may have stopped or at least delayed that attack. Can you see why, given that report, why some of us may be concerned, even worried that 'materials purge' may be another issue or instance of a governmental agency compromising national security under the pressure of political correctness?"* The Judiciary Committee knew the purge was covertly conducted. Because the FBI knew the process would not stand up to scrutiny, it refused to identify the individuals overseeing it when queried by the Committee. Of the five unnamed people in charge of purging content, three were subject matter experts (SMEs) who stood to gain (which is illegal). The three SMEs may not have been US citizens. Rep Gohmert raised this point, on p. 30: *"And, again, the reason I am bringing these things up is because we have got people, we know there are three subject matter experts that your office has refused to identify who have gone through and purged these materials. We were not even told whether they were US citizens, whether they are one of these people that would have gotten the award, that didn't get the award that had all these other suspected problems."* On p.37, Rep Gohmert continued: *"They also said material was pulled from the curriculum if even one component was deemed to, one, include factual errors; two, be in poor taste; three, be stereotypical and; for, four, lack precision. And then we had also gotten—one of the lines that had been purged simply says in training, other self-described jihadist groups can differ with al-Qaeda and like-minded groups in targeting tactical preference and their ultimate political goals, although many jihadist groups overlap in terms of target tactics and goals. And apparently that was found to be offensive to say that there were some jihadist groups that overlap in terms of target because apparently that fits the criteria of being stereotypical. And I want to go back to the subject matter experts. You have mentioned, as we have been told, there were five subject matter experts that were doing this purge and that two of them were interagency. But three of them were outside the agency, and we know Imam Magid, the president of the named co-conspirator in the Holy Land Foundation trial, for which there was plenty of evidence, as the Fifth Circuit Court of Appeals said, to substantiate that they were supporting terrorism, even though the Attorney General decided he did not want to pursue them, or his office—he didn't take credit for that decision, but—and, in fact, he left that to an acting U.S. Attorney to say that there wasn't evidence when, actually, he was on the record before the district court and the Fifth Circuit saying there was plenty of evidence there."* https://www.govinfo.gov/content/pkg/CHRG-112hhrg74121/pdf/CHRG-112hhrg74121.pdf

3   Yuri Bezmenov, "Deception Was My Job," G. Edward Griffin's 1984 interview, Soviet Subversion of the Free World Press, 1984, YouTube https://www.youtube.com/watch?v=AhAzGLb1j40; beginning 1:07:20, *Bezmenov: "Ideological subversion* is the process which is legitimate, overt, and open . . . There is nothing to do with espionage . . . The main emphasis of the KGB is not in the area of intelligence . . . only about 15% of time, money, and manpower is spent on espionage as such. The other 85% is a slow process, which we call either *ideological subversion,* or *active measures,* Активные мероприятия [*aktivniye meropriyatiya*] in the language of the KGB, or *psychological warfare.* What it basically means is to change the perception of reality of every American, to such an extent, that despite the abundance of information, no one is able to come to sensible conclusions, in the interests of defending themselves, their families, their community, and their country."

4   While this paper uses the popular term "*deep state,*" because this paper explains the purge in terms of political warfare, the more precise term is "*counter-state.*" For a more detailed analysis of political warfare, see in Higgins and Coughlin's "*Defeating the Islamic Movement Inside the United States: A Strategic Plan,*" 2016 and "*Re-Remembering the Mis-Remembered Left: The Left's Strategy and Tactics To Transform America,*" 2016.

5   Crossfire Hurricane was a deep state effort to purposefully subvert the electoral process, then a presidential candidate, then a president elect, and finally a sitting president, with the assistance of foreign nationals with foreign allegiances through constructed narratives supported by manufactured evidence.

6   For a detailed initial analysis of the substance of the issues associated with the purge and the *CVE,* see Part VII "Catastrophic Failures" of *Catastrophic Failure: Blindfolding America in the Face of Jihad, CSP Press,* 2015.

7   "Deracinate," *Merriam-Webster Dictionary;* "1: uproot; 2: to remove or separate from a native environment or culture," https://www.merriam-webster.com/dictionary/deracinate

8   National Strategy for Countering Domestic Terrorism, National Security Council, The White House, June, 2021: https://www.whitehouse.gov/wp-content/uploads/2021/06/National-Strategy-for-Countering-Domestic-Terrorism.pdf

9   "*Farhana Khera Letter to John Brennan,*" Assistant to the President for Homeland Security and Counterterrorism and Deputy National Security Advisor, The White House, signed by, among others, numerous organizations known to be associated with the Muslim Brotherhood, PDF document dated 19 October 2011. "We urge you to create an interagency taskforce, led by the White House, tasked with the following responsibilities: 2. Purge *all* federal government training materials of biased materials; 3. Implement a mandatory re-training program for FBI agents, U.S. Army officers, and all federal, state and local law enforcement who have been subjected to biased training; 4. Ensure that personnel reviews are conducted and all trainers and other government employees who promoted biased trainers and training materials are effectively disciplined; 5. Implement quality control processes to ensure that bigoted trainers and biased materials are not developed or utilized in the future."

10   James Barrett, "Loretta Lynch Vows to Prosecute those Who Use 'Anti-Muslim' Speech the 'Edges Towards Violence'," *DailyWire,* December 4, 2015, 2015, https://www.dailywire.com/news/loretta-lynch-vows-prosecute-those-who-use-anti-james-barrett; see also *Muslim Advocates* Tagline—Freedom and Justice for All—an MB Indicator, https://unconstrainedanalytics.org/wp-content/uploads/2019/12/Muslim-Advocates-Tagline-Freedom-Justice-for-All-an-MB-Indicator-r.pdf

11   "MB Announces Establishment of Political Party: Freedom and Justice," *IkhwanWeb,* February 21, 2011, https://ikhwanweb.com/article.php?id=28077; see also Freedom & Justice a Muslim Brotherhood Indicator, https://unconstrainedanalytics.org/wp-content/uploads/2019/12/Freedom-Justice-a-Muslim-Brotherhood-Indicator-r.pdf

12   For example, see Sayyid Qutb, Milestones, *Salimiah,* (Kuwait: International Islamic Federation of Student Organizations. 1978 [written 1966]), 30, 31. Cite hereafter as Qutb, *Milestones,* Salimiah edition. See also *Muslim Brotherhood Freedom & Justice is Milestones F & J,* https://unconstrainedanalytics.org/wp-content/uploads/2019/12/Muslim-Brotherhood-Freedom-Justice-is-Milestones-F-and-J-r.pdf

13   *United States of America vs. Holy Land Foundation,* United States District Court for Northern District of Texas, Dallas Division, (Case 3:04-cr-00240, Document 656–2), 29 March 2007.

14 Explanatory Memorandum: On the General Strategic Goal for the Group," Mohamed Akram, May 22, 1991, Government Exhibit 003–0085/3:04-CR-240-G U.S. v. HLF, et al., United States District Court, Northern District of Texas, https://unconstrainedanalytics.org/wp-content/uploads/2019/12/HLF-Evidence-Explanatory-Memorandum-seachable-Muslim-Botherhood-NA-1991-r.pdf.

15 *John Brennan Letter to Farhana Khera*, the White House, November 3, 2011, (*Brennan Letter*). https://unconstrainedanalytics.org/wp-content/uploads/2019/12/November-3–2011-John-Brennan-Response-Letter-to-Farhana-Khera-r.pdf

16 Khera Letter, *https://unconstrainedanalytics.org/wp-content/uploads/2019/12/October-19–2011-Farhana-Khera-Letter-to-John-Brennan-r.pdf*

17 See Footnote 4 for the reading of the statements: Testimony of FBI Director Mueller, *Federal Bureau of Investigation, HEARING Before the Committee on the Judiciary*, House of Representatives, One Hundred Twelfth Congress, Second Session, Serial No. 112–151, U.S. GPO, May 9, 2012, 30, 37.

18 *Explanatory Memorandum*: On the General Strategic Goal for the Group," Mohamed Akram, May 22, 1991, Government Exhibit 003–0085/3:04-CR-240-G U.S. v. HLF, et al., United States District Court, Northern District of Texas, https://unconstrainedanalytics.org/wp-content/uploads/2019/12/HLF-Evidence-Explanatory-Memorandum-seachable-Muslim-Botherhood-NA-1991-r.pdf, p.24.

19 "United Front" is a political warfare term from the past that *Unconstrained Analytics, Inc* seeks to rehabilitate. In 2016, it was used to explain the actual relationship between the Islamic Movement and Neo-Marxist organizations in *"Defeating the Islamic Movement Inside the United States: A Strategic Plan,"* in 2019, the concept of united fronts was further developed from the perspective of the Left in *Re-Remembering the Mis-Remembered Left: The Left's Strategy and Tactics To Transform America*, and then, later in 2019, how "hate speech" narratives execute out of a converged united front effort in the memo *"Warning on Racism."*

20 Kareem Shora E-Mails with list of prominent Muslim Brotherhood affiliations, January 2010, *Judicial Watch FOIA* to DHS Regarding January 2010 Meeting, Judicial Watch, March 16, 2010. http://www.judicialwatch.org/files/documents/2010/dhs-napolitano-jan-meeting-docs-1.pdf.

21 Countering Violent Extremism (CVE) Working Group, Homeland Security Advisory Council, Spring 2010, "U.S. Department of Homeland Security, Homeland Security Advisory Council," May 26, 2010 (modified August 3, 2010):https://www.dhs.gov/xlibrary/assets/hsac_cve_working_group_recommendations.pdf

22 "UCMO Joined National Faith Groups and Asked Congress to Increase Funding for NSGP to Make Faith Communities Safter. Congress Approves $180 Million," USCMO Press Release, January 14, 2021: https://uscmo.org/2021/01/14/uscmo-joined-national-faith-groups-and-asked-congress-to-increase-federal-funding-for-nsgp-to-make-faith-communities-safer-congress-approves-180-million/

23 An Introduction to the Department of Homeland Security Nonprofit Security Grant Program, YouTube, February 11, 2021: https://www.youtube.com/watch?v=pa-d7vbjKgY

24 DHS? FEMA Nonprofit Security Grant Program (NSGP) Information, Secure Community Network: https://www.securecommunitynetwork.org/resources/dhs-grant-funds-information

25 Michael G. Masters, Biographical Summary, Degree-Choice Blogspot. https://degree-choice.blogspot.com/2018/05/michael-g-masters.html

26 E. Dyer, "Pentagon Memo Fishing for Counterterrorism Training Standards Leaned Heavily on *WIRED* Reporter's Assertions," *Daily Caller*, November 30, 2011: https://dailycaller.com/2011/11/30/pentagon-memo-fishing-for-counterterrorism-training-standards-leaned-heavily-on-wired-reporters-assertions/

27   Secretary of State Hillary Clinton, "Remarks at the Organization of the Islamic Conference (OIC) High-Level Meeting on Combating Religious Intolerance," Given at the Center for Islamic Arts and History, Istanbul, Turkey, *United States Department of State Release,* July 15, 2011. https://2009–2017.state.gov/secretary/20092013clinton/rm/2011/07/168636.htm, accessed July 21 2011.

28   NPR published "*Terrorism Training Casts Pall Over Muslim Employee,*" Dina Temple-Raston, NPR, July 18, 2011.

29   CAIR demands "CAIR Asks CIA to Drop Islamophobic Trainer," American Muslim News Brief, CAIR, July 18, 2011: https://www.cair.com/cair_asks_cia_to_drop_islamophobic_trainer.

30   NPR published "*Terrorism Training Casts Pall Over Muslim Employee,*" Dina Temple-Raston, NPR, July 18, 2011.

31   *Countering Violent Extremism (CVE) Working Group,* Homeland Security Advisory Council, Spring 2010, "U.S. Department of Homeland Security, Homeland Security Advisory Council," May 26, 2010 (modified August 3, 2010)" https://www.dhs.gov/xlibrary/assets/hsac_cve_working_group_recommendations.pdf

32   *Redacted—Unclassified—E-Mail Postponement Announcement:* https://unconstrainedanalytics.org/wp-content/uploads/2019/12/July-22–2011-REDACTED-UNCLASSIFIED-E-Mail-from-CIA-Postponement-Announcement-Conference-on-Homegrown-Radical-Extremism-r.pdf

33   *JournoList,* sometimes called the J-List, is a *Google Group* composed of prominent left-wing academics, political activists, and journalists. In the 2008 presidential election, journalists on the *JournoList*—including reporters from *Time, Newsweek, The Associated Press, Reuters, The Washington Post, The New York Times, Politico, Bloomberg, Huffington Post, PBS,* and *NPR*—coordinated and colluded in their reporting of the 2008 presidential election in support of Barrack Obama and far-left-leaning candidates.

34   J.E. Dyer, "Pentagon Memo Fishing for Counterterrorism Training Standards Leaned Heavily on *WIRED* Reporter's Assertions," *Daily Caller,* November 30, 2011: https://dailycaller.com/2011/11/30/pentagon-memo-fishing-for-counterterrorism-training-standards-leaned-heavily-on-wired-reporters-assertions/

35   Keach Hagey, "Unlike Weigel, Ackerman Keeps Job," *Politico,* July 20, 2010: https://www.politico.com/story/2010/07/unlike-weigel-ackerman-keeps-job-039974#ixzz0ufuJOdHC

36   "Unlike Weigel, Ackerman Keeps Job," https://www.politico.com/story/2010/07/unlike-weigel-ackerman-keeps-job-039974#ixzz0ufuJOdHC

37   Mohamed Elibiary, "M. Elibiary—FBI Training, the Ackerman Expose & American Muslim Community Concerns," *Muslim Matters,* September 18, 2011.

38   Spencer Ackerman, "Video: FBI Trainer Says Forget 'Irrelevant' al-Qaeda, Target Islam," *Wired Magazine,* September 20, 2019.

39   Spencer Ackerman, "Exclusive: Senior U.S. General Orders Top-to-Bottom Review of Military's Islam Training, Spencer Ackerman," *WIRED* Magazine, April 24, 2012.

40   "CAIR Commends Pentagon for Dropping Islamophobic Course," *CAIR Presser,* April 25, 2012: https://www.prnewswire.com/news-releases/cair-commends-pentagon-for-dropping-islamophobic-course-148918715.html

41   Ackerman *WIRED* attack on JFSC, "U.S. Military Taught Officers: Use 'Hiroshima' Tactics for 'Total War' on Islam," Spencer Ackerman, *WIRED Magazine,* May 10, 2012.

42   "CAIR Asks Pentagon to Dismiss Officer Who Taught 'Total War' on Islam," *CAIR Presser,* May 10, 2012: https://myemail.constantcontact.com/CAIR-Asks-Pentagon-to-Dismiss-Officer-Who-Taught—Total-War—on-Islam—-Anti-Sharia-Amendment-Dies-in-Iowa-Legislature.html?soid =1103010792410&aid=lMMnTYlqD4U

43 "Countering Violent Extremism (CVE) Training Guidance & Best Practices," Office for Civil Rights and Civil Liberties, U.S. Department of Homeland Security, October 7, 2011 (modified October 11, 2011):https://www.dhs.gov/xlibrary/assets/cve-training-guidance.pdf

44 Countering Violent Extremism (CVE) Training—Do's and Don'ts, Office of Civil Rights and Civil Liberties, U.S. Department of Homeland Security, October 2011 (estimated date): https://www.scribd.com/document/293418782/Countering-Violent-Extremism-CVE-Training#

45 "Facts on FBI Director Candidates," Key Issues in Islamophobia, CAIR, October 11, 2017: http://www.islamophobia.org/articles/205-facts-on-fbi-director-candidates.html

46 For example, see *Catastrophic Failure: Blindfolding America in the Face of Jihad*, pp.321–332.

47 President Obama's "Remarks by the President to the UN General Assembly," September 25, 2012 (at the 1:14 mark on "President Obama Remarks to the United Nations General Assembly," [2012])" C-SPAN User Clip created May 12, 2013.

48 President Obama, "President Obama: The Full 60 Minutes' Interview," October 12, 2012.

49 Khera Letter, https://unconstrainedanalytics.org/wp-content/uploads/2019/12/October-19–2011-Farhana-Khera-Letter-to-John-Brennan-r.pdf

50 Ibid.

51 Spencer Ackerman, "FBI Crime Maps Now 'Pinpoint' Average Muslims," *WIRED Magazine*, October 24, 2011: https://www.wired.com/2011/10/fbi-geomaps-muslims

52 ACLU Letter to FBI Director Robert Mueller, ACLU, October 4, 2011: https://www.aclu.org/files/assets/sign_on_letter_to_dir_mueller_re_radicalization_report_10.4.11.pdf

53 Ibid.

54 Spencer Ackerman, 'New Evidence of Anti-Islam Bias Underscores Deep Challenges for FBI's Reform Pledge,' *WIRED MAGAZINE*, Sept. 23, 2011: http://www.wired.com/dangerroom/2011/09/fbi-islam-domination/all/1

55 Major Stephen Coughlin, "'To Our Great Detriment,' Ignoring what Extremists say about Jihad," Joint Military Intelligence College—JMIC (now the National Intelligence University) in furtherance of his Master of Science Strategic Intelligence, July 2007, p.4.

56 The Staff Package, Mayorga Memorandum, October 14, 2011: https://unconstrainedanalytics.org/wp-content/uploads/2019/12/STAFF-ACTION-Package-October-14–2011-Violent-Extremist-Briefers-ASD-Mayorga-OSD-SACCP-JS-JSAP-TAB-A-r-.pdf

57 The Staff Package, Mayorga Memorandum, TAB A—The Ackerman Article, October 5, 2011. (NOTE: *"The Staff Package"* refers to ASD Mayorga's Memorandum, the associated TAB A—Ackerman article, the associated OSD SACCP, and the Joint Staff JSAP): https://unconstrainedanalytics.org/wp-content/uploads/2019/12/STAFF-ACTION-Package-October-14–2011-Violent-Extremist-Briefers-ASD-Mayorga-OSD-SACCP-JS-JSAP-TAB-A-r-.pdf

58 The Staff Package, Attachment: TAB A: Spencer Ackerman's *Wired.com* article refers to Ackerman's, "Justice Department Official: Muslim 'Juries' Threaten 'Our Values'," *WIRED Magazine*, Oct. 5, 2011, https://www.wired.com/2011/10/islamophobia-beyond-fbi/

59 Khera Letter: https://unconstrainedanalytics.org/wp-content/uploads/2019/12/October-19–2011-Farhana-Khera-Letter-to-John-Brennan-r.pdf

60 The Staff Package: Mayorga Memorandum, October 14, 2011. https://unconstrainedanalytics.org/wp-content/uploads/2019/12/STAFF-ACTION-Package-October-14–2011-Violent-Extremist-Briefers-ASD-Mayorga-OSD-SACCP-JS-JSAP-TAB-A-r-.pdf

61 Explanatory Memorandum: On the General Strategic Goal for the Group," Mohamed Akram, May 22, 1991, Government Exhibit 003–0085/3:04-CR-240-G U.S. v. HLF, et al., United States District Court, Northern District of Texas, https://unconstrainedanalytics.org/wp-content/uploads/2019/12/HLF-Evidence-Explanatory-Memorandum-seachable-Muslim-Botherhood-NA-1991-r.pdf, 21. In full, from "4. Understanding the Role of the Muslim Brotherhood in North America," the sentence is; "The *Ikhwan* must understand that their work in America is a kind of *grand Jihad* in eliminating and destroying the Western civilization from within and "sabotaging" its miserable house by their hands and the hands of the believers so that it is eliminated and God's religion is made victorious over all other religions."

62 The Staff Package, OSD SACCP, October 17, 2011. https://unconstrainedanalytics.org/wp-content/uploads/2019/12/STAFF-ACTION-Package-October-14–2011-Violent-Extremist-Briefers-ASD-Mayorga-OSD-SACCP-JS-JSAP-TAB-A-r-.pdf

63 Ibid.

64 Spencer Ackerman, "New Evidence of Anti-Islam Bias Underscores Deep Challenges for FBI's Reform Pledge," *WIRED Magazine*, Sept. 23, 2011: http://www.wired.com/dangerroom/2011/09/fbi-islam-domination/all/1.

65 Stephen Coughlin, "America at the Crossroads—2010," February 19, 2010 as posted on YouTube as "Steve Coughlin's Speech on Jihad and Islam for Freedom Defense Initiative," at CPAC, posted by *UAC4America* on YouTube, February 21, 2010: https://www.youtube.com/watch?v=Ty0xe8OyPjY

66 Ackerman innuendo in 'New Evidence'—Sept 23, 2011—Refuted by his own Source America at the Crossroads plus," PDF from presentations Ackerman published: https://unconstrainedanalytics.org/wp-content/uploads/2019/12/Ackerman-innuendo-in-New-Evidence-Sept-23–2011-Refuted-by-his-own-Source-America-at-Crossroads-plus-r.pdf

67 Ibid.

68 Ibid.

69 Stephen Coughlin, *"Catastrophic Failure: Blindfolding America in the Face of Jihad,"* CSP Press, 2015, 20–21, 69–75, 383–399. Part VII "Catastrophic Failures" breaks down Major Hasan's e-mails to Al-Awlaki.

70 *"Final Report of the William H. Webster Commission"* on *The Federal Bureau of Investigation, Counterterrorism Intelligence, and the Events at Fort Hood, Texas, on November 5, 2009,* 19 July, 2012. https://unconstrainedanalytics.org/wp-content/uploads/2019/12/Final-Report-of-the-William-Webster-Commission-FBI-on-Events-of-Fort-Hood-July-19–2012.pdf

71 "Protecting the Force: Lessons from Fort Hood," Report on the DoD Independent Review, Office of the Secretary of Defense, Department of Defense, 15 January 2010, https://unconstrainedanalytics.org/wp-content/uploads/2019/12/Protecting-the-Force-Lessons-from-Fort-Hood-OSD-January-15–2010.pdf

72 "Countering Violent Extremism—Additional Actions Could Strengthen Training." GAO Report to the Committee on Homeland Security and Government Affairs, United States Senate, GAO-13–79, October 18, 2012, https://www.gao.gov/assets/650/649616.pdf

     Of 24,700 who attended 8,424 provided feedback

     54 cited political bias   .2% of the 24,700 (or .6% for the 8,424)
     12 cited offensive   .05% of the 24,700 (or .1% of the 8,424)
     11 cited inaccurate   .04% of the 24,700 (or .1% of the 8,424)

73 Spencer Ackerman, "Justice Department Official: Muslim 'Juries' Threaten 'Our Values'," *WIRED Magazine,* Oct. 5, 2011: https://www.wired.com/2011/10/islamophobia-beyond-fbi/

74   Oussama Jammal, Speech Given at the "FBI Inventing Terrorists Through Entrapment" forum, 18th Annual MAS ICNA Convention, McCormick Place, Chicago, Illinois, December 28, 2019.

4: "How Obama Enabled the Persecution of Christians"

1   Mario Diaz, "Praying for the Body of Christ in Afghanistan," Concerned Women for America, Sept. 17, 2021: https://concernedwomen.org/praying-for-the-body-of-christ-in-afghanistan/

2   RNS: "Media ministry offers 'lifeline' to fearful Afghans as Taliban kill Christians," Aug. 17, 2021: shttps://religionnews.com/2021/08/17/media-ministry-offers-lifeline-to-fearful-afghans-as-taliban-kill-christians/

3   Open Doors UK, Twitter, Feb. 8, 2022: https://twitter.com/OpenDoorsUK/status/1491313417344499718

4   "Tucker: This is how to humiliate the US," Fox News, Aug. 27, 2021: https://www.foxnews.com/transcript/tucker-carlson-tonight-on-afghanistan-violence-chaos

5   "The Full Text of the NDU Libya Speech," NRO, Mar. 28, 2011: https://www.nationalreview.com/corner/full-text-ndu-libya-speech-nro-staff/

6   "The Rape of Christopher Stevens," RaymondIbrahim.com, Sept. 20, 2012: https://www.raymondibrahim.com/2012/09/20/the-rape-of-christopher-stevens/

7   "Hatred of Christians Unleashed in Libya," RaymondIbrahim.com, Mar. 5, 2013: https://www.raymondibrahim.com/2013/03/05/hatred-of-christians-unleashed-in-libya/

8   "Open Season on Christians in Libya," RaymondIbrahim.com, Mar. 4, 2014.https://gloria.tv/post/B7P1AkTKvgUR1GE3EemkDNZ7a

9   Raymond Ibrahim, "ISIS Slaughters Ethiopian Christians, Vows to Slaughter Western Christians," Christian Post, Apr. 20, 2015: https://www.christianpost.com/news/isis-slaughters-ethiopian-christians-vows-to-slaughter-western-christians.html

10   Raymond Ibrahim, "Largest Massacre of Christians Ignored in Syria," RaymondIbrahim.com, Nov. 21, 2013: https://www.raymondibrahim.com/2013/11/21/largest-massacre-of-christians-in-syria-ignored/

11   رصتنم دلاخ ؟نويحيسملا فاخي اذامل :نولءاست ناوخإلا, ["The Brotherhood Asks: Why Are Christians Afraid?"] El Watan News, May 30, 2012: https://www.elwatannews.com/news/details/10238

12   "Arab Spring Egypt's 'Legal' Persecution of Christians," RaymondIbrahim.com, May 29, 2013: https://www.raymondibrahim.com/2013/05/29/arab-spring-egypts-legal-persecution-of-christians/

13   "In Pictures: Savage Islamic Attack on St. Mark Cathedral Allowed by Egyptian Forces," RaymondIbrahim.com, April 9, 2013: https://www.raymondibrahim.com/2013/04/09/scandal-morsi-government-permits-savage-attack-on-st-mark-cathedral/

14   "Obama to Egyptian Christians: Don't Protest the Brotherhood," RaymondIbrahim.com, Jun. 25, 2013: https://www.raymondibrahim.com/2013/06/25/obama-to-egyptian-christians-dont-protest-the-brotherhood/

15   "Statement by the Press Secretary on Violence in Egypt," ObamaWhiteHouse.gov, Oct. 10, 2011: https://obamawhitehouse.archives.gov/the-press-office/2011/10/10/statement-press-secretary-violence-egypt

16   Pete Winn, "State Department Purges Religious Freedom Section from Its Human Rights Reports," CNS News, Jun 7, 2012: https://www.cnsnews.com/news/article/state-department-purges-religious-freedom-section-its-human-rights-reports

17   Ibid.

18   "Why Is President Obama Silent on Religious Freedom in Saudi Arabia?" *Charisma News*, Mar. 3, 2014: https://www.charismanews.com/world/43327-why-is-president-obama-silent-on-religious-freedom-in-saudi-arabia

19   Sarah Kaplan, "Has the world 'looked the other way' while Christians are killed?" *Washington Post*, Apr. 7, 2015: https://www.washingtonpost.com/news/morning-mix/wp/2015/04/07/has-the-world-looked-the-other-way-while-christians-are-killed/

20   "US Failed to Attend UN Security Council Session of Mideast Christians," *WorldTribune.com*, Apr. 3, 2015: http://www.worldtribune.com/2015/04/03/u-s-failed-to-attend-un-security-council-session-on-genocide-of-mideast-christians/

21   Kirsten Powers, "How long will President Obama stay silent on genocide?" *USAToday.com*, Mar. 15, 2016: https://www.usatoday.com/story/opinion/2016/03/14/genocide-christians-middle-east-islamic-state-isil-daesh-obama-column/81769056/

22   "Press Briefing by Press Secretary Josh Earnest, *ObamaWhiteHouse.com*, Feb. 29, 2016: https://obamawhitehouse.archives.gov/the-press-office/2016/02/29/press-briefing-press-secretary-josh-earnest-2292016

23   Matt Lew and Rich Lardner, "House passes resolution condemning IS atrocities as genocide," *APnews.com*, Mar. 14, 2016: https://apnews.com/fe27d841e3684195807a9a874e356ddd

24   Ali Ghraib, "Obama still won't refer to the Armenian genocide by name. He should end the charade," *TheGuardian.com*, Apr. 23, 2015: https://www.theguardian.com/commentisfree/2015/apr/23/obama-armenian-genocide-end-the-charade

25   William Bigelow, "Mainstream Media Refuses to Condemn Obama for Broken Promise on Armenian Genocide," *Breitbart.com*, Apr. 23, 2015: https://www.breitbart.com/the-media/2015/04/23/mainstream-media-refuses-to-condemn-obama-for-broken-promise-on-armenian-genocide/

26   Juliet Eilperin, "Obama calls idea of screening Syrian refugees based on religion 'shameful,' defends White House strategy," *Washington Post*, Nov. 16, 2015: https://www.washingtonpost.com/news/post-politics/wp/2015/11/16/obama-calls-idea-of-screening-syrian-refugees-based-on-religion-shameful-defends-white-house-strategy/?noredirect=on

27   Patrick Goodenough, "So Far: Syrian Refugees in U.S. Include 2,098 Muslims, 53 Christians," CNSnews, Nov. 17, 2015: https://www.cnsnews.com/news/article/patrick-goodenough/syrian-christians-are-greatest-peril-least-likely-be-admitted

28   Patrick Goodenough, "Record 499 Syrian Refugees Admitted to US So Far in May Includes No Christians," *CNSnews*, May 23 2016: https://www.cnsnews.com/news/article/patrick-goodenough/may-brings-biggest-monthly-number-syrian-refugee-arrivals-conflict

29   Phillip Connor, "US admits record number of Muslim refugees in 2016," *Pew Research Center*, Oct. 5, 2016: https://www.pewresearch.org/fact-tank/2016/10/05/u-s-admits-record-number-of-muslim-refugees-in-2016/

30   Patrick Goodenough, "Federal Judge Concerned About Small Number of Christians Among Syrian Refugees Admitted to US," *CNSnews*, Nov. 7, 2016: https://www.cnsnews.com/news/article/patrick-goodenough/federal-judge-concerned-about-small-number-christians-among-syrian

31   Raymond Ibrahim, "Christians Persecuted by Muslims Even in the West," *Gatestone Institute*, Oct. 20, 2015: https://www.gatestoneinstitute.org/6701/christians-persecuted-in-west

32   Raymond Ibrahim, "Muslim Refugees Drown Christian Refugees for Being 'Infidels,'" *RaymondIbrahim.com*, Apr. 17, 2015: https://www.raymondibrahim.com/2015/04/17/refugee-muslims-drown-christian-refugees-for-being-infidels/

33   WikiLeaks. *Asian American Candidates, Muslim American Candidates:* https://wikileaks.org/podesta-emails/emailid/28660

34   Timothy C. Morgan, "Sister Momeka: Liberate Christian Lands from ISIS," *ChristianityToday.com,* May 15, 2015: https://www.christianitytoday.com/news/2015/april/iraqi-christian-leader-denied-us-visa.html

35   "Revs. Rodriguez & Moore Call on the U.S. State Department to Reverse Its Decision to Deny a VISA to Iraq's 'Mother Teresa,'" *PRNewswire,* Apr. 30, 2015: https://www.prnewswire.com/news-releases/revs-rodriguez—moore-call-on-the-us-state-department-to-reverse-its-decision-to-deny-a-visa-to-iraqs-mother-teresa-300075380.html

36   Institute for Global Engagement. https://www.facebook.com/permalink.php?story_fbid=973859 425988072&id=137613622945994

37   Cathy Burke, "Outraged Newsmax TV Viewers Help Bring Iraqi Nun to US," *Newsmax.com,* May 8, 2015: https://www.newsmax.com/Headline/Johnnie-Moore-nun-granted-visa/2015/05/08/id/643594/

38   Peter Run, "Is Nigeria doomed to follow Sudan's example?" *ABC.net,* Apr. 21, 2011: https://mobile.abc.net.au/news/2011–04–21/is-nigeria-doomed-to-follow-sudane28099s-example3f/97708?pfm redir=sm&pfm=sm

39   For President Buhari's role, see Raymond Ibrahim, "New Revelation: Previous US Administration Facilitated Christian Genocide in Nigeria," *Gatestone Institute,* Dec. 23, 2018: https://www.gatestoneinstitute.org/13447/obama-christian-genocide-nigeria

40   Samuel Ogundipe, "Nigeria: How Obama Plotted My Defeat in 2015—Goodluck Jonathan," *AllAfrica.com,* Nov. 20, 2018: https://allafrica.com/stories/201811200464.html

41   Joseph DeCaro, "Muslim Group Demands Christian Prez Convert, or Resign," *Worthy News,* Aug. 11, 2012: https://www.worthynews.com/11679-muslim-group-demands-christian-prez-convert-or-resign

42   Ryan Mauro, "Finally: U.S. Names Boko Haram as Foreign Terrorist Organization," *Clarion Project,* Nov. 14, 2013: https://clarionproject.org/finally-us-names-boko-haram-foreign-terrorist-organization/

43   Elizabeth, Harrington, "'Religion Is Not Driving Extremist Violence' in Nigeria, Says Obama Official, After Church Bombings," *CNSnews,* Apr. 10, 2012: https://www.cnsnews.com/news/article/religion-not-driving-extremist-violence-nigeria-says-obama-official-after-church

44   "Bill Clinton Says Poverty Is Fueling Violence in Nigeria," *NewsOne,* Feb. 4, 2012: https://newsone.com/1872805/bill-clinton-says-poverty-is-fueling-violence-in-nigeria/

45   Steve Peacock, "Obama: Slaughter of Christians a Misunderstanding," *WND,* May 20, 2012: https://www.wnd.com/2012/05/obama-slaughter-of-christians-a-misunderstanding/

46   Lanre Ola, "Nigeria bombs Islamists, U.S. sound alarm," *Reuters,* May 17, 2013: https://www.reuters.com/article/us-nigeria-violence-raids/nigeria-bombs-islamists-u-s-sounds-alarm-idUSBRE94G0AF20130517

47   Michael Carl, "U.S. Blocks Christian Governor from Nigeria Peace Talks," *WND,* Mar. 28, 2014: https://www.wnd.com/2014/03/u-s-blocks-christian-governor-from-nigeria-peace-talks/

5: "Obama's Betrayal of Israel"

1   "Obama's Speech at AIPAC." *NPR,* June 4, 2008: https://www.npr.org/templates/story/story.php?storyId=91150432

2   "Obama Says He Used 'Poor Phrasing' on Jerusalem." *Reuters,* July 13, 2008: https://www.reuters.com/article/us-usa-politics-obama-jerusalem/obama-says-he-used-poor-phrasing-on-jerusalem-idUSN1337076120080713; Ronen, Gil. "Obama Gives Final Burial to 'Undivided Jerusalem' Statement." *Arutz 7,* 14 July 2008: http://www.israelnationalnews.com/News/News.aspx/126832

3   Zimmerman, Eric. "Clinton Says Israel Announcement 'Insulting to the United States." *The Hill,* Mar. 13, 2010. https://thehill.com/blogs/blog-briefing-room/news/86569-clinton-says-israel-announcement-insulting-to-the-united-states; Keinon, Herb, and Hilary Leila Krieger. "'We'll Prevent Future Embarrassments.'" *Jerusalem Post,* Mar. 14, 2010: https://www.jpost.com/Israel/Well-prevent-future-embarrassments

4   Tau, Byron. "Jerusalem Capital Plank Not Included in DNC Platform." *Politico,* Sept. 4, 2012: https://www.politico.com/blogs/politico44/2012/09/jerusalem-capital-plank-not-included-in-dnc-platform-134317

5   "Convention Floor Erupts as Dems Restore References to God, Jerusalem in Platform." *FOX News,* Sept. 5, 2012: https://www.foxnews.com/politics/convention-floor-erupts-as-dems-restore-references-to-god-jerusalem-in-platform

6   Greenfield, Daniel. "Kerry Says Only Muslims, Not Jews, May Pray at Jewish Holy Site." *Front Page Magazine,* Oct. 31, 2014: https://www.frontpagemag.com/point/244226/kerry-says-only-muslims-not-jews-may-pray-jewish-daniel-greenfield

7   Greenfield, Daniel. "Biden's Chanukah Gift to Israel is Seizing Jerusalem for the Islamic Terrorists Killing Jews." *Frontpage Magazine,* Nov 9, 2021: https://www.frontpagemag.com/fpm/2021/11/bidens-chanukah-gift-israel-seizing-jerusalem-daniel-greenfield/

8   Lederman, Josh. "Dropped for Meeting Hamas, Rob Malley Is Now Obama's 'Czar' for Tackling Islamic State." *Times of Israel,* Dec. 11, 2015: https://www.timesofisrael.com/can-one-time-proponent-of-outreach-to-islamists-get-obamas-is-strategy-in-sync/

9   Jalil, Justin. "Congress's Black Caucus Firmly against Netanyahu, Newsweek Says." *Times of Israel,* Mar. 28, 2015: https://www.timesofisrael.com/congresss-black-caucus-firmly-against-netanyahu-newsweek-says/

10   Entous, Adam, and Danny Yadron. "Spy Net on Israel Snares Congress." *Wall Street Journal,* Dec. 29, 2015: https://www.wsj.com/articles/u-s-spy-net-on-israel-snares-congress-1451425210

11   Benjamin J. Rhodes, "The World as It Is: a Memoir of the Obama White House." *The World as It Is: a Memoir of the Obama White House,* Random House, 2018, p. 146.

12   "AIPAC: Obama Administration Peddling 'Inaccuracies' about Us." *Times of Israel,* Aug. 12, 2015: https://www.timesofisrael.com/aipac-obama-administration-peddling-inaccuracies-about-us/

13   Puder, Joseph. "Obama's Shift from AIPAC to J Street." *Front Page Magazine,* Sept. 25, 2013: https://www.frontpagemag.com/fpm/205428/obamas-shift-aipac-j-street-joseph-puder

14   "In Cleveland, Obama Speaks on Jewish Issues." *New York Sun,* Feb. 25, 2008: https://www.nysun.com/national/in-cleveland-obama-speaks-on-jewish-issues/71813/

15   Harel, Amos, and Avi Issacharoff. "Hamas Boosting Anti-Aircraft Arsenal with Looted Libyan Missiles." *Haaretz,* Oct. 27, 2011: https://www.haaretz.com/1.5203865

6: "How Obama Funded the Murder of Israelis"

1   Ruthie Blum, "Widow of Terrorist Who Committed Deadly Jerusalem Truck-Ramming Attack to Receive $760 Lifetime Monthly Allowance From Palestinian Authority," *Algemeiner.com,* Jan. 11, 2017: https://www.algemeiner.com/2017/01/11/widow-of-terrorist-who-committed-deadly-jerusalem-truck-ramming-attack-to-receive-760-lifetime-monthly-allowance-from-palestinian-authority/.

2   Dan Diker, "Understanding Israel's Assessment of ISIS-Inspired Terrorism." *The Jerusalem Post,* Jan. 12, 2017: https://www.jpost.com/Opinion/Understanding-Israels-assessment-of-ISIS-inspired-terrorism-478163.

3   Itamar Marcus and Nan Jacques Zilberdik. "PA: Terrorist Who Killed Four in Truck Ramming Attack Died for Allah: PMW Analysis." *Palestinian Media Watch,* Jan. 10, 2017: https://palwatch. org/page/11467.

4   Matthew Lee, "US Sent $221 Million to Palestinians in Obama's Last Hours," *Associated Press,* Jan. 23, 2017: https://apnews.com/b8446cbf5b504b1abaf49eb0d646367b/US-sent-$221-million-to-Palestinians-in-Obama's-last-hours.

5   Lieber, Dov. "PA Payments to Prisoners, 'Martyr' Families Now Equal Half Its Foreign Budgetary Aid." *The Times of Israel,* July 31, 2017: https://www.timesofisrael.com/pa-payments-to-prisoners-martyr-families-now-equal-half-its-foreign-aid/.

6   Anna Ahronheim, "2017 Numbers: Terrorists Slayed 20 Israelis, 3,617 Palestinians Arrested," *The Jerusalem Post,* Jan. 7, 2018: https://www.jpost.com/Arab-Israeli-Conflict/Terrorists-killed-20-Israelis-in-2017-533008.

7   David Israel, "Terrorist Who Murdered Salomon Family: I Picked a House with Sounds of Laughter," *The Jewish Press,* Oct. 4, 2018: https://www.jewishpress.com/news/eye-on-palestine/palestinian-authority/terrorist-who-murdered-salomon-family-i-picked-a-house-with-sounds-of-laughter/2018/10/04/.

8   "Defense Ministry: Terrorists Will Get NIS 10 Million Each from PA," *The Times of Israel,* May 6, 2018: https://www.timesofisrael.com/defense-ministry-terrorists-will-get-nis-10-million-each-from-pa/.

9   Steven Stotsky, "Does Foreign Aid Fuel Palestinian Violence?" *Middle East Forum,* 2008: https://www.meforum.org/1926/does-foreign-aid-fuel-palestinian-violence/.

10   "U.S. Foreign Aid to the Palestinians," *Congressional Research Service,* Mar. 18, 2016: https://www.everycrsreport.com/files/20160318_RS22967_2711096fe48c81141d951aaab19d3bcca0e7fe71.pdf.

11   Adam Kredo, "Obama Admin Provided Iranian Terror Orgs With $37.4M in Cash," *Washington Free Beacon,* Sept. 13, 2016: https://freebeacon.com/national-security/report-obama-admin-provided-iranian-terror-orgs-37–4-million-cash/.

12   Saeed Ghasseminejad, "Iranian Officials: Obama-Era Prisoner Release Was 'Ransom,'" *Foundation for Defense of Democracies,* Oct. 24, 2018: https://www.fdd.org/analysis/2017/03/03/iranian-officials-obama-era-prisoner-release-was-ransom/.

13   "Statement from the President on the Designation of the Islamic Revolutionary Guard Corps as a Foreign Terrorist Organization," *The White House,* The United States Government, Apr. 8, 2019: https://www.whitehouse.gov/briefings-statements/statement-president-designation-islamic-revolutionary-guard-corps-foreign-terrorist-organization/.

14   Pete Kasperowicz, "State Department Can't Say Who in Iran Got Another $1.3 Billion," *Washington Examiner,* Aug. 22, 2016: https://www.washingtonexaminer.com/state-department-cant-say-who-in-iran-got-another-13-billion.

15   "The Obama Administration Secretly Sought to Give Iran Access to the US Financial System," *Associated Press,* June 6, 2018: https://www.cnbc.com/2018/06/06/the-obama-administration-secretly-sought-to-give-iran-access-to-the-us-financial-system.html.

16   Eli Lake, "U.S. Taxpayers Are Funding Iran's Military Expansion," *Bloomberg.com,* June 9, 2016: https://www.bloomberg.com/view/articles/2016–06–09/u-s-taxpayers-are-funding-iran-s-military-expansion.

17   Adam Kredo, "Obama Admin Provided Iranian Terror Orgs With $37.4M in Cash," *Washington Free Beacon,* Sept. 13, 2016: https://freebeacon.com/national-security/report-obama-admin-provided-iranian-terror-orgs-37–4-million-cash/.

18 Sen. Ashish Kumar. "Iran Admits Giving Hamas Technology for Missiles," *Washington Times,* Nov. 21, 2012: https://www.washingtontimes.com/news/2012/nov/21/iran-admits-giving-hamas-technology-for-missiles/.

19 Carol E. Lee and Jay Solomon. "A Tally of Iran Sanctions Relief Includes More Than $10 Billion in Cash, Gold," *The Wall Street Journal,* Dec. 30, 2016: https://www.wsj.com/articles/a-tally-of-iran-sanctions-relief-includes-more-than-10-billion-in-cash-gold-1483112751.

20 "New Hamas Leader Says It Is Getting Aid Again from Iran," *Associated Press,* Aug. 29, 2017: https://www.cnbc.com/2017/08/29/new-hamas-leader-says-it-is-getting-aid-again-from-iran.html.

21 Michael Bachner, "Iran Said Increasing Hamas Funding to $30m per Month, Wants Intel on Israel." *The Times of Israel,* Aug. 5, 2019: https://www.timesofisrael.com/iran-agrees-to-increase-hamas-funding-to-30-million-per-month-report. /

22 "Iran Provided Most of Hamas' Weapons," *Israel Ministry of Foreign Affairs,* Aug. 31, 2014: https://mfa.gov.il/MFA/ForeignPolicy/Iran/SupportTerror/Pages/Iran-provided-most-of-Hamas-weapons-31-Aug-2014.aspx.

23 "Chaya Salomon." *One Family:* https://www.onefamilytogether.org/chaya-salomon/

7: "Benghazi Betrayal and the Brotherhood Link"

1 Statement of Pete Hoekstra Before the House Committee on Homeland Security Subcommittee on Oversight and Management Efficiency, U.S. House of Representatives, September 22, 2016: https://docs.house.gov/meetings/HM/HM09/20160922/105384/HHRG-114-HM09-Wstate-HoekstraP-20160922.pdf.

2 Ibid.

3 Remarks by the President at Cairo University, 6–04–09: https://obamawhitehouse.archives.gov/the-press-office/remarks-president-cairo-university-6–04–09.

4 "Terrorism: Muslim Brotherhood," *Jewish Virtual Library:* https://www.jewishvirtuallibrary.org/the-muslim-brotherhood.

5 "Muhammad Mursi During Election Campaign: Jihad Is Our Path, Death for the Sake of Allah Is Our Most Lofty Aspiration, The Shari'a Is Our Constitution," *Middle East Media Research Institute (MEMRI),* June 27, 2012: https://www.memri.org/reports/muhammad-mursi-during-election-campaign-jihad-our-path-death-sake-allah-our-most-lofty.

6 Clare Lopez, "History of the Muslim Brotherhood Penetration of the U.S. Government," *Gatestone Institute,* April 15, 2013: https://www.gatestoneinstitute.org/3672/muslim-brotherhood-us-government.

7 James Risen, Mark Mazzetti, Michael S. Schmidt, "U.S.-Approved Arms for Libya Rebels Fell into Jihadis' Hands," *New York Times,* December 5, 2012: http://www.nytimes.com/2012/12/06/world/africa/weapons-sent-to-libyan-rebels-with-us-approval-fell-into-islamist-hands.html; Jeffrey Sparshott, "Group Gets U.S. License to Fund Syria Rebels," *Wall Street Journal,* July 31, 2012: http://online.wsj.com/article/SB10000872396390444405804577561482242140956.html; Elise Labott, "Obama authorized covert support for Syrian rebels, sources say," CNN, August 1, 2012: http://www.cnn.com/2012/08/01/us/syria-rebels-us-aid/index.html; David Enders, "Syrian rebels say Americans, Britons helped train them in Jordan," *McClatchy Newspapers,* December 14, 2012: http://www.mcclatchydc.com/2012/12/14/177474/syrian-rebels-say-americans-britons.html.

8 Citizens Commission on Benghazi, *Accuracy in Media (AIM):* https://www.aim.org/benghazi/declaration-of-the-citizens-commission-on-benghazi/.

9   How America Switched Sides in the War on Terror: An Interim Report by the Citizens' Commission
     On Benghazi," April 22, 2014: https://www.aim.org/benghazi/wp-content/uploads/2014/04/CCB-
     Interim-Report-4-22-2014.pdf; "Betrayal in Benghazi: A Dereliction of Duty," by the Citizens'
     Commission on Benghazi, June 29, 2016: https://www.aim.org/wp-content/uploads/2016/06/
     AIM-Citizens-Commission-on-Benghazi-FINAL-REPORT-June-2016.pdf.

10   CCB June 2016 report, "Betrayal in Benghazi: A Dereliction of Duty."

11   "Shariah: The Threat to America. An Exercise in Competitive Analysis, Report of Team B II,"
     Center for Security Policy, 2010: http://shariahthethreat.org/, on Kindle, iPad, or at http://www.
     amazon.com/Shariah-America-Exercise-Competitive-Analysis/dp/098229476X.

12   Ibid.

13   Kerry Picket, "Muslim advocacy groups influence heavily on U.S. national security protocol
     and lexicon," *Washington Times,* September 24, 2012: http://www.washingtontimes.com/blog/
     watercooler/2012/sep/24/picket-muslim-advocacy-groups-influence-heavily-us/.

14   CCB June 2016 report, "Betrayal in Benghazi: A Dereliction of Duty."

15   Ibid.

16   Ibid.

17   Ambassador (Ret.) Yoram Ettinger, "Yoram Ettinger: President Biden's Middle East Policy," *Jewish
     World News,* August 5, 2021. https://jewishworldnews.org/Yoram-ettinger-president-bidens-middle-
     east-policy/

18   Daniel Greenfield, "Biden's Anti-Israel 'Point Man' Behind Plan to Fund Terrorists," *Front Page
     Magazine,* April 9, 2021: https://www.frontpagemag.com/fpm/2021/04/bidens-anti-israel-point-
     man-behind-plan-fund-daniel-greenfield/

19   Jonathan Schanzer, "Israel Imperiled: Threats to the Jewish State," Joint Hearing before House
     Foreign Affairs Committee Subcommittee on Terrorism, Nonproliferation, and Trade and the
     Subcommittee on the Middle East and North Africa, April 19, 2016: https://docs.house.gov/
     meetings/FA/FA18/20160419/104817/HHRG-114-FA18-Wstate-SchanzerJ-20160419.pdf

20   U.S. Council of Muslim Organizations (USCMO): http://uscmo.org/founding_members/

21   Million Muslim Votes Summit, July 20, 2020: https://www.youtube.com/watch?v=Z9rCpAkPuY4

22   Clare M. Lopez, "Joe Biden Calls for Jihad Against America," *World View Weekend,* 28 July 2020.
     From a well-known hadith, [177] 78—(49) by Sahih Muslim, one of the two most authoritative
     of all hadith collectors: http://admin.worldviewweekend.com/news/article/joe-biden-calls-jihad-
     against-america

23   Holy Land Foundation trial documents, ATTACHMENT A List of Unindicted Co-conspirators—
     Page 1, IN THE UNITED STATES DISTRICT COURT FOR THE NORTHERN DISTRICT
     OF TEXAS DALLAS DIVISION. *Investigative Project on Terrorism (IPT):* https://www.
     investigativeproject.org/documents/case_docs/423.pdf#page=5

24   Ibid.

25   Farooq Mitha, Emgage USA Board Member, Virginia: https://emgageusa.org/board-member/
     farooq-mitha/

26   U.S. Department of Defense, Farooq A. Mitha: https://www.defense.gov/About/Biographies/
     Biography/Article/2580009/Farooq-a-mitha/

27   Explanatory Memorandum.

28   President Ronald Reagan, "A Time For Choosing" speech in support of Barry Goldwater's presidential
     campaign, 1964: https://www.americanrhetoric.com/speeches/ronaldreaganatimeforchoosing.htm

8: "Obama's Russia Collusion"

1   Stanley Ann Dunham Soetoro, Metapedia.org entry, https://en.metapedia.org/wiki/Stanley_Ann_Dunham_Soetoro. Also, Barack Obama, Sr., wrote an article titled "Problems Facing Our Socialism" in the *East African Journal* in 1965: https://prestopundit.wordpress.com/2008/04/10/problems-facing-our-socialism-by-barak-h-obama/.

2   YouTube.com, video of Hillary Clinton, March 24, 2010: https://www.youtube.com/watch?v=AKoCwHGJ1To. She states, "One of the fears that I hear from Russia is that somehow the United States wants Russia to be weak. That could not be farther from the truth. Our goal is to help strengthen Russia."

3   Kaitlyn Schallhorn, "Obama-era Russian Uranium One Deal: What to Know," *Fox News,* February 8, 2018: https://www.foxnews.com/politics/obama-era-russian-uranium-one-deal-what-to-know

4   Diana West, "Ka-Boom: Putin, Barack and Hillary's Skolkovo," *Diana West blog,* March 3, 2017: http://dianawest.net/Home/tabid/36/EntryId/3507/Ka-Boom-Putin-Barack-and-Hillarys-Skolkovo.aspx

5   Michael McFaul, *From Cold War to Hot Peace* (Kindle), p. 256–290. McFaul offers many details of meetings in which Obama and his Secretaries of State met secretly with Russian leaders in the absence of witnesses.

6   Yahoo News video feed of 2012 Presidential Debate, "Romney and Obama on Russia": https://video.search.yahoo.com/yhs/search;_ylt=AwrWmjyTlppddzQAPwsPxQt.;_ylu=X3oDMTEyOGZqOXJqBGNvbG8DZ3ExBHBvcwMxBHZ0aWQDQjg5MjJfMQRzZWMDc2M-?p=obama+scolds+romney+on+russia&fr=yhs-pty-pty_weather&hspart=pty&hsimp=yhs-pty_weather

7   Ibid., p. 339.

8   Ibid., p. 340.

9   Ibid., p. 347.

10   Ibid., p. 259.

11   Scott Wilson, *Washington Post,* March 25, 2014.

12   Anne R. Pierce, *A Perilous Path: The Misguided Foreign Policy of Barack Obama, Hillary Clinton and John Kerry* (New York: Post Hill Press, 2016), p. 109.

13   Ibid.

14   McFaul also discusses this in greater detail in his book, cited above.

15   Pierce, p.110.

16   McFaul, pp.353–354.

17   Pierce, p. 115. Also see, Paul N. Schwartz, "Russian INF Treaty Violations: Assessment and Response," *Center For Strategic & International Studies,* October 14, 2014: https://www.csis.org/analysis/russian-inf-treaty-violations-assessment-and-response

18   KH. Sabirov, *What is Communism?* (Moscow: Progress Publishers, 1987), p.283.

19   *The Jeff Nyquist Radio Show,* the full audio can be downloaded for free from iTunes. https://www.iheart.com/podcast/256-jeff-nyquist-show-31007622/episode/tom-fife-and-anne-leary-interviews-39542021/

20   Philip Bump, "Robert Gates Thinks Joe Biden Hasn't Stopped Being Wrong for 40 Years," *The Atlantic,* Jan. 7, 2014. https://www.theatlantic.com/politics/archive/2014/01/robert-gates-thinks-joe-biden-hasnt-stopped-being-wrong-40-years/356785/

9: "Obama's Enabling of Jihad and Stealth Jihad"

1   Rachel Cox, "Fort Hood Gunman Says Uniform 'Represents An Enemy of Islam,'" *KWTX.com*, July 9, 2013.

2   Manny Fernandez, "Fort Hood Gunman Told Panel That Death Would Make Him a Martyr," *New York Times*, August 12, 2013.

3   Ibid.

4   "Hasan: 'Illegal war' provoked Fort Hood rampage," *Associated Press*, August 22, 2013.

5   "Hasan: 'I switched sides,'" *CNN*, August 6, 2013.

6   "Doctor: Fort Hood Suspect Didn't Want Deployment," *Associated Press*, August 20, 2013.

7   Fernandez, op. cit.

8   Nick Allen, "Fort Hood gunman had told US military colleagues that infidels should have their throats cut," *Telegraph*, November 8, 2009.

9   James C. McKinley Jr. and James Dao, "Fort Hood Gunman Gave Signals Before His Rampage," *New York Times*, November 8, 2009.

10 Michael Graczyk, "No defense from suspect in Fort Hood shooting," *Associated Press*, August 21, 2013.

11 Susan Crabtree, "Fort Hood victims see similarities to Benghazi," *Washington Times*, October 18, 2012.

12 "Hasan: 'Illegal war' provoked Fort Hood rampage," op. cit.

13 Angela K. Brown, "Victims want Hood shooting deemed terror attack," *Associated Press*, October 19, 2012.

14 "Mueller: FBI didn't drop the ball on Ft. Hood shooter," *CBS News*, August 22, 2013.

15 Daniel Bardsley, "Fort Hood killer 'does not represent Muslims': American security chief," *The National*, November 9, 2009.

16 "General Casey: diversity shouldn't be casualty of Fort Hood," *Reuters*, November 8, 2009.

17 "FBI removes hundreds of training documents after probe on treatment of Islam," *FoxNews.com*, February 21, 2012.

18 "CAIR: Jesse Jackson, ICNA Endorse Letter on Anti-Islam FBI Training," *Council on American-Islamic Relations* press release, August 6, 2010.

19 Andrew C. McCarthy, "Director Mueller, Say No to CAIR: A Muslim Brotherhood Tentacle Targets Robert Spencer," *National Review*, August 10, 2010.

20 Roger L. Simon, "Real Blog War: CAIR Goes After Robert Spencer," *PJ Media*, August 9, 2010.

21 Spencer Ackerman, "FBI Teaches Agents: 'Mainstream' Muslims Are 'Violent, Radical,'" *Wired*, September 14, 2011.

22 Andrew C. McCarthy, "Why They Can't Condemn Hamas," *National Review*, August 28, 2010; "Nihad Awad," Investigative Project on Terrorism, August 4, 2010.

23 "Hizballah's Brash U.S. Supporters," IPT News, November 18, 2010; Reza Aslan, "Obama's Middle East policy Is a Failure," *Huffington Post*, October 29, 2010.

24 Josh Gerstein, "Mag says W.H. Islam envoy misquoted; writer denies," *Politico*, February 16, 2010; Joel Mowbray, "Islamic Hall of Shame," *FrontPageMagazine.com*, May 30, 2005.

25 Muhammed Ibn Ismail Al-Bukhari, *Sahih al-Bukhari: The Translation of the Meanings*, translated by Muhammad M. Khan, Darussalam, 1997, vol. 9, book 88, no. 6922.

26 A. Guillaume, *The Life of Muhammad: A Translation of Ibn Ishaq's Sirat Rasul Allah*, Oxford University Press, 1955, pp. 674–676.

27 Spencer Ackerman, "FBI Teaches Agents: 'Mainstream' Muslims Are 'Violent, Radical,'" *Wired*, September 14, 2011.

28 Ibid.

29 Ibid.

30 "FBI drops lecture that was critical of Islam," *Associated Press,* September 16, 2011.

31 Salam al-Marayati, "The wrong way to fight terrorism," *Los Angeles Times,* October 19, 2011.

32 "Community to Brennan re FBI training," *Muslim Advocates,* October 19, 2011.

33 "Community to Brennan re FBI training," *Muslim Advocates,* October 19, 2011.

34 Ibid.

35 Ibid.

36 Ibid.

37 Federal Bureau of Investigation, "The Radicalization Process: From Conversion to Jihad," May 10, 2006.

38 "Community to Brennan re FBI training," *Muslim Advocates,* October 19, 2011.

39 Ian Fisher, "A Tale of War: Iraqi Describes Battling G.I.'s," *New York Times,* December 5, 2003.

40 "Commander of the Khobar Terrorist Squad Tells the Story of the Operation," Middle East Media Research Institute Special Dispatch Series No. 731, June 15, 2004.

41 "Al-Qa'ida Internet Magazine, "Sawt Al-Jihad Calls to Intensify Fighting During Ramadan—'the Month of Jihad,'" Middle East Media Research Institute, Special Dispatch No. 804, October 22, 2004.

42 AlMaghrib Institute et al., Letter to John Brennan, October 19, 2011.

43 Letter of John Brennan to Farhana Khera, November 3, 2011, in AWR Hawkins, "Emerson, IPT Expose Brennan Letter: FBI Training 'Substandard and Offensive' to Muslims," *Breitbart,* February 8, 2013.

44 Ibid.

45 Ibid.

46 Ibid.

47 Ibid.

10: "Obama's Enabling of ISIS"

1 "VOA: ISIS Shows Signs of Strengthening in Syria, Iraq," *Shafaq News,* November 7, 2021.

2 David Remnick, "Going the Distance," *New Yorker,* January 27, 2014.

3 Dan Merica, "ISIS is neither Islamic nor a state, says Hillary Clinton," *CNN,* October 7, 2014.

4 Missy Ryan, "Islamic State threat 'beyond anything we've seen': Pentagon," *Reuters,* August 21, 2014.

5 Michael Zennie, "Somali-American who died fighting for ISIS cleaned planes for Delta Airlines at Minneapolis airport before he joined terrorist group," *Daily Mail,* September 3, 2014.

6 Ibid.

7 "Transcript: President Obama's remarks on the execution of journalist James Foley by Islamic State," *Washington Post,* August 20, 2014.

8 Brittany M. Hughes, "State Dept. on Beheading of U.S. Journalist: 'This Is Not About the United States,'" *CNS News,* August 21, 2014.

9 "Crowd Gathers to Show Support of ISIS Takeover of Mosul," *Middle East Media Research Institute,* June 12, 2014.

10 "Obama: ISIL is 'unique in its brutality'—full transcript," *Chicago Sun-Times,* September 10, 2014.

11 Greg Giroux, "Obama Confirms Kassig Beheaded by Islamic State," *Bloomberg,* November 16, 2014.

12 Andrew Kirell, "State Dept Spokeswoman Marie Harf: We Can't Beat ISIS Just by Killing Them," *Mediaite,* February 17, 2015.

13 Patrick Goodenough, "Kerry: Extremism Not Linked to Islam; Factors Include Deprivation, Climate Change," *CNS News,* October 17, 2014.

14 Patrick Goodenough, "Kerry: Potential Terror Recruits Need 'More Economic Opportunities,'" *CNS News,* September 30, 2013.

15 Ibid.

16 Ibid.

17 Ibid.

18 Ibid.

19 Ibid.

20 Ibid.

21 Pam Key, "Fox Host to WH Spox: People With Shrapnel in Their Shoulders Don't Think This Is a Narrative Battle," *Breitbart,* September 19, 2016.

22 Abu Muhammad al-Adnani ash-Shami, op. cit.

23 Jordan Schachtel, "Daily Jihad: Obama's 'Vetted' Free Syrian Army Joining Forces with Islamic State Terror Group," *Breitbart,* September 9, 2014.

24 "Christians Massacred by 'Free' Syrian Army Terrorists (Rebels)," *OrthodoxNet.com,* August 24, 2013.

25 Joseph DeCaro, "Free Syrian Army Massacre Christian Village," *Worthy News,* July 5, 2013.

26 Lee Stranahan, "'Moderate' Syrian Rebels Post Videos of Attack on Christian Town," *Breitbart,* September 7, 2013.

27 "Frustration drives Arsal's FSA into ISIS ranks, *Daily Star,* September 8, 2014.

28 Ibid.

29 Scott Wong and Cristina Marcos, "House approves Syria aid," *The Hill,* September 17, 2014.

30 Ibid.

31 Kathleen Hennessey, "Obama outlines strategy to 'ultimately destroy' Islamic State," *Los Angeles Times,* September 5, 2014.

32 Wong and Marcos, "House approves Syria aid," op. cit.

33 Con Coughlin, "US blocks attempts by Arab allies to fly heavy weapons directly to Kurds to fight Islamic State," *Telegraph,* July 2, 2015.

34 Roy Gutman and Duygu Guvenc, "Turkey vows to strike anyone killing civilians in planned free zone," *McClatchy,* July 27, 2015.

35 Edwin Mora, "Benghazi Commission: Obama Admin Gun-Running Scheme Armed Islamic State," *Breitbart,* November 30, 2015.

36 Nancy A. Youssef, "Exclusive: Obama Refuses to Hit ISIS's Libyan Capital," *The Daily Beast,* February 18, 2016.

37 Ibid.

38 Damien Gayle and Simon Tomlinson, "ISIS issues direct threat to Obama in new beheading video after Japanese hostage says jihadis will execute him and Jordanian airman within 24 hours unless jailed female terrorist is released," *MailOnline,* January 27, 2015.

39 Lachlan Markay, "Islamic State Hacks CENTCOM Twitter Feed as Obama Talks Cybersecurity," *Washington Free Beacon,* January 12, 2015.

40 Jamie Tarabay and Gilad Shiloach, "ISIS Supporters Shaken By U.S. Killing of Abu Sayyaf, Vow Revenge," *Vocativ,* May 16, 2015.

41   Hannah Roberts, "ISIS threatens to send 500,000 migrants to Europe as a 'psychological weapon' in chilling echo of Gaddafi's prophecy that the Mediterranean 'will become a sea of chaos,'" *MailOnline,* February 18, 2015.

42   Aaron Brown, "'Just wait . . . ' Islamic State reveals it has smuggled THOUSANDS of extremists into Europe," *Express,* November 18, 2015.

43   Manasi Gopalakrishnan, " 'Islamic State' reportedly training terrorists to enter Europe as asylum seekers," *DW,* November 14, 2016.

44   Jacob Bojesson, "German Intel Agency Says Hundreds of Jihadis Arrived Among Refugees," *Daily Caller,* July 5, 2017.

45   Julia Edwards, "U.S. to accept 10,000 Syrian refugees: White House," *Reuters,* September 10, 2015.

46   Patrick Goodenough, "Record 499 Syrian Refugees Admitted to US So Far in May Includes No Christians," *CNS News,* May 23, 2016.

47   Daniel Greenfield, "How Hillary and Obama Caused the Orlando ISIS Attack," *FrontPage Magazine,* June 22, 2016.

48   Ari Lieberman, "Obama's ISIS Lies Exposed," *FrontPage Magazine,* June 21, 2016.

49   Alyssa Canobbio, "Two Weeks After Calling Islamic State 'Contained,' Obama Says It Poses 'Serious Threat to All of Us,'" *Daily Caller,* November 24, 2015.

50   Jeffrey Goldberg, "The Obama Doctrine," *The Atlantic,* April 2016.

51   Caroline Glick, "The Obama Doctrine, Unplugged," *FrontPage Magazine,* March 18, 2016.

52   Daniel Greenfield, "Obama Wants to Defeat America, Not ISIS," *FrontPage Magazine,* November 18, 2015.

53   Oli Smith, "Christians claim Obama 'ABANDONED' them to sick ISIS jihadis—and back Trump election win," *Express,* November 6, 2016.

11: "The Iran Deal"

1   Andrea Mitchell, Abigail Williams, and Cassandra Vinograd, "Iran Nuclear Deal: Tehran, World Powers Agree to Historic Pact," *NBC News,* July 14, 2015.

2   Ibid.

3   Erin McClam, "Iran Nuclear Deal: President Obama Says Deal Makes World 'Safer and More Secure,'" *NBC News,* July 14, 2015.

4   Mitchell, Williams, and Vinograd, "Iran Nuclear Deal."

5   Ali Wambold, "Fatal Flaw in the Iran Deal," *New York Sun,* August 11, 2015.

6   Ibid.

7   "Iran's Khamenei hails his people for demanding death to America and Israel," *Times of Israel,* July 18, 2015.

8   Ibid.

9   Ibid.

10   Ibid.

11   "Sectarian, Tribal Wars Protecting Israel: Leader," *Press TV,* July 18, 2015.

12   Ibid.

13   Ibid.

14   Ibid.

15   Adam Kredo, "Iran: 'We Will Trample Upon America,'" *Washington Free Beacon,* July 20, 2015.

16   Robert Spencer, "Iran's Supremo Tweets Picture of Obama Committing Suicide," *Jihad Watch,* July 25, 2015.

17   "Iran Hits Out at Kerry's 'Empty Threats,'" *AFP,* July 25, 2015.

18 Adam Kredo, "Iran: Nuke Deal Permits Cheating on Arms, Missiles," *Washington Free Beacon,* July 27, 2015.

19 Ibid.

20 Tim Hume, "Iran Test-Fires New Generation Long-Range Ballistic missiles, state media report," *CNN,* October 11, 2015.

21 Arthur MacMillan, "Iran conducts new missile tests defying US sanctions," *Agence France-Presse,* March 8, 2016.

22 Jon Gambrell, "Iran fires 2 missiles marked with 'Israel must be wiped out,'" *Associated Press,* March 9, 2016.

23 Elad Benari, "Iran: The Americans Had 'No Option' Besides a Deal," *Israel National News,* September 12, 2015.

24 Ibid.

25 Amir Taheri, "Obama Just Made Iran's Brutal Regime Stronger," *New York Post,* January 24, 2016.

26 Goldberg, "Kerry Warns Congress."

27 Ibid.

28 "Iran says will ban US experts from UN nuclear inspections," *Associated Press,* July 30, 2015.

29 Khamenei's Advisor Ali Akbar Velayati: Inspectors Will Not Be Allowed into Iranian Military Sites," *Middle East Media Research Institute* (MEMRI), July 31, 2015.

30 Michael R. Gordon, "John Kerry Wins Gulf States' Cautious Support for Iran Deal," *New York Times,* August 3, 2015.

31 Guy Benson, "Wow: AP Confirms Secret Side Deal Allows Iran to Inspect Itself at Key Nuclear Site," *Townhall.com,* August 19, 2015.

32 Ibid.

33 Mitchell, "'Side Deal.'"

34 Patrick Goodenough, "WH 'Confident' in IAEA's Reported Plan to Let Iran Inspect Its Own Suspect Nuclear Site," *CNS News,* August 20, 2015.

35 George Jahn, "Correction: Iran-Nuclear story," *Associated Press,* August 28, 2015.

36 Cheryl Rofer, "How the AP Got the Iran Inspections Story Wrong," *War on the Rocks,* August 24, 2015.

37 Kimberly Dozier, "Satellites Show Mystery Construction at Iran's Top-Secret Military Site," *Daily Beast,* February 8, 2016.

38 Joint Comprehensive Plan of Action, p. 3.

39 Ibid., p. 9.

40 Elizabeth Chuck, "Benjamin Netanyahu to Lester Holt: Iran Nuclear Deal Poses Threat to U.S., Israel," *NBC News,* July 15, 2015.

41 Joint Comprehensive Plan of Action, p. 43.

42 Goldberg, "Kerry Warns Congress."

43 "Journalist Offers Inside Look at Modern Life in Iran," *PBS NewsHour,* March 24, 2015.

44 Joint Comprehensive Plan of Action, p. 3.

45 Patrick Goodenough, "Iran Deal Includes Loophole in Sanctions 'Snapback' Mechanism," *CNS News,* July 14, 2015.

46 Joint Comprehensive Plan of Action, p. 15.

47 Ibid.

48 Joint Comprehensive Plan of Action, p. 20.

49 Ibid.

50 Ibid.

51   Ibid.; Nicole Duran, "Obama Admits Iran Deal Could Fund terror," *Washington Examiner,* July 15, 2015; Chuck Ross, "Obama Admits Iran Will Likely Use Sanctions Relief Money to Fund Military, Terrorism [VIDEO]," *Daily Caller,* August 5, 2015

52   Raf Sanchez, "Barack Obama Admits Iran Nuclear Deal Will Mean More Money for Terror Groups," *Telegraph,* August 5, 2015.

53   Avi Issacharoff, "Boosted by Nuke Deal, Iran Ups Funding to Hezbollah, Hamas," *Times of Israel,* September 21, 2015.

54   David Lawder, "Iran to receive $1.7 billion from the US in a claim settlement," *Reuters,* January 17, 2016; Joel Schechtman and Yeganeh Torbati, "White House dropped $10m claim in Iran prison deal," *AOL.com,* January 27, 2016.

55   Maayan Groisman, "Iran offers financial reward for families of potential Palestinian 'intifada martyrs,'" *Jerusalem Post,* February 24, 2016.

56   Michael Rubin, "White House Making Up Iran Data?," *Commentary,* March 6, 2016

12: "Obama's Illegal Marxist Immigrant Amnesty Movement"

1   Youngro Lee, "To Dream or Not to Dream: A Cost-Benefit Analysis of the Development, Relief, and Education for Alien Minors (Dream) Act." *Cornell Journal of Law and Public Policy,* Fall 2006: https://scholarship.law.cornell.edu/cgi/viewcontent.cgi?article=1107&context=cjlpp

2   Robert Siegel and Selena Simmons-Duffin, "How Did We Get To 11 Million Unauthorized Immigrants?" *NPR,* March 3, 2017: https://www.npr.org/2017/03/07/518201210/how-did-we-get-to-11-million-unauthorized-immigrants

3   Mohammad Fazel Zarandi, Jonathan S. Feinstein, Edward H. Kaplan, "Yale Study Finds Twice as Many Undocumented Immigrants as Previous Estimates," *Yale Insights,* Sept. 21, 2018: https://insights.som.yale.edu/insights/yale-study-finds-twice-as-many-undocumented-immigrants-as-previous-estimates

4   Emil Schepers, "Working Class Position on Immigration," *Communist Party USA website,* May 1, 2016: https://www.cpusa.org/party_voices/working-class-position-on-immigration/

5   Mark Krikorian, "If I Want to Make Changes, I Have to Infiltrate the System," *National Review,* Oct. 23, 2015: https://www.nationalreview.com/corner/if-i-want-to-make-changes-i-have-to-infiltrate-the-system/

6   Photo: Luis Gutierrez, *Unity* supplement, 1987.

7   Trevor Loudon, "Enemies Within," *Internet Movie Database:* https://www.imdb.com/title/tt6048414/reviews?ref_=tt_urv

8   Herman Baca, "Part One: President Obama & the Gang of Eight's 'Comprehensive Immigration Reform,'" *San Diego Free Press,* March 10, 2013: https://sandiegofreepress.org/2013/03/part-one-president-obama-the-gang-of-eights-comprehensive-immigration-reform/#.XfqX_uhKjIV

9   David Bacon, ""El Valiente. Chicano," *In These Times,* Aug. 12, 2009: http://inthesetimes.com/working/entry/4738/el_valiente_chicano

10   Bert Corona, "Bert Corona: 1918–2001: Labor Organizer," *Brief Biographies:* https://biography.jrank.org/pages/3057/Corona-Bert-1918–2001-Labor-Organizer-El-Paso-Childhood.html

11   Harvey Klehr, *The Communist Experience in America: A Political and Social History,* Transaction Publishers, Jan. 31, 2010, p. 119–120.

12   "The Nationwide Drive Against Law Enforcement Intelligence Operations," Hearings before the Subcommittee to Investigate the Administration of the Internal Security Act, Senate Internal Security Subcommittee, Sen. Judiciary Committee, 94th Congress, 1st Session, July 14, 1975; David Bacon, *In These Times,* "El Valiente Chicano," Aug. 12, 2009: http://inthesetimes.com/working/entry/4738/el_valiente_chicano

13 Mario T. Garcia, *Memories of Chicano History: The Life and Narrative of Bert Corona,* University of California Press, Feb. 1, 1995, p. 325.

14 Bert Corona Leadership Institute, "Bert Corona profile," May, 2010: http://web.archive.org/web/20080705233158/http://www.bcli.info/profile.htm

15 Lloyd Billingsley, "Union Card for Green Card: The Radical Vanguard in the Los Angeles Labor Movement," *Enter Stage Right,* Aug. 14 2000: http://www.enterstageright.com/archive/articles/0800lalabour.htm

16 "Bert Corona Facts," Your Dictionary, Feb. 5, 2020: https://biography.yourdictionary.com/bert-corona

17 John Haer, "Timeless Values, New Ideas," *Democratic Left,* January/February, 1986, p. 9–11: https://democraticleft.dsausa.org/files/sites/6/2019/01/DL_1986_V014_01_final.pdf

18 Elise Foley, "Antonio Villaraigosa: Obama Should Follow California on Secure Communities Immigration Program," *Huffington Post,* Aug. 9, 2012: https://www.huffpost.com/entry/antonio-villaraigosa-obama-secure-communities-_n_1762177

19 Richie Calbuzz Ross, "Untold Story: How the Latino Vote Hit Critical Mass," *Calbuzz,* Nov. 15, 2010: http://www.calbuzz.com/tag/maria-elena-durazo/

20 City News Service, "San Diego Lawmakers Battle Effort to Overturn Law Granting Undocumented Immigrants to Get a Driver's License," *ABC 10 News,* July 10, 2018: https://www.10news.com/news/la-councilman-denounces-effort-to-overturn-ab-60

21 Michael A. Memoli, *Los Angeles Times,* "Villaraigosa praises Obama for immigration policy change," June 15, 2012: https://www.latimes.com/politics/la-xpm-2012-jun-15-la-pn-villaraigosa-obama-deportations-20120615-story.html

22 ObamaCA, "California State Senator Gil Cedillo Supports Barack Obama," *YouTube,* Jan. 15, 2008: https://www.youtube.com/watch?v=qPBLXKcdWTQ

23 Robin Abcarian, "Obama Gets Major Labor Endorsement," *Los Angeles Times,* Jan. 16, 2008: https://www.latimes.com/nation/la-na-labor16jan16-story.html

24 Ibid.

25 David Bacon, "Obama Gets Major Labor Endorsement," *In These Times,* Aug. 12, 2009: http://inthesetimes.com/working/entry/4738/el_valiente_chicano

26 Bruce Gaston, "Obama Transition Team Extends Diversity Outreach To Afro-Latinos," *Redding News Review,* Jan. 12, 2008: http://reddingnewsreview.com/newspages/2009newspages/Obama_tran_team_09_091000001.htm

27 Renee Nal, "Obama consults with SEIU's Eliseo Medina before debating on immigration," *YouTube,* Jan. 24, 2018: https://www.youtube.com/watch?v=5h_cC6tQkAM

28 "Eliseo Medina on Immigration Reform and Activism," *DSA website,* Feb. 13, 2014: https://www.dsausa.org/democratic-left/eliseo_medina_on_immigration_reform_and_activism/

29 Evelina Alarcon, "Northern California PWW banquet raises $11,000," *Peoples Weekly World,* Dec. 7. 2001.

30 "Eliseo Medina Board Member," *Mi Familia Vota,* accessed Dec.18, 2019: https://www.mifamiliavota.org/people/eliseo-medina/Eliseo

31 SEIU, "SEIU's Eliseo Medina on the Progressive Community and Comprehensive Immigration Reform," *YouTube,* June 3, 2009: https://www.youtube.com/watch?v=ZM1A-71R8TU

32 George Ramos, "Bert Corona; Labor Activist Backed Rights for Undocumented Workers," *Los Angeles Times,* Jan. 17, 2001: https://www.latimes.com/archives/la-xpm-2001-jan-17-me-13397-story.html

33 David Bacon, "El Valiente. Chicano," *In These Times,* Aug. 12, 2009.

34   Michael Yates, "The dubious legacy of César Chávez," *Left Business Observer,* 2009: http://www. leftbusinessobserver.com/YatesOnUFW.html

35   Fred Hirch, "Ginny Hirsch," *Social Policy Magazine,* 2003: https://www.thefreelibrary.com/ Ginny+Hirsch.-a0107041413

36   Ray Stern, "Cesar Chavez's Rabid Opposition to Illegal Immigration Not Covered in New Movie," *Phoenix New Times,* March 28, 2014: https://www.phoenixnewtimes.com/news/cesar-chavezs-rabid-opposition-to-illegal-immigration-not-covered-in-new-movie-6643666

37   Dennis Havesi, "Paul Du Brul, Writer and Leader in Fight to Ban Lead Paints, Dies," *New York Times,* Dec. 20, 1987: https://www.nytimes.com/1987/12/20/obituaries/paul-du-brul-writer-and-leader-in-fight-to-ban-lead-paints-dies.html?pagewanted=1; Paul DuBrul Memorial Facebook page, "Remembering Paul DuBrul (1938–1987)," Dec. 18, 2018: https://www.facebook.com/pages/category/Writer/Paul-DuBrul-Memorial-1931479330240237/

38   Miriam Pawel, "Former Chavez Ally Took His Own Path," *Los Angeles Times,* Feb. 15, 2006: https:// www.latimes.com/business/la-me-medina11jan11-story.html

39   "Third Party Conferene in D.C.," *Democratic Left,* July/August 1995, p.22: https://democraticleft. dsausa.org/files/sites/6/2018/12/DL_1995_V023_04_final.pdf

40   Nancy Cleeland, "AFL-CIO Calls for Amnesty for Illegal U.S. Workers," *The Los Angeles Times,* Feb. 17, 2000: http://www.sci.sdsu.edu/salton/AFL-CIOAmnestyForIllegals!html

41   "Eliseo Medina Board Member," *Mi Familia Vota,* accessed Dec.18, 2019: https://www. mifamiliavota.org/people/eliseo-medina/Eliseo

42   Mark Gruenberg, "Medina, Other Immigration Reform Fasters, Step Aside for Reinforcements," *Peoples World,* Dec. 4, 2013: https://peoplesworld.org/article/medina-other-immigration-reform-fasters-step-aside-for-reinforcements/

43   Hillary Clinton Campaign press release, "Dolores Huerta, Eliseo Medina Join Hillary for California as Senior Advisors; Gabriel Rodriguez Announced as Latino Outreach Coordinator," *P2016 Race for the White House,* May 17, 2016: http://www.p2016.org/clinton/clinton051716prca.html

44   Hillary Clinton Campaign press release, "Immigration reform," *HillaryClinton.Com,* 2016: https:// www.hillaryclinton.com/issues/immigration-reform/

13: "Obama's Damage to Border Security"

1   "Remarks by the President at Law Enforcement Briefing on Immigration," *The White House,* May 13, 2014: https://obamawhitehouse.archives.gov/realitycheck/photos-and-video/video/2014/05/13/president-obama-speaks-immigration-reform?page=5#transcript

2   May, Caroline. "Sen. Sessions Releases Lengthy Timeline Of Obama Administration's Dismantling Of Immigration Law." *Breitbart News,* Feb. 16, 2015: https://www.breitbart.com/politics/2015/02/16/sen-sessions-releases-lengthy-timeline-of-obama-administrations-dismantling-of-immigration-law/

3   CNSNews.com Staff. "AG Nominee Lynch: Illegal Aliens Have 'The Right' to Work In U.S." *CNS News,* Jan. 29, 2015: https://www.cnsnews.com/news/article/cnsnewscom-staff/ag-nominee-lynch-illegal-aliens-have-right-work-us

4   Vadum, Matthew. "Sessions: Obama dismantling the immigration system." *FrontPageMag,* Feb. 17, 2015: https://archives.frontpagemag.com/fpm/sessions-obama-dismantling-immigration-system-matthew-vadum/

5   "President Obama's record of dismantling immigration enforcement 2009–2015," Federation for American Immigration Reform, 2017: https://www.fairus.org/issue/publications-resources/president-obamas-record-dismantling-immigration-enforcement

6 Vadum, "Sessions"

7 Federation for American Immigration Reform.

8 May.

9 Von Spakovsky, Hans A. "Trump's Immigration Actions Reverse Obama's Open Borders Policy," *Heritage Foundation*, Jan. 26, 2017: https://www.heritage.org/immigration/commentary/trumps-immigration-actions-reverse-obamas-open-borders-policy

10 Lemons, Stephen. "Congressional Hispanic Caucus Asks Barack Obama to Terminate 287(g) Program." *Phoenix New Times*, Sept. 30, 2009: https://www.phoenixnewtimes.com/news/congressional-hispanic-caucus-asks-barack-obama-to-terminate-287-g-program-6502298

11 Federation for American Immigration Reform.

12 *Ibid.*

13 May.

14 Delahunty, Robert J. and Yoo, John C. "Dream On: The Obama Administration's Nonenforcement of Immigration Laws, the DREAM Act, and the Take Care Clause." *Texas Law Review*, vol. 91:871 of 2013, p.783: http://texaslawreview.org/wp-content/uploads/2015/08/DelahuntyYoo.pdf

15 Binder, John. "Leaked Memo: DACA Amnesty Is 'Critical Component of Democratic Party's Future Electoral Success.'" *Breitbart News*, Jan. 11, 2018: https://www.breitbart.com/politics/2018/01/11/leaked-memo-daca-amnesty-is-critical-component-of-democratic-partys-future-electoral-success/

16 May.

17 Vadum.

18 Federation for American Immigration Reform.

19 May.

20 Ibid.

21 Ibid.

22 Ibid.

23 Bryan, Susan Montoya. "Past projects show border wall building is complex, costly." *Associated Press*, Jan. 12, 2019: https://apnews.com/ab1b07e15e6f4e9a9274b576ff3a1d45

24 Federation for American Immigration Reform.

25 Vadum, Matthew. "Illegals for Biden." *FrontPageMag*, March 26, 2021: https://www.frontpagemag.com/fpm/2021/03/illegals-biden-matthew-vadum/

26 Hackman, Michelle. "U.S. in Talks to Pay Hundreds of Millions to Families Separated at Border." *Wall Street Journal*, Oct. 28, 2021: https://www.wsj.com/articles/biden-administration-in-talks-to-pay-hundreds-of-millions-to-immigrant-families-separated-at-border-11635447591?mod=e2tw

27 Rodriguez, Sabrina. "Mayorkas to Cubans, Haitians: Do not come to the U.S." *Politico*, July 13, 2021: https://www.politico.com/news/2021/07/13/mayorkas-cubans-haitians-499531

28 Vadum, Matthew. "New rule bans immigrants from being a 'public charge.' *The Epoch Times*, Aug. 12, 2019: https://www.theepochtimes.com/new-rule-bans-immigrants-from-being-a-public-charge_3039473.html

14: "ObamaGate: The Coup Attempt Against President Trump"

1 Halon, Yael, "Ex-Independent Counsel Robert Ray predicts prosecutions from Durham probe: 'Political scandal of the highest order'" (May 24, 2020), *Fox News*. https://www.foxnews.com/media/robert-ray-durham-investigation-prosecutions-michael-flynn-predictions

2 Solomon, John, "The FBI documents that put Barack Obama in the 'Obamagate' narrative" (June 2, 2020), *Just the News*. https://justthenews.com/accountability/russia-and-ukraine-scandals/fbi-documents-put-barack-obama-obamagate-narrative?utm_campaign=external-news-aggregators&utm_medium=news-app&utm_source=smartnews.com

3   Federal Bureau of Investigation, Closing Communication, Crossfire Razor Foreign Agents Registration Act—Russia; Sensitive Investigative Matter (January 4, 2017).

4   Solomon, John, "FBI found no 'derogatory' Russia evidence on Flynn, planned to close case before leaders intervened" (May 26, 2020), *Just the News*. https://justthenews.com/accountability/russia-and-ukraine-scandals/fbi-found-no-derogatory-russia-evidence-flynn-planned

5   Singman, Brooke, "Flynn not masked in report on key calls with Russian ambassador: source" (May 21, 2020), *Fox News*. https://www.foxnews.com/politics/flynn-not-masked-report-on-key-calls-with-russian-ambassador

6   White, Chris, "Obama National Security Advisor Susan Rice Reportedly Requested 'Unmasking' of Trump Officials" (April 3rd, 2017), Law&Crime. https://lawandcrime.com/high-profile/obama-national-security-advisor-susan-rice-reportedly-requested-unmasking-of-trump-officials/

7   Golding, Bruce, "Joe Biden may have 'personally raised' idea to investigate Michael Flynn" (June 24, 2020), *New York Post*. https://nypost.com/2020/06/24/biden-may-have-personally-raised-idea-to-investigate-flynn/

8   Re, Gregg, "Obama knew details of wiretapped Flynn phone calls, surprising top DOJ official in meeting with Biden, declassified docs show" (May 7, 2020), *Fox News*. https://www.foxnews.com/politics/obama-knew-details-of-wiretapped-flynn-phone-calls-surprising-top-doj-official-new-docs-show

9   "Peter Strzok's Notes Confirm Obama Personally Ordered Hit on Michael Flynn" (Uploaded by The Federalist). https://www.scribd.com/document/466809620/Peter-Strzok-s-Notes-Confirm-Obama-Personally-Ordered-Hit-On-Michael-Flynn

10   Ignatius, David, "Why did Obama dawdle on Russia's hacking?" (January 12, 2017), *Washington Post*. https://archive.is/iwAPN

11   Dunleavy, Jerry, "Fully declassified Susan Rice email reveals reluctance to share 'sensitive' Russia information with Michael Flynn" (May 19, 2020), *Washington Examiner*. https://www.washingtonexaminer.com/news/fully-declassified-susan-rice-email-reveals-reluctance-to-share-sensitive-russia-information-with-michael-flynn

12   Isikoff, Michael, "Exclusive: Obama says in private call that 'rule of law is at risk' in Michael Flynn case" (May 8, 2020), *Yahoo News*. https://news.yahoo.com/obama-irule-of-law-michael-flynn-case-014121045.html

15: "Obama's Enabling of Racial Strife and Domestic Terror"

1   Barack Obama, "2004 Democratic National Convention Keynote Address." July 27, 2004. American Rhetoric Online Speech Bank. https://www.americanrhetoric.com/speeches/convention2004/barackobama2004dnc.htm

2   A. Southall, 2020. *Obama Vows to Push Immigration Changes*. The Caucus. https://thecaucus.blogs.nytimes.com/2010/10/25/in-appeal-to-hispanics-obama-promises-to-push-immigration-reform/>

3   "Biden Tells African-American Audience GOP Ticket Would Put Them 'Back in Chains.'" *CBS News*. August 12, 2012. https://www.cbsnews.com/news/biden-tells-african-american-audience-gop-ticket-would-put-them-back-in-chains/.

4   2008. Pew Research. November 13, 2008. https://www.pewresearch.org/politics/2008/11/13/section-2-the-president-elects-image-and-expectations/#optimism-about-race-relations.

5   Gallup, Inc. 2019. "Race Relations." https://news.gallup.com/poll/1687/race-relations.aspx.

6   "How Americans See the State of Race Relations." 2019. *Pew Research Center's Social & Demographic Trends Project*. April 9, 2019. https://www.pewsocialtrends.org/2019/04/09/how-americans-see-the-state-of-race-relations/

7   Gallup, Inc. 2019. "Race Relations." https://news.gallup.com/poll/1687/race-relations.aspx

8   David Hunn, "The Justice Department's Soft Side: How One Federal Agency Hopes to Change Ferguson." *St. Louis Post-Dispatch*. https://www.stltoday.com/news/local/govt-and-politics/the-justice-departments-soft-side-how-one-federal-agency-hopes-to-change-ferguson/article_591a2e64–7dd1–5008-b300–0ab9ad8b9168.html

9   "Documents Obtained by Judicial Watch Reveal Justice Department Sent Community Relations Service Agents to Ferguson at the Request of the NAACP." 2014. *Judicial Watch*. November 20, 2014. https://www.judicialwatch.org/press-releases/documents-obtained-judicial-watch-reveal-justice-department-sent-community-relations-service-agents-ferguson-request-naacp/

10   David Hunn, n.d. "The Justice Department's Soft Side: How One Federal Agency Hopes to Change Ferguson." *St. Louis Post-Dispatch*. https://www.stltoday.com/news/local/govt-and-politics/the-justice-departments-soft-side-how-one-federal-agency-hopes-to-change-ferguson/article_591a2e64–7dd1–5008-b300–0ab9ad8b9168.html

11   "[USC02] 42 USC CHAPTER 21, SUBCHAPTER VIII: COMMUNITY RELATIONS SERVICE." n.d. Uscode.House.Gov. https://uscode.house.gov/view.xhtml?path=/prelim@title42/chapter21/subchapter8&edition=prelim

12   Edward Kennedy, 2009. "Text—S.909—111th Congress (2009–2010): Matthew Shepard Hate Crimes Prevention Act." Www.Congress.Gov. April 28, 2009. https://www.congress.gov/bill/111th-congress/senate-bill/909/text

13   Ryan Lovelace. "The Department of Social Justice." 2014. *National Review*. December 8, 2014. https://www.nationalreview.com/2014/12/department-social-justice-ryan-lovelace/

14   "Documents Obtained by Judicial Watch Reveal Justice Department Sent Community Relations Service Agents to Ferguson at the Request of the NAACP." 2014. *Judicial Watch*. November 20, 2014. https://www.judicialwatch.org/press-releases/documents-obtained-judicial-watch-reveal-justice-department-sent-community-relations-service-agents-ferguson-request-naacp/

15   "Park Board Member Frances Semler Resigns." Kansas. *The Wichita Eagle*. Jan 22, 2008. https://www.kansas.com/news/article1005142.html; Cashill, Jack. n.d. "Ingram's New Council Proves Itself 4-Star Chamber" July 2007 https://ingrams.com/archive/July_2007/columns/btl.html

16   "Reminder: 'Hands up, Don't Shoot' Is a Fabricated Narrative from the Michael Brown Case." 2020. *Legal Insurrection*. June 4, 2020. https://legalinsurrection.com/2020/06/reminder-hands-up-dont-shoot-is-a-fabricated-narrative-from-the-michael-brown-case/

17   "Feds Urged Police Not to Release Michael Brown 'Robbery' Video." n.d. *NBC News*. August 16, 2014. https://www.nbcnews.com/storyline/michael-brown-shooting/feds-urged-police-not-release-michael-brown-robbery-video-n182346

18   Debra Heine, 2014. "Holder DOJ Behind the Suppression of Michael Brown Robbery Video." *Breitbart*. August 17, 2014. https://www.breitbart.com/blog/2014/08/17/holder-doj-behind-the-suppression-of-michael-brown-robbery-video/

19   OPA. 2015. "Memorandum DEPARTMENT OF JUSTICE REPORT REGARDING THE CRIMINAL INVESTIGATION INTO THE SHOOTING DEATH OF MICHAEL BROWN BY FERGUSON, MISSOURI POLICE OFFICER DARREN WILSON." https://www.justice.gov/sites/default/files/opa/press-releases/attachments/2015/03/04/doj_report_on_shooting_of_michael_brown_1.pdf

20   "Attorney General Holder Delivers Update on Investigations in Ferguson, Missouri." 2015. www.Justice.Gov. March 4, 2015. https://www.justice.gov/opa/speech/attorney-general-holder-delivers-update-investigations-ferguson-missouri

21   "End the Anti-Cop Witch Hunt." n.d. Greenfield, Daniel. *Front Page Magazine*. Dec 30, 2015. https://archives.frontpagemag.com/fpm/end-anti-cop-witch-hunt-daniel-greenfield/

22   Investor's Business Daily. 2015. "Holder Already Lowered 'Standard Of Proof' in Civil Rights Probes." *Investor's Business Daily*, March 2, 2015. https://www.investors.com/politics/editorials/holder-already-lowered-standard-of-proof-in-civil-rights-probes/

23   "Who Is Funding Black Lives Matter." n.d. McGirt, Ellen. *Fortune Magazine*. August 8, 2016. https://fortune.com/2016/08/08/funding-black-lives-matter-ford/

24   Valerie Richardson, 2016. "Black Lives Matter Cashes in with $100 Million from Liberal Foundations." *Washington Times*. August 16, 2016. https://www.washingtontimes.com/news/2016/aug/16/black-lives-matter-cashes-100-million-liberal-foun/

25   "Patrick Gaspard." n.d. Www.Influencewatch.Org. https://www.influencewatch.org/person/patrick-gaspard/

26   "George Soros's Foundation Is Spending $220 Million to 'Dismantle Systemic Racism' in U.S." 2020. *The Daily Wire*. July 13, 2020. https://www.dailywire.com/news/george-soross-foundation-is-spending-220-million-to-dismantle-systemic-racism-in-us

27   Matthew Desmond, "Where Have The Riots Gone?" n.d., *The Atlantic*. April 3, 2018. https://www.theatlantic.com/magazine/archive/2018/02/matthew-desmond-riots/552542/.

16: "An Ex-President's Post-Presidential War on America"

1   Paul Sperry, "How Obama is scheming to sabotage Trump's presidency" (February 11, 2017), *New York Post*. https://nypost.com/2017/02/11/how-obama-is-scheming-to-sabotage-trumps-presidency/

2   Peter Baker, "How Trump's Election Shook Obama: 'What if We Were Wrong?,'" (May 30, 2018), *New York Times*. https://www.nytimes.com/2018/05/30/us/politics/obama-reaction-trump-election-benjamin-rhodes.html

3   Ian Schwartz, "Krauthammer: Obama's Legacy Is Toast, Will End Up Being a 'Parenthesis in American History'" (November 11, 2016), *Real Clear Politics*. https://www.realclearpolitics.com/video/2016/11/11/krauthammer_obamas_legacy_is_toast_will_end_up_being_a_parenthesis_in_american_history.html

4   "Obama receives rock star welcome in Germany as he appears alongside Merkel and says 'we can't hide behind a wall'" (May 25, 2017). *Associated Press* and *Daily Mail*. https://www.dailymail.co.uk/news/article-4541136/Obama-receives-rock-star-welcome-Germany.html

5   Andrew Kaczynski, "Joe Biden once said a fence was needed to stop 'tons' of drugs from Mexico" (May 10, 2019), *CNN*. https://www.cnn.com/2019/05/10/politics/kfile-biden-drugs-fence-2006/index.html

6   Edward-Isaac Dovere, "How Obama not so subtly undercuts Trump" (May 25, 2019), *Politico*. https://www.politico.com/story/2017/05/25/how-obama-undercuts-trump-238814

7   Transcript: Obama's Speech at the 2018 Nelson Mandela Annual Lecture (July 17, 2018), *NPR*. https://www.npr.org/2018/07/17/629862434/transcript-obamas-speech-at-the-2018-nelson-mandela-annual-lecture

8   Edward-Isaac Dovere, "Obama on Trump: 'We see the utter loss of shame'" (July 17, 2018), *Politico*. https://www.politico.com/story/2018/07/17/barack-obama-trump-criticism-725977

9   Andrew Meldrum, "Obama delivers veiled rebuke to Trump in Mandela address" (July 17, 2018), *Associated Press*. https://apnews.com/9c415f558c874ddba99ef23f2cd040f5/Obama-delivers-Mandela-address-on-values-in-rebuke-to-Trump

10   Graeme Wood, "What ISIS Really Wants" (March 2015), *The Atlantic*. https://www.theatlantic.com/magazine/archive/2015/03/what-isis-really-wants/384980/

11 Op. cit., fn. 2.

12 Barack Obama, (May 8, 2018), Facebook post. https://www.facebook.com/barackobama/posts/10155854913976749

13 Alexander Fulbright, "Netanyahu: Iran brazenly lied about nuclear program, has made plans to revive it" (April 30, 2018), *The Times of Israel*. https://www.timesofisrael.com/pm-iran-lied-about-nuclear-plans-continued-to-expand-program-after-deal/

14 "Netanyahu: Iran cheated on nuclear accord, so no point in preserving it" (April 30, 2018), *DEBKAfile*. https://www.debka.com/netanyahu-reported-preparing-address-to-the-nation/

15 United Nations Security Council Resolution 2231 (Adopted July 20, 2015). https://www.securitycouncilreport.org/atf/cf/%7B65BFCF9B-6D27–4E9C-8CD3-CF6E4FF96FF9%7D/s_res_2231.pdf

16 "Final Assessment on Past and Present Outstanding Issues regarding Iran's Nuclear Programme, Report by the Director General" (December 2, 2015), *International Atomic Energy Agency Board of Governors*. https://www.iaea.org/sites/default/files/gov-2015–68.pdf

17 Maegan Vazquez, "Kerry says Trump's Iran strategy 'very dangerous and ill-advised'" (September 9, 2018), *CNN*. https://www.cnn.com/2018/09/09/politics/john-kerry-iran-deal-dangerous-cnntv/index.html

18 John Kerry, "John Kerry: Diplomacy Was Working Until Trump Abandoned It" (January 9, 2020), *New York Times*. https://www.nytimes.com/2020/01/09/opinion/john-kerry-trump-iran.html?action=click&module=Opinion&pgtype=Homepage

19 David Larter, "Experts: Iran's arrest of U.S. sailors broke international law" (January 27, 2016), *NavyTimes*. https://www.navytimes.com/news/your-navy/2016/01/27/experts-iran-s-arrest-of-u-s-sailors-broke-international-law/

20 "John Kerry: Some Iran sanctions relief likely to go to terrorists" (January 21, 2016), *CBS News*. https://www.cbsnews.com/news/john-kerry-some-iran-sanctions-relief-likely-to-go-to-terrorists/

21 Lia Eustachewich, "Kerry admits to meeting Iranian officials over nuclear deal" (September 12, 2018), *New York Post*. https://nypost.com/2018/09/12/kerry-admits-to-meeting-iranian-officials-over-nuclear-deal/

22 Donald J. Trump @realDonaldTrump (May 8, 2018), Twitter post. https://twitter.com/realDonaldTrump/status/993815373190492160

23 Emily Shugerman, "John Kerry predicts Trump administration 'won't last the year,' according to report" (January 25, 2018), *The Independent*. https://www.independent.co.uk/news/world/americas/us-politics/trump-john-kerry-predicts-out-of-white-house-one-year-israel-a8178771.html

24 18 U.S. Code § 953, Private correspondence with foreign governments (June 25, 1948, ch. 645, 62 Stat. 744; Pub. L. 103–322, title XXXIII, § 330016(1)(K), Sept. 13, 1994, 108 Stat. 2147), *Cornell Law School—Legal Information Institute*. https://www.law.cornell.edu/uscode/text/18/953

25 Transcript: Former President Obama's speech at the University of Illinois (September 7, 2018), *Politico*. https://www.politico.com/story/2018/09/07/obama-university-of-illinois-speech-811130

26 "Obama speech at University of Illinois draws huge interest" (September 4, 2018), *Associated Press*. https://www.chicagotribune.com/news/breaking/ct-obama-speech-university-of-illinois-speech-20180904-story.html

27 Jackson Brooks, "Obama's Final Numbers" (Posted on September 29, 2017 | Updated on September 24, 2018), *FactCheck.org*. https://www.factcheck.org/2017/09/obamas-final-numbers/

28 Jackson Brooks, "Trump's Numbers October 2019 Update" (Posted on October 11, 2019), *FactCheck.org*. https://www.factcheck.org/2019/10/trumps-numbers-october-2019-update/

29 Barack Obama'@BarackObama (October 1, 2018), Twitter post. https://twitter.com/BarackObama/
    status/1046803503988006912/photo/1?ref_src=twsrc%5Etfw%7Ctwcamp%5Etweetembed%7C
    twterm%5E1046803503988006912&ref_url=https%3A%2F%2Fthehill.com%2Fhomenews%2F
    campaign%2F409294-obama-announces-endorsement-for-ocasio-cortez

30 Rashida Tlaib @RashidaTlaib (March 28, 2019), Twitter post. https://twitter.com/RashidaTlaib/
    status/1111413716057128960/photo/1

31 David Kramer, "Obama Acquiesces to Russia on Missile Defense" (September 18, 2009),
    The Washington Post. https://www.washingtonpost.com/wp-dyn/content/article/2009/09/17/
    AR2009091702303.html

32 "Obama tells Russia's Medvedev more flexibility after election" (March 26, 2012), *Reuters*. https://
    www.reuters.com/article/us-nuclear-summit-obama-medvedev/obama-tells-russias-medvedev-
    more-flexibility-after-election-idUSBRE82P0JI20120326

33 James Risen, "If Donald Trump Targets Journalists, Thank Obama" (December 30, 2016), *New
    York Times*. https://www.nytimes.com/2016/12/30/opinion/sunday/if-donald-trump-targets-
    journalists-thank-obama.html

34 Dan Roberts, "Holder accused of misleading Congress over investigation into journalist leaks"
    (May 29, 2013), *The Guardian*. https://www.theguardian.com/world/2013/may/29/eric-holder-
    congress-journalist-leaks

35 Victor Davis Hanson, "Is the Country Unraveling?" (June 25, 2012), *PJ Media*. https://pjmedia.
    com/victordavishanson/is-the-country-unraveling/?singlepage=true

36 Grace Panetta, "Obama attributes the world's problems to 'old people not getting out of the way,'
    warning politicians that they are not in office to 'prop up' their 'self importance'" (December 16,
    2019), *Business Insider*. https://www.businessinsider.com/obama-blames-old-people-not-getting-
    out-of-the-way-for-world-problems-2019–12

37 Maureen Groppe, "Biden insists his presidency is not a third Obama term; his staff picks
    suggest otherwise" (June 16, 2021), *USA TODAY*. https://www.usatoday.com/story/news/
    politics/2021/06/16/most-bidens-top-white-house-staff-worked-obama-and-female/7706857002/

38 Daniel Chaitin, "Obama envisions creating 'a million young Barack Obamas' during speech in
    Japan" (March 25, 2018). *Washington Examiner*. https://www.washingtonexaminer.com/news/
    obama-envisions-creating-a-million-young-barack-obamas-during-speech-in-japan

39 Renae Reints, "Barack Obama Says United States Is 'Shrouded With Hate, Anger, Racism'"
    (November 20, 2018), *Fortune*. https://finance.yahoo.com/news/barack-obama-says-united-
    states-201203563.html

40 Obama Foundation Scholars Program Website. https://www.obama.org/scholars/

41 TEDWomen 2019 Speakers Webpage. https://tedwomen2019.ted.com/speakers#colette-pichon-
    battle

42 "White House to Recognize Colette Pichon Battle as "Champion of Change for Climate Equity"
    (July 15, 2016), Gulf Coast Center for Law & Policy Webpage. https://www.gcclp.org/single-
    post/2016/07/15/White-House-to-Recognize-Colette-Pichon-Battle-as-"Champion-of-Change-
    for-Climate-Equity"

43 "Vision & Mission," Gulf Coast Center for Law & Policy Webpage. https://www.gcclp.org/mission-
    vision

44 Gulf South for a Green New Deal, Gulf Coast Center for Law & Policy Webpage. https://www.
    gcclp.org/gulf-south-for-a-green-new-deal

45 The forum chosen by Obama Fellow Colette Pichon Battle for her interview, Radical Imagination, describes itself as "a platform to study, analyze, foment, broadcast and promote the radical ideas that emerge from social movements." *Radical Imagination Webpage*. http://radicalimagination.org/about/

46 "Climate Migrants" (Season 1, Episode 5: November 18, 2019), *Radical Imagination*. https://radicalimagination.us/episodes/climate-migrants

47 Gulf South for a Green New Deal Policy Platform(2019), *Gulf Coast Center for Law & Policy Webpage*. https://f051d680-6bda-4883-b0d9-76edcc6ecdae.filesusr.com/ugd/6ac318_4a76df6a0cd949508798d3cbd66e3e62.pdf

48 Colette Pichon Battle Transcript (December 2019), TEDWomen 2019. https://www.ted.com/talks/colette_pichon_battle_climate_change_will_displace_millions_here_s_how_we_prepare/transcript?language=en#t-682222

49 Alice Barbe @BarbeAlice (March 8, 2019), Twitter post. https://twitter.com/BarbeAlice/status/1104014756246183936

50 Alice Barbe @BarbeAlice (December 17, 2019), Twitter post. https://twitter.com/BarbeAlice/status/1206985418090143744

51 "Put the meeting at the heart of the migration issue" (March 2019), Tribune Fonda N° 241. https://fonda.asso.fr/ressources/mettre-la-rencontre-au-coeur-de-lenjeu-migratoire

52 Danielle Holly, "The Obama Foundation's Financials Don't Match Its Rhetoric" (October 1, 2018), *Nonprofit Quarterly*. https://nonprofitquarterly.org/the-obama-foundations-financials-dont-match-its-rhetoric/

53 Benjamin Schneider, "The Obama Center: Caught in an Old David vs. Goliath Drama" (June 8, 2018), *CityLab*. https://www.citylab.com/equity/2018/06/the-obama-center-caught-in-an-old-david-v-goliath-drama/561878/

54 Brian Montopoli, "Obama Versus the 'Fat Cats'" (December 13, 2009), *CBS News*. https://www.cbsnews.com/news/obama-versus-the-fat-cats/

55 Op. cit., fn. 24.

56 Tony Owusu, "Barack Obama Is Now Among 10 Highest-Paid Public Speakers" (September 25, 2017), *The Street*. https://www.thestreet.com/investing/highest-paid-public-speakers-14315669

57 Cheryl Chumley, "Obama Foundation's newest director a tax haven hiding fat cat" (November 9, 2017), *Washington Times*. https://www.washingtontimes.com/news/2017/nov/9/obama-foundations-newest-director-paradise-papers-/

58 Max Abelson, "Obama Goes from White House to Wall Street in Less Than One Year" (September 18, 2017), *Bloomberg*. https://www.fa-mag.com/news/obama-goes-from-white-house-to-wall-street-in-less-than-one-year-34715.html?section=43&page=2

59 Margaret Abrams, "Barack and Michelle Obama net worth 2019: How much is the former US President worth along with his wife?" (December 12, 2019), *ES. Insider*. https://www.standard.co.uk/insider/alist/barack-and-michelle-obama-net-worth-2019-how-much-is-the-former-us-president-worth-along-with-his-a4178561.html

60 Dan Western, "Barack Obama Net Worth" (Last Updated: 2021), *Wealthy Gorilla*. https://wealthygorilla.com/barack-obama-net-worth/

61 Mary Hanbury, "The Obamas just took a luxurious cruise with Oprah and Bruce Springsteen on this billionaire producer's yacht" (April 17, 2017), *Business Insider*. https://www.businessinsider.com/obamas-on-david-geffens-yacht-with-celebrity-guests-2017-4

62 Ethan Sacks, "Barack Obama Angering Many on Left with Extravagant Vacations" (June 27, 2017), *InsideHook*. https://www.insidehook.com/article/politics/extravagant-obama-vacations-angering-left

63 Sean Neumann, "Barack & Michelle Obama Just Bought a $11.75M, 7-Bedroom Martha's Vineyard Estate: Reports" (December 6, 2019), *People*. https://people.com/home/barack-michelle-obama-buy-marthas-vineyard-mansion/

64 Sam Dangremond, "See Photos of the Obamas' New House" (April 19, 2018), *Town & Country*. https://www.townandcountrymag.com/leisure/real-estate/news/g2535/obama-new-house-photos/

65 "Michelle Obama Rents Amazing Hollywood Hills Home" (July 10, 2019), *TMZ*. https://www.tmz.com/2019/07/10/michelle-obama-rents-hollywood-hills-home-los-angeles/

66 Op. cit., fn. 6. See also Caplan, Joshua. "Barack Obama Lectures World on Racial, Wealth Inequality in South Africa" (July 17, 2018), *Breibart*. https://www.breitbart.com/politics/2018/07/17/barack-obama-preaches-wealth-redistribution-in-south-africa/

67 Full text: President Obama's DNC speech (July 27, 2016), *Politico*. https://www.politico.com/story/2016/07/dnc-2016-obama-prepared-remarks-226345

68 Op. cit., fn. 36.

17: "Why Obama Should Have Been Impeached"

1 Ben Shapiro, *The People Vs. Barack Obama: The Criminal Case Against the Obama Administration* (Threshold Editions: 2014), pp. 4, 8.

2 Andrew McCarthy, *Faithless Execution: Building the Political Case for Obama's Impeachment* (Encounter Books: 2014).

3 Obama Administration's Abuse of Power, Hearing Before The Committee on The Judiciary House of Representatives One Hundred Twelfth Congress (September 12, 2012). https://www.govinfo.gov/content/pkg/CHRG-112hhrg75846/html/CHRG-112hhrg75846.htm

4 Greg Corombos. "Prosecutor: Top 7 reasons to impeach Obama" *WND*, June 10, 2014). https://www.wnd.com/2014/06/prosecutor-top-7-reasons-to-impeach-obama/

5 Andrew McCarthy, "Understanding Adam Schiff's 'Bribery' Theory" *National Review*, November 21, 2019. https://www.nationalreview.com/2019/11/bribery-and-impeachment/

6 Obama Administration's Abuse of Power, Hearing Before The Committee on The Judiciary House of Representatives One Hundred Twelfth Congress (September 12, 2012). https://www.govinfo.gov/content/pkg/CHRG-112hhrg75846/html/CHRG-112hhrg75846.htm

7 *Nat'l Labor Relations Bd. v. Noel Canning*, 134 S. Ct. 2550 (2014). https://casetext.com/case/natl-labor-relations-bd-v-canning

8 Joseph Klein, "Obama's Most Flagrant Violation of the Constitution Yet," *FrontPage Magazine*, September 7, 2016. https://archives.frontpagemag.com/fpm/obamas-most-flagrant-violation-constitution-yet-joseph-klein/

9 *Kendall v. United States*, 37 U.S. 524, (1838). https://www.law.cornell.edu/supremecourt/text/37/524

10 Jan Ting, "Obama's Own Words Refute His Stand on Immigration Authority" *New York Times*, July 8, 2015. https://www.nytimes.com/roomfordebate/2014/11/18/constitutional-limits-of-presidential-action-on-immigration-12/obamas-own-words-refute-his-stand-on-immigration-authority

11 Press Release, Remarks by the President on Immigration—Chicago, IL, The White House Office of the Press Secretary (Nov. 25, 2014). https://obamawhitehouse.archives.gov/the-press-office/2014/11/25/remarks-president-immigration-chicago-il

12 *State of Texas, et al. v. United States of America, et al.* (January 19, 2017, CIVIL NO. B-14–254). https://www.aila.org/File/Related/14122946cg.pdf

13   Remarks by the President on the Supreme Court Decision on U.S. Versus Texas (June 23, 2016). https://obamawhitehouse.archives.gov/the-press-office/2016/06/23/remarks-president-supreme-court-decision-us-versus-texas

14   Obama Tweet: *"If Congress won't act, I will."*—*President Obama on meeting the challenge of #climate change.* https://twitter.com/barackobama/status/366932015439810560?lang=en

15   Paul Roderick Gregory, "Why the Fuss? Obama Has Long Been on Record in Favor of Redistribution," *Forbes*, September 23, 2012, https://www.forbes.com/sites/paulroderickgregory/2012/09/23/why-the-fuss-obama-has-long-been-on-record-in-favor-of-redistribution/#57b4d7e8593a

16   Greg Corombos, Op. cit.

17   Jake Tapper and Dana Bash, "Former deputy chief of mission in Libya: U.S. military assets told to stand down" *CNN*, May 17, 2013. https://www.cnn.com/2013/05/06/politics/benghazi-whistleblower/index.html

18   Gertz, Bill, "Obama-era cash traced to Iran-backed terrorists" *Washington Times*, February 7, 2018. https://www.washingtontimes.com/news/2018/feb/7/inside-the-ring-obama-era-cash-traced-to-iran-back/

19   James Risen, "If Donald Trump Targets Journalists, Thank Obama," *New York Times*, December 30, 2016. https://www.nytimes.com/2016/12/30/opinion/sunday/if-donald-trump-targets-journalists-thank-obama.html

20   Letter from The Reporters Committee for Freedom of the Press. https://www.rcfp.org/wp-content/uploads/imported/Media-coalition-letter-re-AP-subpoena.pdf

21   Dan Roberts, "Holder accused of misleading Congress over investigation into journalist leaks" (May 29, 2013), *The Guardian*. https://www.theguardian.com/world/2013/may/29/eric-holder-congress-journalist-leaks

22   "Journalists or Criminals?" Attorney General Eric Holder's Testimony before the Committee and the Justice Department's National Security Leak Investigative Techniques, House Committee on the Judiciary Majority Staff Report to Chairman Bob Goodlatte (July 31, 2013). https://fas.org/irp/congress/2013_rpt/hjc-holder.pdf

23   Bill Mears, "Inside the hunt for a leaker: State Dept., search warrants and Fox News" CNN, May 30, 2013. https://www.cnn.com/2013/05/30/politics/inside-hunt-leaker/index.html

24   Editorial Board, "Another Chilling Leak Investigation," *New York Times*, May 21, 2013. https://www.nytimes.com/2013/05/22/opinion/another-chilling-leak-investigation.html

25   Remarks by the President at Cairo University, June 4, 2009. https://obamawhitehouse.archives.gov/the-press-office/remarks-president-cairo-university-6-04-09

26   Remarks by the President to the UN General Assembly, September 25, 2012. https://obamawhitehouse.archives.gov/the-press-office/2012/09/25/remarks-president-un-general-assembly

27   Remarks at the Organization of the Islamic Conference (OIC) High-Level Meeting on Combating Religious Intolerance, July 15, 2011. https://2009-2017.state.gov/secretary/20092013clinton/rm/2011/07/168636.htm

28   Rich Lowry, "The Benghazi Patsy," *Politico*, May 9, 2013. https://www.politico.com/story/2013/05/the-benghazi-patsy-091101

29   Controversial Filmmaker Nakoula Arrested for Probation Violations.https://jonathanturley.org/2012/09/28/controversial-filmmaker-nakoula-arrested-for-probation-violations/

30   Remarks by the President in State of the Union Address (January 27, 2010). https://obamawhitehouse.archives.gov/the-press-office/remarks-president-state-union-address

31   CITIZENS UNITED, APPELLANT v. FEDERAL ELECTION COMMISSION. https://www.law.cornell.edu/supct/pdf/08-205P.ZO

32   Stephen Dinan and Seth McLaughlin, "Emails show IRS' Lois Lerner specifically targeted tea party," *Washington Times*, September 12, 2013. https://www.washingtontimes.com/news/2013/sep/12/emails-ois-lerner-specifically-targeted-tea-party/

33   Sidney Powell, "IRS Shocker: Filing Reveals Lerner Blackberry Destroyed" *The Observer*, August 25, 2014. https://observer.com/2014/08/irs-shocker-filing-reveals-lerner-blackberry-destroyed/

34   Erik Wasson, "Obama: Not 'even a smidgen of corruption' behind Internal Revenue Service targeting," *The Hill*, February 2, 2014. https://thehill.com/policy/finance/197224-obama-not-a-smidgen-of-corruption-behind-irs-targeting

35   Linchpins of Liberty, et al., Plaintiffs-vs- UNITED STATES OF AMERICA, et al., Defendants. http://media.aclj.org/pdf/17.10.25-Proposed-Consent-Order-FILED.pdf

36   *Hosanna-Tabor Evangelical Lutheran Church and School v. Equal Employment Opportunity Commission*, 565 U.S. 171 (2012). https://www.law.cornell.edu/supremecourt/text/10–553

37   Obama Administration's Abuse of Power, Hearing Before The Committee on The Judiciary House of Representatives One Hundred Twelfth Congress (September 12, 2012). https://www.govinfo.gov/content/pkg/CHRG-112hhrg75846/html/CHRG-112hhrg75846.htm

38   *Burwell v. Hobby Lobby Stores, Inc.*, 134 S. Ct. 2751 (2014). https://scholar.google.com/scholar_case?case=5322529599500468186

39   Tim Johnson, "Secret court rebukes NSA for 5-year illegal surveillance of U.S. citizens," *Miami Herald*, May 26, 2017. https://www.miamiherald.com/news/nation-world/national/article152948259.html

40   Charlie Savage, "N.S.A. Gets More Latitude to Share Intercepted Communications," *New York Times*," January 12, 2017. https://www.nytimes.com/2017/01/12/us/politics/nsa-gets-more-latitude-to-share-intercepted-communications.html

41   Jordan Sekulow, *Unprecedented Unmasking and Political Bias: ACLJ Uncovers Major Political Bias from Ambassador Power in the Final Days of Obama Administration*.https://aclj.org/government-corruption/unprecedented-unmasking-and-political-bias-aclj-uncovers-major-political-bias-from-ambassador-power-in-final-days-of-obama-administration

42   UNITED STATES SURVEILLANCE COURT, https://int.nyt.com/data/documenthelper/1338-carter-page-fisa-documents-foi/844b27afa687de0dbee7/optimized/full.pdf

43   Department of Justice Office of the Inspector General, "Review of Four FISA Applications and Other Aspects of the FBI's Crossfire Hurricane Investigation" (as revised December 11, 2019), p. vi. https://www.justice.gov/storage/120919-examination.pdf

44   Ibid., pp. viii-ix.

45   Ibid., p. xi.

46   Adam Goldman and Charlie Savage, "Horowitz Hearing Highlights: Watchdog Warns Against Exonerating F.B.I. in Russia Inquiry, Pointing to Flaws," *New York Times*, December 11, 2019. https://www.nytimes.com/2019/12/11/us/politics/fbi-ig-hearing.html

47   Survey of Presidential Leadership.https://www.politico.com/f/?id=0000015a-4d99-d5b6-a35f-ffff4eae0001

48   Beth Walton, "Goodwin talks Trump, Obama and the election," *Citizen Times*, May 26, 2017. https://www.citizen-times.com/story/news/local/2017/05/26/doris-kearns-goodwin-talks-trump-obama-and-2016-election/335931001/

18: "Obama's Revisionist 'Promised Land'"

1   Dov Lipman, "Obama's Revisionist 'Promised Land,'" *JNS.org*, November 26, 2020. https://www.jns.org/opinion/obamas-revisionist-promised-land/